203 Home-Based Businesses That Will Make You Rich

*The Complete Guide to
Financing and Running
a Fabulously Successful
Home-Based Business*

Tyler G. Hicks

THREE RIVERS PRESS
NEW YORK

Published by Three Rivers Press, New York, New York.
Member of the Crown Publishing Group, a division of Random House, Inc.
www.randomhouse.com

THREE RIVERS PRESS and the Tugboat design are registered trademarks of Random House, Inc.

Originally published by Prima Publishing, Roseville, California, in 1998.

Investment decisions have certain inherent risks. Any investment a reader may make based on the information in this book must be at the reader's sole risk. You should carefully research or consult a qualified financial adviser before making any particular investment.

Furthermore, while efforts have been made to make this book complete and accurate as of the date of publication, in a time of rapid change, it is difficult to ensure that all information is entirely accurate, complete, or up-to-date. Although the publisher and the author cannot be held liable for any inaccuracies or omissions in this book, they are always grateful for suggestions for improvement.

Printed in the United States of America

Library of Congress Cataloging-in-Publication Data

Hicks, Tyler Gregory.
 203 home-based businesses that will make you rich : the complete guide to financing and running a fabulously successful home-based business / Tyler G. Hicks.
     p.   cm.
  Includes index.
    1. Home-based businesses—Management.   2. New business enterprises—Management.   I. Title.
 HD62.38.H53   1998
 658'.041—dc21   98-20425
                                                                      CIP

ISBN 0-7615-1259-4

10 9 8 7 6

First Edition

CONTENTS

INTRODUCTION: HOW TO USE THIS BOOK

Have you been downsized from your job? Or do you still have a job but you hate it? Has a business of your own been a lifelong dream? Or is an independent income—free from the control of others—your goal in life?

If you answer *yes* to any of these questions, this book is for you. Why? Because this book shows you how to:

1. **Pick** a home-based business you like and succeed in it.
2. **Find** a low-cost, lean way to start that business.
3. **Generate** substantial income quickly from your home.
4. **Build** a strategic cash reserve for your future.
5. **Have** plenty of free time to do what you richly enjoy.
6. **Expand** your business to bring in more money.

Over the years I've shown thousands of Beginning Wealth Builders—BWBs in my shorthand notation—how to start and succeed in their own home-based business. And these happy BWBs—many of whom are stay-at-home moms (or dads)—voluntarily write me thousands of glowing letters telling me that the ideas I gave them really do work! Now I'm ready to show you how you can do the same—starting this very instant on your own kitchen table or in your garage or basement. You can even start your own business in a trailer, motor home, boat, or mountain cabin!

Businesses I think you might use to build your wealth are what I call "paper businesses," that is:

- **Businesses** that can be run from a simple desk at home—made by putting a plywood door on two low-cost (or salvaged) filing cabinets.
- **Businesses** that do not need a big payroll—or any payroll at all—because you have independent contractors work for you on an hourly or per-job basis; they're paid for what they do, nothing more (no medical plans, no pensions, no sick leave, etc.).

- **Businesses** that you can run single-handedly at the start, and that you can continue to run that way for as long as you wish—as long as you're satisfied with an income of up to about $400,000 a year as sole owner, with your income rolling in year after year.
- **Businesses** that don't require a factory, heavy machinery, minerals in the ground, or any other large investment of any kind.
- **Businesses** that can be run from your self-built desk using just paper, stamps, a pen, a typewriter or computer, a telephone, and—if you wish—a fax machine.
- **Businesses** that you can start on little cash—just a few hundred dollars for most of them.
- **Businesses** that recently took on a new short name—SOHO, for small office/home office—that are being catered to by some of the world's largest companies that sell phones, copy machines, and other equipment that gives you complete work-at-home flexibility.

The businesses you just read about have other attractive features that will appeal to many of today's aspiring BWBs. These features are attractive to:

1. **Stay-at-home mothers** or fathers who must care for young children.
2. **Handicapped people** of all ages and genders who can't get out to a job because they don't have the needed mobility, but who seek the positive healing power a successful business brings to both the wallet and mind.
3. **Poor credit-history BWBs** who have a less-than-perfect credit report because of past illness, divorce, job loss, or bad advice on repaying student loans; these folks believe they deserve to be rich, and they seek a better life using creative solutions to their problems.
4. **Ex-military personnel** who can't find a suitable job in what seems like an alien world; they seek extra-income opportunities in a successful business of their own that they manage wisely.
5. **Former prison inmates** with little employment history to use in finding work; this book—full of insider's how-to success strategies for success at home—could be their last-chance success guide.

6. **Minority individuals** who face job discrimination—even in today's so-called tolerant world; in this book, they'll find the best places to offer their home business products or services and network with others who can help them succeed.

7. **Career changers**—young or experienced—who want to do an about-face in their lives and switch to a new and larger source of income for themselves, using breakthrough thinking.

8. **New workers** who early on recognize that they don't want to get into the corporate rat race; instead they want a business of their own that could make them rich—as everyone who develops creative ideas and solutions to people's problems is entitled to be.

9. **Unemployed people** who were downsized, laid off, given early retirement, or otherwise fired from their "steady, lifetime" job.

10. **Retirees** who've found they can't play golf seven days a week, can't travel 365 days a year, can't live "outside the loop" of the work world and want to get back into the action of the real world.

So if you're one of these people, come with me—your good and dependable friend—and I'll show you how to grow rich in your own business today. I'll guide you every step of the way—in person, by mail, by phone, or by fax. Call me and I'll personally answer on the first ring. Your questions will be answered quickly and clearly. You'll start to bring in a steadily rising income—month after month.

You can get rich in your own home business today. A new millionaire is created every few minutes in the United States—every day! Most of these new millionaires are self-made people who own their own businesses. You too can reach millionaire status. This book shows you exactly how to reach that income level, giving you step-by-step directions and providing you with business moxie and smart techniques that will work for you every time you use them. So if you're ready to start getting rich, I'm ready to show you how. Just turn to Chapter 1—now!

Tyler G. Hicks

HOW YOU CAN MAKE
A FORTUNE AT HOME

Do YOU WANT to start your own business at home? You *can*—if you use the ideas I give you in this book! Plenty of today's most successful companies were started at home and grew into billion-dollar businesses. Here are a few examples—you've probably heard of some of these companies.

- **One of the largest specialty-bread bakers** in the United States was founded in the suburban kitchen of a woman seeking a better bread for her ill son.
- **A big recycled-metals exporter** ships his recovered metals all over the world from his home; he never sees what he exports!
- **Four of the world's largest computer companies** began at home—two in garages, one in a barn on a farm, the fourth in a college dormitory room.
- **A reader of our newsletter** started a mail-order exporting business while in jail, selling children's clothing all over the world, preparing himself for an honest, productive career on his release.
- **One of the biggest newsletter publishing companies** in the world was started on a kitchen table at home with $1,000 and did $300,000 in business in its first year. Today it grosses more than $100 million a year—from a single office building.
- **A home-based book publisher** has annual sales of $300 million from his home. And he has no plans to move into an office—his sales are high enough as it is!

There are thousands of other successful companies in almost every field that started—and prospered—at home. And *you* can do the same, starting right now! Here's how *you* can make your fortune at home—just take these ten easy steps:

1. **Decide** what business you want to run from your home.
2. **Prepare** a short business plan telling what you'll do.
3. **Choose** your sources of supply or expertise.
4. **Select** ways to publicize and advertise your business.
5. **Raise** money to start your business, after figuring your needs.
6. **Register** your business as required by local regulations.
7. **Start** your business by taking the first step in your plan.
8. **Test** various marketing methods—ads, mail, TV, Internet.
9. **Introduce** new products or services whenever you can.
10. **Expand** your business to the income level you seek.

There you have your ten-step plan for success in any home business. Let's look at each of these steps in detail and see how you can use this plan in your new home business!

Decide What Business You Want to Run from Your Home

To be successful in any home business, you *must enjoy your business!* Why do I say this? For several important reasons, namely:

- **Making money** can become boring if you don't enjoy what you're doing.
- **Bored business owners** transmit negative messages to their customers, leading to declining sales.
- **Your whole life** takes on a depressing tone when you don't enjoy what you're doing for a living.

Contrast this with the person who enjoys his or her home business. When you enjoy what you're doing, you'll find:

- **Making money** is a joy when you have fun at what you're doing in your business.

- **You do a better job** when you enjoy your work; your customers sense your enjoyment and become more loyal to you—that is, they spend more money.
- **Your business prospers** while you have fun and your employees have a pleasant working atmosphere.

To decide what business you want to run in your own home, just follow two easy steps:

1. **List what you enjoy** as a career, your leisure-hour turn-ons, any hobbies you like, and volunteer work you do for "the fun of it."
2. **Examine your list** to see if there are any potential businesses there for you.

Here's a real-life example of how one Beginning Wealth Builder (BWB) converted her likes and interests into a home business:

Judy S. always liked making her own cosmetics, having started doing this as a teenager. For years she collected formulas for the oils, spices, and scents she used in preparing her cosmetics. She loved the feel of her skin after she applied one or more of her favorite cosmetics.

When Judy told her friends about her cosmetics they all wanted to try them. Soon Judy had a working home business selling her cosmetics to friends. These people told others and the orders began to pile in. Many of the people placing orders asked Judy how they too could make their own cosmetics and where they could buy the ingredients.

Judy prepared a twelve-page catalog listing the ingredients for homemade cosmetics and how much they cost. She sent this to her customers. Orders poured in—so many that Judy had to hire a part-time assistant and get low-cost storage space in a nearby warehouse. Today Judy's home business is booming—via her mail-order catalog sales of cosmetics and their ingredients.

You, too, can do the same—starting with what you enjoy doing. Go over your list and see what potential businesses it contains. And if you can't figure out what business would be good for you, call, write, or fax me for help. You'll find my phone and fax numbers, and my business address, in the last line of this book. When you call I'll answer on the first ring. You *do* have a friend in Ty Hicks!

Prepare a Short Business Plan Telling What You'll Do

Most BWBs shy away from doing a business plan. Why? Because it entails writing. And they hate writing.

But a two-page business plan can tell you more about yourself and your future than you might ever think. And writing such a plan can be fun because it will show you what you'll be doing for the next few years—and how much money you'll be earning.

Knowing how much some BWBs dislike preparing their business plan, I will prepare—completely free of charge— an Executive Summary for a business plan for those who subscribe to my newsletter, *International Wealth Success*, for two years or more. (For a description of my newsletter, turn to the back of this book.) Just ask for the Executive Summary Form when you send your subscription payment or call in your credit card order. It will be sent with your first issue of our newsletter.

Your Executive Summary is a 300- to 400-word description of a business, summarizing its key features. Such a summary will often be enough for you to get a loan or grant to finance your business. And a well-written Executive Summary can serve as the short business plan we suggest you prepare. All I need from you are the key details about your business; first call me to discuss specifics at (516) 766-5850; then you can mail the details, or fax them to me at (516) 766-5919. I need the details in writing before I can prepare the Executive Summary.

A reader, calling from Arizona, told me:

"The short business plan (just one page) I prepared using your suggestions as a guide—got me the business loan I needed. The banker told me it was the best such business plan he had ever seen. 'I wish everyone came in here with a business plan like yours,' he said. And our business is doing great, using the loan we got based on the Executive Summary and loan application."

So don't let the suggestion to write a business plan turn you off. You can get it written—painlessly—if you know the details of your business. My Executive Summary Form is an easy way to get your business plan written. As long as you can give details about the business, you can get the plan written.

As a final strong reason for writing a business plan, take a look at these statistics:

Studies by several business development groups show that some 80 percent of businesses that prepared a business plan before starting were still in business five years later. But only 20 percent of businesses that started without a business plan were still in business five years later! So if you want to be in business for a long time, write your plan.

Choose Your Sources of Supply or Expertise

In your home business you will sell either products or services. If your business sells products—such as books, newsletters, perfume, soap, and so on—you will need a source of supply. For example, for each of these products your supplier would be:

- Books—book publisher
- Newsletters—newsletter publisher
- Perfume—perfume manufacturer
- Soap—soap manufacturer

In a service business you sell expertise—knowledge of certain topics, laws, or rules. Thus, your experts might be:

- Attorneys—for legal expertise
- Accountants—for tax and business expertise

- Engineers—for design expertise
- Health professionals—for health-care expertise
- Hobby specialists—for hobby advice
- Sports experts—for instructions on playing

These experts give your customers or clients advice for a fee. You don't need any "hard assets"—such as a factory, apartment house, bowling alley, hotel, or tennis court—to earn your fee. You deal in words, many of which will be spoken. The spoken words are often followed up by a brief written summary—which your expert prepares.

To choose your supplier—either of products or expertise—follow these easy steps:

1. **Determine the best sources** of supply for your products or services—do this by consulting directories of products in your local public library; for experts, consult your local bar, accounting, medical, or other association for the names of qualified people.
2. **Contact at least three suppliers** and ask for quotes on the product or products you want to sell in your business; these will be mailed or faxed to you in a few days.
3. **Ask the association** you contact for the names of three specialists in the field you're calling about. Contact the specialists; describe what you'd like them to do for you for a fee; ask for a quote on their price for the service you plan to offer.
4. **Select your suppliers or experts** and work out an agreement with them for providing the items or services you need; provide a written agreement covering your arrangement; have your supplier sign off on it; put it in your file for your business.

Here's a real-life example of how this approach worked in a successful home business—and we've seen it work in various parts of the country and the world:

A housewife who wanted to stay home with her young children became interested in the liquidation business. In this business you buy excess or unwanted merchandise from a firm or individual seeking to get rid of it. Then you turn around and sell it to a firm or person needing the item. Your profit is the difference between the two prices.

This capable and astute housewife located jewelry that a manufacturer wanted to sell off at a low price. She agreed to buy the jewelry and then began looking for a buyer. Within a month she reported grossing some $200,000 in sales. And all of this was done by phone from home—and she was still available to care for her children! She searched for sellers and buyers using tools like those we suggested above.

While quick earnings of this amount are unusual, you *can* get started earning income in your own home business when you have competent suppliers. Build *your* sources of good products or services and customers will soon start ordering from you. Result? You'll soon be earning money in your own home business! And the sky will be your only limit.

Select Ways to Publicize and Advertise Your Business

You can get free publicity that will help put your business on the map in your area by:

1. **Telling people** that you're in business and ready to deliver reliable products or services.
2. **Giving the location** of your business, or its mailing address, telephone number, and Internet address if you're online.
3. **Informing potential customers** of any special services you might offer—such as custom design, construction, tailoring, etc.—that set you apart from other people in your business.

Free publicity costs little more than the price of a first-class stamp plus an envelope and a sheet of standard business-size paper. Here's how you can get thousands of dollars' worth of free publicity for your home business:

1. **Write a news release** announcing the opening of your new business, its address, telephone number, and online address, if any. (You can use a post office box as your address if you don't want people coming to your home.) If you

need help writing your news release, I'll be glad to help you—if you supply the essential information to me. Also, ask for our helpful booklet "How to Write a News Release," which is free when you subscribe to our newsletter, *International Wealth Success*, for two years or more. Just ask for the booklet when you send your check or money order for $48 to IWS, Inc., P.O. Box 186, Merrick, NY 11566-0186. Or you can call the phone number listed in Chapter 12 to order by credit card.

2. **Have your news release printed**, double-spaced, on one or two sheets of paper. You can also photocopy your news release if you're sending out just fifty or so copies.

3. **Send your news release** to newspapers and magazines whose readers might be interested in your products or services. If you can include a photograph or drawing with your news release, do so. Why? You will get more space if both your illustration and words are included. When your news release includes product or service prices, you'll probably receive some paid orders soon after your news release appears.

When you're ready to advertise, consider using those publications from which you got the largest response to your news release. Why? Because a large response indicates that the readers of the publication are interested in your products or services. To maximize your ad results:

1. **Start with classified ads.** They cost the least, and the response to them is often greater, per dollar spent, than to display ads.

2. **Run as many classified ads as you can afford** for as long as they earn more than their cost plus product or service cost and delivery charge.

3. **Experiment with 1-inch display ads**, such as that shown in Figure 1-1, which pull strongly for us, month after month.

4. **Expand into larger display ads** in those publications from which your 1-inch ads pull well. What is a good pull? When you bring in three, or more, times your ad cost, you'll make money! But you can still make money at a lower ratio, especially when you work from home. Figure 1-2

Figure 1-1. A typical 1-inch display ad.

shows a typical full-page ad we use for my home-based
publishing business. This ad is run in those magazines
where the 1-inch ad has produced profitable results.

To show you how ads can build your home business, here's
a real-life example from a reader who called to tell me:

"I decided to have a statue of a golfer made to sell to the golf-
ing public. I had it designed and made in pewter. It's 6 inches
high and shows a male golfer at the end of his swing. Advertising it in a local weekly paper cost me $507 for one week. I sold
500 statues at about $50 ($49.95) each, bringing in $24,975 from
my home. The checks and money orders poured in. I ran to the
manufacturer and asked if they could turn out 500 units in the
four to six weeks I promised in the ad. They said they could.
Now I'm ready to have a statue made of a female golfer to sell
the same way. With so much interest in golf worldwide, my
future is unlimited! By the way, my cost—in the mail—is about
$23 per statue, not including my ad cost."

To me, this is a great example of what you can do in
your own home business when you develop a needed product or service. You can do much the same with a product or
service you buy. But your profit will usually not be as high.

Raise Money to Start Your Business, After Figuring Your Needs

You need money to start any business—even your own home
business. But the fortunate aspects of home businesses are:

How to MAKE BIG MONEY as a FINANCIAL BROKER/FINDER/BUSINESS BROKER/BUSINESS CONSULTANT

Become a FINANCIAL CONSULTANT/FINDER/BUSINESS BROKER/CONSULTANT! Some people call this the "best business anyone can get into!" Would YOU like to become a Financial Broker/Finder/Business Broker? You can! How? Read on!

If YOU like money, if YOU have ever had some type of job in business, if YOU want to help others, and if YOU like people, YOU can become a Financial Broker. All YOU need to do to start YOUR future in this great career is to use the IWS FINANCIAL BROKER/FINDER/BUSINESS CONSULTANT KIT: It shows YOU the how, where, when, and way of this money-laden career. Here's why YOU need this great KIT. It gives YOU the ideas, methods, forms, and steps which YOU can use to get started. Here are some of the specific topics covered in detail in this great KIT!

- How to prepare your business announcement
- Developing a list of financial and business brokers
- Typical business loan application forms
- How to start your own financial broker office
- Where to locate your business
- Doing business from your home
- How to get your letterhead and business cards
- How, and where, to contact money sources
- What to charge your clients for your help
- Finding clients all over the world
- 2,500 sources of business loans for you
- How to be a financial broker anywhere without a state or city license (this method has never been covered in print before – so far as we can determine)
- Typical financial broker/finder/business broker forms (113 pages of forms covering every aspect commonly met –from placement and processing agreements to financial statements for borrowers to commercial financing forms. You get a total of 41 forms, many of which YOU can use directly without changing a word!)
- Complete guide to becoming a highly paid business broker in your spare time
- Fees you can collect as a business broker
- Starting with NO license, NO test, NO exams
- Which industries pay the biggest fees to YOU
- How to become a highly paid business consultant (income to $1,000 a day!)
- Kinds of problems financial brokers/finders/business brokers solve (get paid big to suggest ideas)
- Get contracts for annual consulting fee
- How to become a highly paid finder in your spare time (turn leisure into BIG cash)
- What finders do – and where – and for what
- How much to charge for being a finder
- Typical finder-fee agreement you can use today
- How to pick a good plant site
- Taking a company public – Regulation 'A' offerings
- Terms used in the Regulation; what they mean
- How to write a selling prospectus
- Samples of forms to be used for Reg 'A'
- Irrevocable appointment of you as an agent
- Offering stock through underwriters
- Registering with the SBC for the offering
- Loan packages – how to prepare them for approval
- SBIC - Small Business Investment Companies – what they do, how you can use them
- Advertising and office mailing flier for your firm
- Typical bank letter of credit, typical surety bond for a business loan
- Plus four membership certificates in two colors suitable for framing and mounting in your office or den
- Much, much more to help YOU get started

Here's what some of the users say about this great FINANCIAL BROKER/FINDER/BUSINESS BROKER/CONSULTANT Kit:

"Received Financial Broker Kit yesterday morning. Using info in it, closed deal for $463,750 yesterday afternoon. Thank you. Best regards." Tennessee

"My financial brokerage business grossed $45,000 in first year. I am now working on starting a finance company." Virginia

"It was through your letter that I became a part-time financial broker, have been one for six months and have enjoyed several commissions!" Massachusetts

"...went out and borrowed $10,000 and bought a business brokerage representing small business opportunities. I was recently (1 year later) offered $25,000 for half of my brokerage." Pennsylvania

"My fee between two findings is $180,000." Montana

"I am underway and doing quite well. I have completed one merger deal and placed 2 loans for $75,000." Massachusetts

This great KIT contains 12 speed- read books, a total of some 500 ages, 4 ready-to-frame membership certificates and costs only $99.50. Send your check or money order TODAY!

ABOUT THE AUTHOR

Tyler G. Hicks is the president of INTERNATIONAL WEALTH SUCCESS, INC., as well as the president of a large lending organization in New York. He is internationally recognized as the foremost expert on making money from scratch and is the best-sellingauthor of many books, including *How to Get Rich on Other People's Money, How to Start a Business on a Shoestring and Make Up to 500,000 a Year* and *How to Borrow Your Way to Real Estate Riches*. Over 2 million people have read some of his books. He will provide free consultation for every buyer of this kit.

FREE CONSULTATION!

Yes, I do like money! And this sounds like the kind of business I've been looking for. Enclosed is $99.50 for the FINANCIAL BROKER/FINDER/BUSINESS BROKER/BUSINESS CONSULTANT KIT. (Air mail outside North America: add $60; there is no postage for surface – sea shipment.) I can consult with Ty Hicks as a Bonus for buying the KIT.

Name:____________________

Street:____________________

City: ____________________

State ____________________

Credit Card No.__________ Expiration Date________

Signature__________ Telephone No.________

Call (516) 766-5850 day or night to order by credit card.

SEND YOUR PAYMENT TO:

IWS, INC.
24 CANTERBURY RD.
ROCKVILLE CTR.
NY 11570

Figure 1-2. A typical full-page ad.

1. **You can get started on very little cash**—often just $100 can get you into a position where money is coming in regularly, helping you pay bills and invest in new promotions and ads to bring in more money to fuel your growth.
2. **You can get by with little more than a telephone** at the start because you can farm out printing, faxing, and computer work at low cost.
3. **You can use hourly workers** who you pay only when they work and who don't get any medical coverage, vacations, or sick pay—saving you big bucks in your cost of doing business.

To raise money for your home business, look to these often-used sources. If none suit you, then see the end of this section for an almost sure-fire source of business money for you, my good friend. Here are five frequently used money sources:

1. **Credit-card lines of credit.** Many credit cards offer a line of credit of $1,000, $2,000, $5,000—or more. You can take this much cash against your credit card and use it for any purpose you wish—such as starting your own home business. Thousands of my readers have done—and are doing—this successfully for all types of home businesses. You can too! Just tap into your line of credit on your credit card—provided that you're sure you can repay all the money you borrow in a timely manner.
2. **Relatives and friends** can be a convenient source of loans to finance your new home business. Just be certain to set up the loan in a businesslike manner with a promissory note and a schedule for repayment of the loan at the going interest rate in your area.
3. **Bank loans are a popular source of money** to start a home business. However, banks often won't lend money for startup businesses. The bank may, however, be ready to loan for furniture, home improvement, vacation, education, debt consolidation, and more. If you have a need for money for one of these acceptable purposes, you can often combine it with the amount you need for your business startup and have your application approved. I'll never forget applying for a business loan and having the banker

say, "Mr. Hicks, don't you need some new furniture? I'm sure you do, because the loan committee loves to make loans for new furniture!" I got the hint and got the new furniture, plus startup money for my business.

4. **Credit unions throughout the country** are now making business loans. And their requirements are usually less stringent than banks. So check out your local credit union in the yellow pages of your telephone book. Call and ask about membership requirements and the types of loans they make. You may find they are happy to work with you. Further, your membership in any credit union is free.

5. **Private lenders** make loans to BWBs (Beginning Wealth Builders) at varying interest rates—usually equal to, or a little above, the going rate in the area. Many private lenders will make their loan decision based on their impression of the potential borrower. Thus, if you have a good, short business plan (Step 2, above) that you can send to a private lender, your chances of getting the loan you need are much better.

If none of the above lenders, or any of the many others discussed in Chapter 11 of this book, will finance your home business, try another potential source—me. I function as a private lender and offer loans around the country (where allowed by local regulations). My company's interest rate is just a simple 6 percent, and our loans go for a maximum of seven years. We need some type of collateral on each loan, but we're willing to work with the borrower. To get our way of thinking, we suggest that you subscribe to our newsletter, though it is not a requirement. Our only requirement is that the loan be used for active business purposes.

Among the thousands of letters and calls I get from readers, there are many that tell of successful financing of a business project. I received this phone call from a reader in North Carolina, who said:

"I have $1,000 per month positive cash flow from six apartment units and five houses I took over using my credit cards and a loan from a small bank. Getting these units really gave me much greater confidence!"

Don't you think that an extra $1,000 per month positive cash flow—that is, pure money in your pocket—would give *you* much greater confidence? I'm sure it would!

Register Your Business As Required by Local Regulations

Local business regulators—such as the county clerk, the sheriff, and others—want to be able to locate you in the event that they have a question about your business. So if you operate under an assumed name—such as Ace Services—the regulators insist that you register your business. Then if there's a question about Ace Services they can look you up and write you a letter or give you a call.

But if you operate your business under your own name— say John or Jane Smith—you need not register. Why? Because you'll have an address and—usually—a telephone at which they can reach you.

Registering your business is simple. Just get a form from your county clerk or other official in your area in charge of this, and fill it out. You pay a nominal fee—anywhere from $5 to $50, depending on the locality—and your business will be registered. Then you can open a bank account after you get your federal identification number (fed ID) from the Internal Revenue Service. You get this number free of charge by calling your local IRS office and asking for the form that must be filled out. You will also be provided—free of charge—one or more valuable booklets on running your business in a tax-acceptable way. If you have an accountant— which you eventually should—he or she will do much of this work for you.

When you operate your business under your own name, your Social Security number is your federal ID number for bank and tax purposes. In other words, you can open your business bank account under your own name when you operate your business under that name.

Most BWBs who start a home business operate under their own names for the first few months. Then they convert to an assumed name—sometimes called the "doing business as" (DBA) name—as a sole proprietorship. Later, as their business grows, they may convert to a corporation.

You must—of course—have access to an attorney to get answers to any business-related legal questions you may have. To be certain you are making the right decision, you must discuss the above suggestions with your attorney. We recommend that you follow his or her directions if they are different from those above.

Start Your Business by Taking the First Step in Your Plan

You'll be nervous—that I can guarantee! But don't let nervousness stop you. Your nervousness is a good reaction. Why? Because it will alert you to possible problems. You'll avoid doing foolish things because being nervous makes you more alert, more careful, more sensible.

And what might your first step—and the next few—be? Here are the typical early steps a BWB takes on his or her first few days in business:

1. **Register** the business with local regulators.
2. **Find** a place to do business at home—a private room.
3. **Contact** money sources for the funds you need.
4. **Make** your first sales contact—by mail, phone, fax, or Internet.
5. **Sell** your product or service to your first customers.

To show you how quickly and easily you can get started, here's what a reader from Missouri told me on the phone recently:

"I read *101 Great Mail-Order Businesses* in two hours. The next morning I wrote a newsletter on how to teach kids to play baseball. I priced it at $15 and made a mailing to 600 parents of kids who play baseball. I made $2,200 in one-and-a-half weeks. Not bad for a college student who plays baseball himself!"

This college student works out of his dorm room—his present home. And he'll continue working from his home as long as he's in school—and will shift his office to his regular home with his parents when the semester ends.

He was very nervous at the start. Questions kept popping into his mind—questions like these:

- **Will anyone want** to read my newsletter?
- **Is the $15 price** too high for most parents?
- **Do I really have** enough to say to keep the newsletter going for years?
- **Can I work** efficiently out of my dorm room?

His newsletter boomed. Today his business is stronger than ever because he started his business despite nervousness. You—too—can do the same! Just take charge of yourself, your life, and your business—and get started. You'll be amazed—and delighted—with the results. Taking money to the bank every day never gets boring.

Test Various Marketing Methods for Best Results

In your own business you'll almost certainly sell a product or service. And most BWBs start by selling a product. The selling method you choose depends on what you're offering to the public. A good way to choose your selling method is this:

Look in magazines, on TV, in newspapers, and on the Internet for ads for similar products or services. Note what types and sizes of ads are used. Then design a similar—but better—ad for your product or service.

Test your ad by running it a few times and keeping careful track of your responses and sales.

Here's a real-life example of this technique at work. You can use a similar approach for your business.

Mary L. wanted to sell recipes by mail order. So she started by checking large-circulation weekly newspapers' classified ads. She found dozens of firms advertising recipes for all types of exotic dishes. She then called me and asked, "How can my recipes compete with all those others that are advertised?" and "Won't mine get lost among all the others that are in those papers?" My answers? "You can compete with the other recipes by advertising unusual dishes—ones that are not currently advertised," I told her. "Your recipes won't get lost among the others if they're for dishes that are not offered by other firms. The very fact that so many recipes are advertised shows that the ads pull in money. If they didn't, the ads would soon disappear!"

Mary L. took my advice and ran small classified ads for her unique recipes. Since she was worried about competing, and nervous about not getting back the money she spent on the ads, she priced her recipes $1 below the competition—$4 for five recipes, instead of $5. She received an avalanche of orders from her first ad. Soon thereafter she raised her price to $5, and the orders continued to pour in.

What was Mary L. doing here? She was using the proven technique for getting started in any home business. That technique is called *innovative imitation*. What you do using this technique is:

1. *Imitate* what other companies are already doing in their ads and product offerings;
2. *Innovate* to make your ads and products better than those of other successful competing businesses.

By imitating you're avoiding having to spend big bucks on research. The other companies did that for you. For example, the large number of recipe ads in the national weekly newspapers tells you that other advertisers researched the pulling powers of these papers and found them strong and worth their ad dollars for recipe sellers. So you don't have to spend money trying to learn which papers pull best.

When you innovate—that is, put a new twist or attraction on a product—you beat out the competition. Mary L. sold five unique recipes for $4. She beat out the competition because their recipes weren't unique and they cost $1 more for the same number of recipes. You too can do the same with the product or service that you sell from home.

Mary L. then tested other marketing outlets. She tried ads for her recipes in women's magazines, on local TV, and the Internet. None of these ads pulled as well, for the money spent, as her weekly newspaper ads did. So she shifted her ad budget to weekly papers, based on her tests of the other outlets. Result? Her business boomed! Try testing—it will work for you!

Introduce New Products or Services Whenever You Can

You can start with one product or service working in your own home. If you want your business to grow and bring in more money, it will be necessary to add other products or services as time goes by. Why? Because your first product or service will usually plateau at a certain income level and stay there, or start to decline.

Introduce a new product or service related to the first and your business will boom out. Why? Because you can sell to your original customers. They'll be happy to buy from you. Here's another real-life example from a recent Rhode Island reader who expanded his home-based real estate business by adding new units to his holdings:

> "I talked to you briefly last night (on the phone). I read two of your books one year ago by accident. Then I ventured out to buy my first fourplex with no money down. Thanks a bunch for those books. I now have twenty units in my portfolio. I gross $98,000 a year with a net of $30,000. I am now seriously considering quitting my job to do this full time (from home). The biggest miracle is that I've been in this country (the United States) fifteen years and was starting to feel unsure about what to do with the rest of my life, when I read these (your) books. Thanks a bunch."

If this reader had stayed with just his first four units, his income would be much lower. Introducing new units (products or services) increased his income considerably. Another real-life example from Nevada:

> "My husband and I have been trading (exporting to) with China for ten years. Every year this huge market is growing in scope and there are many opportunities for an entrepreneur to make good money without investing a great deal of money. Recently we sold a product for $25,000; our investment was $3,000 for a trip to China to introduce the buyer (to this additional product)."

So you see, introducing new products works in every home-based business to increase sales. You—too—can do the same.

Expand Your Business to the Income Level You Seek

How much income do you want? You should know the answer to this question. And the real answer is not "As much as I can get." Your answer should be a specific number—based on sitting down and figuring out how much money would make you happy in life.

Is your desired income $100,000, $150,000, or $250,000? Only you can answer that. But I can give you one number. That number is the maximum amount one person with an assistant can earn in a home business—based on my experience and observation of thousands of home businesses around the world. It appears to me that $500,000 a year is about the most one person—with an assistant—can earn in a home-based business. Beyond this number you—generally—must rent an office, warehouse, or factory outside the home. So, if you believe my maximum number, that will be the largest income you can expect in your home business without renting outside space. Here is a good example of how much some people earn at home. This came from Texas by phone to me:

> "I have over $3 million in property I got in two years on zero cash down. I started with a property that was about to be demolished; I fixed it up and sold it off for a good profit. Now I want to start a

gym. My real estate gives me a positive cash flow (PCF) of $25,000 to $30,000 per month (that's $300,000 to $360,000 a year).

And—good friend of mine—I'm sure you know that PCF is money-in-fist—that is, cash in your hand after all expenses (including mortgages) are paid! So this BWB comes close to my $500,000 number. And PCF can make you rich—faster than you might think.

When you expand your business to bring in more income, follow these simple rules:

1. **Stay in a business you know.** The other person's business always looks easier to run and more profitable than yours. But the truth is that he or she has almost the same business problems you do. And your business looks easier and more profitable to him or her!
2. **Be cautious about spending** on equipment and inventory for your expansion. Try to outsource instead of buying new equipment—i.e., lease instead of buying until you're sure your expanded business can support the equipment you want to buy.
3. **Use temporary help at the start.** Avoid taking on permanent employees until you're sure you can keep them on the payroll. While it's true you can fire people when work slows down, you do have a responsibility to keep people on as long as you can. Layoffs are always painful.
4. **Give good customer service** at all times. This binds your new customers to you. They'll return to buy more—again and again. And this—after all—is why you're in business—to make sales that keep you and your customer happy!

You *can* succeed in your own home business! I see people doing it every day of the week. Just like these readers who contacted me from Illinois to say:

"My husband and I have been selling perfumes from home for fifteen years. Because of the low overhead at home, we are able to sell at well below the cost a department store would charge a customer. And we've been able to take our business with us when we moved to three other cities. My husband has had steady employment in the business and I went back to school for my medical degree."

This letter shows you three of the many advantages of a home-based business:

1. You can take it with you.
2. It will provide a steady income for you and your family.
3. You'll have time freedom to do what you want to do while the money keeps rolling in—day after day!

Another reader—this one is from Texas—says the following:

> "I had about fifty responses to my ad in IWS. I have two loans in process right now (as a financial broker), which—if completed (and it appears they will be)—will net me $5,400. I used to work three months for that kind of money. I have learned more from your books than I did in four years of college."

To show you how much faith I have in you and your business, I make this offer to you: I'll gladly consider financing your business via a low-interest loan for up to seven years. There are no up-front charges, fees, or retainers of any kind for such a loan. The only charge you'll ever face is the low-rate interest on the money you have in hand. This is called *simple interest.*

To help you better understand how I view building wealth in your own home-based business starting with little cash, I suggest that you subscribe to my newsletter, *International Wealth Success,* for two years. Send $48 to IWS, P.O. Box 186, Merrick, NY 11566; ask for a business or real estate loan application. We'll send it to you immediately. You'll get a fast answer when you return your completed short application to us. With certain types of collateral we can process a loan in four hours after receiving the application. That's one of the fastest times I've heard of in this business.

Now that you know that you *can* get rich and make a fortune in your own home-based business, let's take a look at one of the most popular home businesses of all—mail order. I've made some $10 million in it—and I want *you* to do better than I've done. And I'm happy to show you how. Just turn to Chapter 2. Your good friend—me—wants to get you started—right now!

MARKET DIRECTLY TO CUSTOMERS AND GROW RICH

SELLING DIRECTLY TO your customers is the rage in business today. Why? There are a number of reasons—and most of them are important to you. Key reasons why direct selling via mail, TV, radio, Internet, and catalog are so important to BWBs today are:

1. **You can sell directly from home.** Your buyer doesn't care where you ship from—just as long as the product or service he or she is buying is a good value for the money.
2. **With a toll-free number and credit-card facility**, people can order from *their* home to *your* home. The order can be placed while a housewife is preparing dinner, or from a cell phone in a car, or from a business office during the workday—that is, from almost anywhere—day, night, holidays. Your customer has the ultimate in shopping convenience. And all customers love shopping convenience—they even buy more because they feel so good about not having to drive to a mall, find a parking space, fight crowds in the walkways, and then stand in long lines at the checkout counter!
3. **People trust direct selling** because the catalog houses— L. L. Bean, Lillian Vernon, Talbot's, etc.—have made ordering safe, fast, efficient, and fun. When you sell direct you benefit from people's greater faith in ordering by mail, phone, fax, or online.

4. **Buyers everywhere—from America to the entire world— have less time.** We're all rushing about trying to do ten things in the time that only five things can be done. Buying directly saves time, fuel, and tempers, and gives people a feeling of power when they say, "Put it on my credit card and ship it to me next-day air, no matter how much it costs!" Result? You earn more in your home business.

5. **All these reasons will get stronger** as time goes by. Why? Because as the population of the world grows and people become richer, more individuals will want the joy, fun, and time-saving advantages of buying direct. And you— I'm sure—are ready to serve their needs—if direct selling by mail order and its many variants turn you on!

Let's, then, put *you* into the direct-selling business of *your* choice. We'll show you how to get started and where you can earn the most money in the shortest time.

Pick What You Want to Sell

You can sell a product or service directly and make money today. Most BWBs start with a product. Why? Because a product is more tangible than a service. You can hold a product, weigh it, use it, etc. A service is a harder sell because it usually doesn't have these features. Here's a good example:

Many BWBs are making big money selling how-to videos directly to customers. They usually sell by mail—either direct mail letters to lists of potential customers, or mail-order ads in magazines or newspapers. A video is a product you can hold in your hand, slip into your VCR, and turn on to watch—in full living color—how to golf better, build a house, cruise the world in a sailboat, cook a delicious meal, and more. You know what you bought because you can see it, feel it, and work it. And if you don't like what you bought, you can return it to your direct seller and ask for a different video, or for a full refund of your money. You're in command at all times. And products such as videos are ideal items for a home-based business to sell. They're light, safe (they don't explode), they're easy to ship (the post office has special cartons for them that you can order), they don't take up much storage space, and buyers love them. Could you ask for a better combination for a lucrative home-based business?

When you sell a service, you usually must deliver it through the action of a human being—either yourself or someone who works with you. While you can supply a service at home, you are more directly involved in its delivery than when you deliver a product via the mail or a courier service—FedEx, United Parcel Service, etc.

Typical home-based services that can build your wealth are: piano or other music lessons, tax-return preparation, educational tutoring, child care in your home, cooking lessons, and writing articles or books. While each of these services involves your participation at the start, some can pay you handsomely. For example, cooking lessons from recognized gourmet cooks can run as high as $1,000 a session for four people. Give a ten-session cooking course over a two-week period and you'll bring in $10,000 with no cost other than some cooking gas, a little electricity, and some pepper and salt. No food? No! Your students bring the food to be cooked! If you give twenty two-week sessions a year of your cooking class and each is sold out, your income will be: 20 sessions × $10,000 = $200,000. Not bad for staying at home and giving lessons on a topic you love. Just be sure to watch your food intake! A good friend of mine—the mother of three children—has been giving cooking lessons in her home for years and has earned big money doing so. You—too—can do the same, if cooking is your turn-on.

To pick what you want to sell, sit down with pencil and paper and list what you like to do. If sports turn you on, try to pick a product or service related to your favorite sport. For example:

You list sports as your favorite pastime. And soccer is your favorite sport. To sell *products* related to soccer you might consider: soccer balls, shoes, uniforms, instruction books, etc. *Services* for soccer could include coaching, refereeing, training, etc.

No matter what you choose, be sure you like your choice. You'll enjoy what you're doing, you'll have more fun, and—incidentally—you'll earn more money from your home-based business. And that—after all—is what you're after in reading this book.

To help you earn more money in your home-based business we'll devote the rest of this chapter to showing how to market directly to your customers and grow rich doing so— right out of your home, no matter where it may be located.

Choose Your Best Selling Methods

The best selling methods—you say—are those that bring in the most money. Right on! But choosing your best selling methods isn't always easy. You'll probably ask yourself these and other questions:

1. **Will this product or service sell by mail?** Or would TV or radio ads be better? What about the Internet? Or magazines or newspapers?
2. **Should I ask for money in my ad or promotion?** Or should I send out sales materials and let my customers order from them in a two-step process?
3. **Should I sell from a street address?** Or would a post office box be better? What about a mail drop where I have a street address and a suite number—taken together the two sound like an office-building address.

How can you get the right answers to these questions for your product or service? There's just one answer. And that is? You must TEST! And how do you test? You follow these easy steps:

1. **Choose your first sales method.** Let's say it's direct mail for decorative borders for motorcycle license plates. You check a mailing-list house and find that there are 1.5 million motorcycle owners available on lists you can rent at $70 per 1,000 names.
2. **Figure out how many sales** you'll have to make to earn a profit from your mailing. Do this by listing all your costs

for each sale—this will be made up of these costs: product, shipping, list rental, postage, direct-mail letters and envelopes, labor, and overhead (rent, light, heat, etc.). (For more on this, see the examples that follow.)

3. **Make a test mailing** or other promotion, keeping careful track of the results. Seek a profit from every mailing you make.

4. **If your first choice for selling doesn't work**, try another method—for example, you might set up a home page on the Internet and sell from it.

Tests can—and do—work. Every major direct-marketing firm uses them in their business. For many smaller firms, testing is the only way to learn if your products will sell. This BWB from Florida found that out, saying:

"I started my mail-order business on April 1 this year. Today (in June), I'm doing $1,600 a month in sales with about $500 of that on credit cards to my merchant account. Thanks for your help."

Another reader says:

"In the past year I've made a profit of over $48,000 buying and selling quality used merchandise through consignment stores. I enjoy all the benefits of being self-employed in a fun business. Many people want me to teach them how to sell successfully using the consignment method." (Consignment selling is where you put an item in a store free of charge—i.e., the store owner does not pay for it—instead the item is put on display with the hope that it will sell. Then the owner collects a commission on the sale—from 10 to 40 percent of the selling price, depending on the deal you work out with the store owner. Your test here is which items, at what prices, move quickly. This reader knows what moves!)

Use Proven Test Goals for Your Direct-Marketing Sales

People call me—again and again—from around the world asking a question that goes like this: "I'm going to run an ad in a newspaper (or magazine, or radio station, or on a TV channel, or on the Internet) that has a circulation of 1 million. What percent response should I expect to get?"

And my answer—again and again—is "You have to test!" But if you don't want to test, here are some of my findings for test ads of many different kinds. Your results may be better—or worse. Here's the answer to that familiar direct-marketing question:

> **Direct-mail letters to a prospect list:** 1 to 2 percent of names mailed will order what's offered. (A *prospect* is a person or organization that has expressed interest in the type of offer you are making.)
> **Classified ads in newspapers:** 0.1 percent of the paper's circulation
> **Classified ads in magazines:** 0.15 percent of the magazine's circulation
> **Space ads in newspapers:** 0.5 percent of the newspaper's circulation
> **Space ads in magazines:** 0.75 percent of the magazine's circulation
> **Radio commercials:** 0.01 percent of the station's listening audience
> **TV infomercial:** 0.5 percent of the TV station's viewing audience on any given day
> **Internet:** 0.1 percent of the number of page requests on a home page per day

While these numbers may seem small, I've seen some ads in magazines that report a return as high as 7 percent—that is, 7 percent of the readers responded with either a request for information, or sent an order for what was advertised. And I've heard of direct-mail lists that pull an 8 percent return on a mailing. Again, you'll never know what your response to a direct-marketing promotion will be until you test! But you now know some of the numbers you may meet in your home-based direct-marketing business. Now let's see how you might apply these numbers in a test for your direct-marketed product or service.

Check the Direct-Marketing Numbers for Your Business

To show you how you can check the numbers of your business using the above guidelines, let's take the real-life example of Jeff, mentioned in Chapter 1, who developed the golfer statue. Here are the details:

- **He ran a half-page space ad** for the statue in a local weekly newspaper with a circulation of 100,000.
- **He received 500 orders** for the statue at $49.95 per statue; his ad cost was $507 for this one-time ad.
- **Total income** was 500 × $49.95 = $24,975. His response rate from the ad was 500 orders ÷ 100,000 circulation = 0.005. This equals 0.5 × 0.01 which is, as given above, a 0.5 percent return for space ads in newspapers.
- **Ad cost per item sold** = $507 ÷ 500 orders = $1.01. This is extremely low. But it does show you how profitable a home-based business can be.

Now let's carry this further to see the income you might earn if this were your product. Here are the details for this excellent item:

- **Income** = $24,975 received in the form of checks and money orders from the ad you ran.
- **Expenses** = $17 each for cost of statute + ad cost of $1.01 per statue sold + $5 shipping cost per statue + $12.49 overhead, estimated at 25 percent of the sales income. Thus, total cost = $35.50.
- **Profit** = $49.95 - $35.50 = $14.45 per statue. With a sale of 500 statues, Jeff's profit = 500 × $14.45 = $7,225.
- **Future sales**: If another 250 statues are sold from this ad, which will probably happen, his profit will be 750 × $14.45 = $10,837.50. And Jeff can go on advertising this statue for as long as he lives because the popularity of golf seems almost endless.

With just this one product, plus a female golfer statue that I suggested Jeff sell, he can easily become a kitchen-table millionaire. Why? Because:

- **People will order** from a post office box; a store is not needed to sell this statue.
- **Manufacturing is done** in a factory remote from the seller's home.
- **Mailing can be done** from any post office, anywhere in the world.
- **People are willing to wait** for the statue; hence shipping is not a rush activity.

To check the numbers for your direct-marketing offer, follow these easy steps early in the life of your business, after choosing what you want to sell:

1. **Test what you think is your best selling method** by running a promotion using it.
2. **Keep careful records** of the results of your marketing test; use the above example as a guide for the costs you must know.
3. **Decide if the marketing method you're using is effective** for your product. Thus, the half-page ad run for the golf statue is effective because the product started earning a profit from day one!

You now know how to check the numbers of your business. By testing early in the life cycle of your business you will quickly learn which is the best selling method for you, and where you should spend future ad and promotion funds. And if ad cost worries you, try subscribing to my newsletter, *International Wealth Success*, mentioned above. With a two-year subscription, you can run one free classified ad per month. The response to your ad will indicate if there's enough interest in your product or service to advertise in other publications that require you to pay for the ad. After running your ad in IWS you might write me to say, as this reader from Maryland did:

"I am very pleased with the response to the ad you have been running for me. I have been able to come up with some good business out of the responses."

Or, you might have the same results as this reader from Colorado did:

> "I have had a fabulous response from my ad. Over the last year I recruited over twenty people into my program."

Now let's look at how you can use each major type of direct marketing to satisfy your belief—and mine—in *yourself*: that you deserve to be rich. We'll give you creative ways of breakthrough advertising that will make you a work-at-home millionaire. Let's start—now!

Use Direct Mail to Sell Your Products or Services

Direct mail has been used to sell products or services for more than 100 years. Many millionaires owe their wealth to direct mail. Using direct mail gives you many advantages, including:

- **Your customer or prospect hears—directly from you**—your good news about the newest products or services he or she can order from you.
- **You can easily keep track of how many orders** your direct-mail campaign brings back to you for each piece of mail you send out.
- **You can easily track your costs** of getting an order, having the item made, and shipping it.
- **You are in control**—you can increase, or decrease, your mailings as your income rises or falls.

Your direct mail can be in a variety of forms, depending on what you think will induce your prospect to buy what you offer. Thus, your direct mail might be:

1. **A letter describing your offer,** its major features, reasons for buying what you offer, and details of your guarantee.
2. **A catalog illustrating and describing the items** you offer for sale; included with your catalog will be a return

envelope for ordering by mail, and other directions for
ordering by phone.

Under each of these two forms of direct mail you can
use a variety of methods to present your offer. For example,
you can have:

- **A two-page letter** with a return ordering coupon plus an
  addressed return envelope for ordering by mail. The return
  coupon can give a telephone number for ordering by phone
  using a credit card.
- **A multi-page letter** (eight, ten, twelve, or more pages) giving, in great detail, a full description of the offer, what
  customers will get, etc. The letter copy is hard-sell, because
  you want good, strong results from this more expensive format. Again, you'll have the return coupon, phone-order
  option, and return envelope.
- **A multi-page letter plus** a two-page, or longer, brochure listing features, and benefits, of the offer. The return coupon
  may include some type of action device where you take a
  stamp-like label and affix it to a circle or square on the return coupon to indicate your acceptance of the offer. Each
  item in the mailing is directed at making it more successful—that is, bring in more money to your bank.

At the start all you really need is a two-page letter plus
an ordering coupon and a reply envelope. If you're selling
printed materials—books, reports, courses, newsletters,
etc.—you may want to include a "buck slip" (so named because it's the size of a dollar bill) describing each book,
report, or newsletter you're offering. These are cheap to
print because you can fit four of them out of one sheet of
8½ × 11-inch paper. The buck slip is even used to sell other
products by mail—tools, appliances, sports gear, and more.
One reader from Massachusetts told me by phone:

> "I made quite a bit of money from your mail-order ideas. I sell
> books by mail. These books are self-help, how-to, and busi-
> ness methods."

Another reader writes from California:

"Only eleven months ago I started in the mail-order business. I decided to market a carpet-cleaning course for novices who want to start a business of their own. My secret carpet cleaning formula really did a job for me! I've sold courses in the U.S., Canada, Mexico, Europe, Africa, Asia, and Australia. All this happened in less than one year! Many of my dealers asked for commercial carpet cleaning equipment also. So I now handle my own brand-name equipment."

Both these BWBs used a two-page letter plus buck slips to promote their products. You—too—can do the same. The product or service you sell by direct mail can make you a successful home-based millionaire. Your key to success is simply this:

Develop your own product or service based on your analysis of what the market seeks, or needs, in the field in which you'll be selling. If you can't develop your own product or service, get the exclusive right to market a product or service that you believe fits the desires or needs of the market you'll serve.

Let's see how this might work for you in various markets that you might want to sell to in your business.

Sports Markets: Develop, or get the rights to, new or better shoes, uniforms, timers, protective equipment, etc.

How-To Markets: Develop, or get the rights to, books, videos, audiotapes, etc., that teach people how to build a house, repair a boat, race a car, and so on.

Mechanics' Markets: Develop, or get the rights to, courses, review manuals, videos, or other instructional materials for licensed trades such as plumbers, electricians, boaters, boiler operators, etc.

Women's Clothing Markets: Develop new designs for outer, or inner, clothing for casual, dress, sports, or other wear. Or get the rights to sell an exclusive design not readily available in local stores.

When you develop your own product or service, you have a unique offer that others cannot duplicate. Further, most of the products or services you develop will be the type you cannot get at the corner store. Why? Because if you could get such a product or service locally you wouldn't even think about developing it! So the key to success in direct marketing is:

Offering a unique product or service you develop, or get the rights to, that is not available locally and is needed by the market you wish to enter. In developing or finding your product or service, you're motivated by your perceived need for either—by buyers you can reach.

One of the best examples of this was told to me by the father of a college student:

"My son is putting himself through college by earning money from a mail-order business he started in his dorm room selling unique cosmetics by mail. I didn't give my son any money to start his business. Instead, he started it on his own and he hasn't asked me for money for college tuition, room, board, or books. I hope his business booms and he offers me a job!"

The key here is the "unique cosmetics sold by mail" aspect of this student's business. If people want to try unique cosmetics, they probably would like to do so in the privacy of their home without anyone knowing they are doing so. Hence, selling such products by mail is a smart idea. And unique cosmetics are those that you probably can't buy at your local department or drug store. As a result, this student's business is booming. No wonder his father would like to apply for a job with him!

Build Wealth on the Wide Range of Sales Potentials with Direct Mail

Almost every product and service used by individuals and businesses is—or has been—sold by direct mail. Here are a few of the products and services being sold in today's market. You—too—can sell any of these—if what you offer is unique in its market:

PRODUCTS	SERVICES
Books	Work-at-home plans
Newsletters	Tax-return preparation
Clothing	Furniture refinishing
Games	Carpet cleaning
Software	Windshield repair
Videos	Astrological advice
Food	Lock installation, repair
Recipes	Business/personal advice
Toys	Gardening instructions
Fishing supplies	Weight-loss guidance
Tennis equipment	Memory strengthening
Golf supplies	Personal shopping
Furniture	Wake-up and date calls
Computers	Dating service
VCRs, TVs, radios	Health improvement
Auto supplies	Time control tips
Boating equipment	Accounting help
Jewelry, diamonds, stones	Beauty aids/consultation

The above list contains only thirty-six suggestions. I'm sure you can come up with hundreds of others. And once you get a product or service you'd like to offer via direct-mail marketing you can get several other related products or services. Then it's easy to use a catalog to promote, and sell, your unique products or services. Let me tell you my story of products and services sold by direct mail, which are— and have been—generating many millions of dollars in sales:

I started my newsletter, *International Wealth Success*, as a business opportunity publication because I thought that I could do a unique job in the field. There were two other newsletters in the business opportunity field at the time and I thought they were rather weak because they were published by writers— that is, people who had never run a successful business but thought they could tell others how to do so. I had run several successful small businesses and had learned how to make money in them. Today *International Wealth Success* is the longest running business opportunity newsletter still under control of its founder. The other two newsletters—by the way—are long since gone, having folded because of various problems caused by their inexperienced owners. When I started *International Wealth Success* I planned to offer the newsletter and backup books and courses to help people get started in a business of their choice. Today we have some seventy books and twenty-five courses—called Kits for short. These products sell all over the world and all have sold many thousands of copies. Revenues have been in the millions. All sales—at the start—were by direct mail, as we're discussing in this chapter. But as TV infomercials, telemarketing, and the Internet developed, we expanded to these forms of direct selling. Today we use all of them, plus classified and space ads.

Our unique approach to the market consists of one-on-one service to our readers. Any reader can call me and I'll answer on the first ring and give him or her direct solutions to any business questions they may have. Readers can visit me in my office in New York City and I'll give face-to-face answers. And all this is at no cost to the reader—if he or she is a subscriber to one of my newsletters. At these visits we've been able to raise money for readers' business ideas. And we've never asked for, nor accepted, one penny for raising money for our readers. Why? Because if one isn't paid he or she is still independent— that is, no one "owns" you! And—as a further service to our readers—we will consider making business or income real estate loans to them at low interest rates (where such loans are permitted by local statutes). Over the years we've made many loans to our readers and every loan has been repaid in full. Again, there are no fees, no points, and no charges of any kind associated with these loans, except the low interest that starts one month after the loan money is received.

Offering these services has allowed our business to grow to the point where we now have a forty-eight-page catalog of our products, which sell throughout the world. And our entire business started at home, the original idea for it having come to me in a flash while I was sitting on a commuter train one rainy February morning, wondering how I could increase my

income. That one idea resulted in more than $10 million in
business while providing jobs and income for many people!

Two entrepreneurs I know of do well by selling how-to
videos and CDs by direct marketing using a catalog. Their
catalog lists some 3,000 how-to videos. And each sale from
the catalog averages nearly $90!

Another direct-marketing entrepreneur friend sells
name labels for envelopes. He sells to the Latin and South
American markets by using small space ads in newspapers
and magazines. These labels are printed with a four-color
illustration of the buyer's choice. This choice is often the
flag of the buyer's country. Business is booming because few
of the countries he deals with have printing facilities that
can handle label printing for envelopes. So if you receive a
letter from a Latin country with a four-color sender's name
label on it, my home-based friend operating out of his apartment in Miami probably printed and sold the label!

Try Postcard Mailings for Faster Tests and Market Penetration

Postcards are becoming increasingly popular for selling by
direct mail. The postcard replaces the conventional letter
in a No. 10 envelope, which has been used for 100 years to
sell by direct mail. Postcard mailings:

1. **Are quick**—you can make such a mailing in a matter of
   hours and get lots of responses from your mailing list in
   just days.
2. **Save postage costs**—the average postcard costs just two-
   thirds of a regular first-class envelope mailing, and the
   card costs less to print.
3. **May receive more attention** by the recipient because they
   can be read quickly without having to fuss with opening
   the envelope and removing the contents to read them.

To use postcard mailings, follow these easy, proven steps, which have made money for lots of postcard direct-mail millionaires:

1. **Choose which products or services you want to sell** by postcard. Items that sell well by postcard are moneymaking plans, books, newsletters, magazines, etc.
2. **Get a list of prospects** for what you're selling. You can do this by renting names of people who've bought similar items by mail, or you can develop your own list by buying small classified ads on the Internet or in magazines and newspapers.
3. **Prepare the offer on the front and back** of the postcard. You can do this yourself or have someone prepare the offer on computer or a typewriter. Since your sales message is short, the wording can be prepared quickly—in just a few minutes.
4. **Make your mailing**—this is easy. You just apply the stamp to each postcard and drop them in a local mailbox. You can mail any time of the day or night; the mail will always be picked up and sent on its way to your prospects.
5. **Wait for the orders to come in.** You can have the orders sent to your home or a post office box—it does not seem to make much difference, as long as your offer interests the people to whom you sent it.
6. **Keep a record of your responses and orders.** You can expect anywhere from 0.5 to 1 percent to as high as a 2 percent response to your postcards. Much depends on your offer and the mailing list you use.

How much can you earn from postcard mailings? That depends in large part on the type of offer you're making, the list you use, and the price of your product. But if you mail 1,000 cards and get a 2 percent return, you'll have twenty orders. And if your item is priced at $30, you'll bring in 20 × $30 = $600. With the postcards costing 25 cents in the mail, your mailing cost will be $250. And with a product cost of $7.50 in the mail, your total costs will be $250 + $150 = $400. This leaves you a profit of $600 - $400 = $200 before overhead. Do this ten times and you'll bring in $2,000; 100 times will bring you $20,000!

Use Low-Cost Classified Ads to Build Your Direct-Marketing Wealth

Classified ads, such as those shown below, are the cheapest way for you to get national, and international, attention for your product or service. You can advertise in some small-circulation magazines and newspapers for only $3 when you use a classified ad. But a good classified ad can earn millions for you! Here are a few examples of money-producing classified ads:

MAKE MONEY AT HOME! Sell how-to books and kits. Free information. IWS, Inc., POB 186, Merrick, NY 11566.

NEED A BUSINESS LOAN? We can supply the lender you need. Write: IWS, Inc., POB 186, Merrick, NY 11566.

GET RICH IN BUSINESS! How? Use our ideas and methods. Write: IWS, Inc., POB 186, Merrick, NY 11566.

HOW TO GET RICH AT HOME. Free information shows you how! Write: IWS, Inc., POB 186, Merrick, NY 11566.

PICK THE INCOME YOU WANT! We'll show you how and where to earn it. Free information today. No selling required. Write: IWS, Inc., POB 186, Merrick, NY 11566.

To earn the most from your classified ads, pick the category of ad carefully. When you look at a magazine's or newspaper's classified ads you'll see that they use a number of eye-catching headings. Typical headings include:

BUSINESS OPPORTUNITIES	MONEY/LOANS AVAILABLE
Agents Wanted	Advertising Services
Books & Courses	Books & Periodicals
Business Services	Buy It Wholesale
Computers & Software	Distributors Wanted
Education & Instruction	Employment Information
Financial	For Inventors
Government Surplus	Help Wanted
Import–Export	Insurance
Inventions Wanted	Investments
Jewelry	Legal Services
Loans by Mail	Low-Interest Credit
Mailing Lists	Mail-Order Opportunities
Miscellaneous	Moneymaking Opportunities
New Products	Of Interest to All
Personal	Printing
Real Estate	Salespeople–Distributors
Songwriters	Start Your Own Business

Some of these headings will have more ads under them than others. If your ad can fit in two or more categories, consider putting the ad in a category that has fewer ads in it. Why? Because your ad will probably get more readership when there are fewer entries. For example, the heading "Legal Services" usually has only one or two entries under it. So:

A BWB decided to publish helpful legal books for "the person in the street"—that is, people who do not know much about the law. So he authorized the writing of a family will kit, a power-of-attorney book, a living trust kit, an estate planning kit, and several similar kits. Using classified ads, he sold some 250,000 of these books through the mail at prices ranging from $40 to $70 each. His income ranges between $250,000 and $300,000 a year. And as the population grows, more people need—and seek—such books. So his business grows every year. You—too—can sell unusual books or periodicals using classified ads to generate inquiries about your product and convert these interested people to a sale by sending them additional materials on your offer.

To make money in direct marketing using classified ads, follow these experience-based tips to your fortune:

- **Start your classified ad with a catchy idea**—such as making money, becoming healthier, living longer, etc.
- **Do not ask for money** in your ad—other than $1 or $2 for postage for heavy items. Asking for larger amounts will usually reduce the number of responses your ad gets.
- **Use a street address** or post office box address for responses, unless you want to spend time answering the telephone. Getting your responses by mail allows you to build a mailing list while acquiring response envelopes that you can sell for 15 cents each to houses specializing in buying active names.
- **Put an income number in your ad** whenever you can—people are more strongly motivated to answer when an ad says "MAKE $1,000 WEEKLY" than when there are no numbers in the ad.
- **Emphasize speedy results.** "MAKE $1,000 WEEKLY IMMEDIATELY," for example, promises fast results. Today, almost everyone seeks speed in their lives.
- **Feature free information** for the person responding. "FREE 20-PG BOOKLET" will generate many more responses than "BOOKLET SHOWS HOW TO . . . ."
- **Close with a selling message**, such as, "MONEY NEVER STOPS" (coming into your business).
- **Use uplifting words** whenever you can, such as PROFITS, GOOD MONEY, STAY HOME, EASY WORK, HIGH MONTHLY INCOME, BOOMING BUSINESS, SKYROCKET YOUR INCOME, GET TONS OF MONEY, UNLIMITED CASH INCOME, etc.
- **Run your ad in publications where similar ads appear.** Why? The other advertisers are spending money to run their ads. If the ads appear month after month, it means that money is being made from the ad. You—too—can make money from your ad!
- **Continue running a moneymaking ad** for as long as you bring in more than the ad costs. You can generate income from the

names you get in three ways: by selling what you're offering; by renting out the names to other direct-marketing firms; and by selling the envelopes and postcards, after the name has been stored in a computer file.

- **Send a catalog of your offers** to people who respond to your classified ad. This will make maximum sales impact. A catalog is usually not thrown away. Instead, people keep it and refer to it again and again—eventually sending you money— which is the whole purpose of your classified ad!
- **Place your ads on local bulletin boards** in stores and malls to get additional coverage. Just cut your classified ad out of the magazine or newspaper in which it appears, have photocopies made of the ad, mount them on a 3 × 5-inch card and tack the card on bulletin boards all over town. Your ad will generate extra income for you at no additional cost!

Some classified ads have generated millions in income. Hopefully, your classified ads will do the same! Then you can write me a letter like the one from this BWB from the Midwest:

"I have been using your methods to create tons of money in the last six months. Just a little tip I picked up in your *101 Great Mail-Order Businesses* book has made me financially independent." On the phone the reader told me, "My wife and I just moved into a beautiful new house—thanks to my mail-order business. And my wife loves working in the business with me." He goes on to write in his letter that he faxed to me "We have recently opened a retail store devoted to improving one's mind, and we specialize in self-help motivational books and newsletters, as well as framed motivational pictures."

And what is this successful BWB doing to "create tons of money"? He publishes a newsletter that helps parents teach their children all kinds of sports—baseball, soccer, lacrosse, hockey, Rollerblading, hiking, etc. His newsletter is priced at $34.95 and is published six times a year. Now he's considering publishing another newsletter—this one will be on motivation for small-business people. Not bad for just six months' work! And many of his subscribers came from small classified ads he ran.

Build Your Direct-Marketing Wealth with Space Ads

Space ads, also called *display ads*, such as the one shown in Figure 2-1, can produce enormous numbers of orders for your products or services. What's more, space ads bring in the names of new buyers to whom you can sell more products or services. And you can rent out these names to other direct-marketing firms to earn "pure money"—that is, money that you just deposit in the bank. You don't have to ship any products or deliver any services. All you need send is a tape or disk containing the names of your customers! And—if you use a mailing-list manager—that person will do the shipping for you.

Some people insist on using full-page space ads, like the one in Figure 2-1. But we've found that smaller ads—half page, quarter page, even 1 inch—can pull profitably at a much lower cost than full-page ads. Our half-page ads (see Figure 2-2) pull again and again. Yet they cost only a little more than half the cost of a full-page ad!

Here are the important characteristics of space ads—full page down to just 1 inch:

- **Use a good headline for your space ad.** Some people say that 75 percent of an ad's pull is in its headline. While you can argue about the number, the point is that your headline is extremely important.
- **Promise your buyers strong results.** Almost everyone in the world seeks a higher income, better looks, more successful personal relations, etc. Promise any of these in your space ad and your results are almost guaranteed to be profitable. See if these headlines could induce you to buy a specific product or service: *Make $100,000 in the Next 10 Weeks—from the Comfort of Your Own Home! Add 3 Inches to Your Biceps in 3 Weeks—With NO Exercise! Get More Dates Than You Can Handle—Before Next Saturday Night! Lose 10 Pounds in 10 Days to Become Lean and Luscious!* Try some headlines for your own product or service. I'll be glad to review them free of charge if you're a subscriber to my newsletter.
- **Use an uplifting illustration in your space ad.** Pick the illustration to emphasize the results your buyer will obtain if he

HOW TO GET
GUARANTEED LOAN MONEY

"I ALMOST LOST MY HOME BEFORE FINDING THIS INSTANT CASH PLAN!"

I NEEDED MONEY BADLY—to pay my bills so I could get rid of the bill collectors banging on my door—day and night!

BUT THE LENDERS WOULDN'T EVEN TALK to me since my credit was so bad! "Get lost!" is what they said, or told me in their eyes. I was desperate. My kids hardly had any food; my car wouldn't go a block without breaking down; the landlord was ready to throw us out of our tiny, unheated house.

I FRANTICALLY RAN AROUND, looking for money. Yet everywhere I turned I got a NO along with a cold, cold shoulder. I couldn't—it seemed—raise a thin dime to pay my bills. What could I do? My wife was ready to leave me, taking our kids with her!

THEN ONE NIGHT, WHILE LYING AWAKE IN BED, I discovered the idea of GUARANTEED LOAN MONEY. I jumped up and madly searched for a pencil and paper to jot down the ideas pouring out of my mind. It seemed like the perfect answer to anyone who:

- Has bad credit
- Has been turned down for a loan
- Doesn't have a good job history
- Needs money so badly "he can smell it"
- Needs personal, business, or real estate loans to make money

BUT BEFORE I STARTED FEELING GOOD, I decided to test out my GUARANTEED LOAN MONEY METHOD to see if it would work. To give it an "acid test" I went back to several lenders who had turned me down in the last few weeks.

TO MY GREAT SURPRISE EACH LENDER SAID YES! That meant each would lend me the money I needed—with almost NO QUESTIONS! I was stunned! The method really does work. Joy hit me!

TO BE DOUBLY SURE THE GUARANTEED LOAN MONEY METHOD WORKS, I had some of my "bad-credit" friends try it. They got the money they needed in hours! After they had been turned down just a few days earlier!

RIGHT AWAY I KNEW I WAS ON TO SOMETHING GOOD. But to be sure, I called friends 3,000 miles away and told them about my GUARANTEED LOAN MONEY METHOD. "Try it out this way," I told them. "Let me know the results you get!"

WITHIN HOURS I GOT EXCITED CALLS saying, "It works! It works! I got the first loan I've ever been able to get in 15 years. And it only took 20 minutes! I love you for what you've done for my family and myself! You should put this method into a book." Now it's available from IWS—the entire method.

USING THIS METHOD YOU SHOULD BE ABLE TO GET:

- Unsecured signature loans for personal use
- Business loans of any type
- Real estate loans of any type
- Any other type of loan needed
- Financing that's "tough to get"

SO IF YOU NEED ANY KIND OF LOAN, you should get a copy of my big, helpful, get-out-of-hock GUARANTEED LOAN MONEY METHOD! And if you order now I'll include FREE a copy of "Diversified Loan Sources" which gives YOU hundreds of money sources for this great Method!

BE POOR NO MORE! Get the cash you need NOW! Let me show you how to get GUARANTEED LOAN MONEY sooner than you ever thought possible.

Send or call TODAY for your GUARANTEED LOAN MONEY METHOD KIT AND BONUS "DIVERSIFIED LOAN SOURCES!"

Enclosed is $100.00. Send me the GUARANTEED LOAN MONEY METHOD plus my free bonus—"Diversified Loan Sources"

NAME

ADDRESS

CITY   STATE   ZIP

To order by credit card please include: Credit Card #   Expiration Date

SIGNATURE   PHONE#

(Send Check or Money Order or charge by phone—516-766-5850.)
Send order to IWS, Inc., 24 Canterbury Rd., Rockville Centre, NY 11570.

Figure 2-1. A typical full-page display ad.

BUSINESS INFORMATION KITS—business and real estate finance, real-estate business, business borrowing, business cash program, financing real estate, grants and fund raising, mail-order direct-mail business, business starting, franchise business.

FINANCIAL BROKER/FINDER/BUSINESS BROKER/BUSINESS CONSULTANT KIT Contents: Financial Broker Guide; Business Broker Guide; Finder Guide; Business Consultant Guide; How to Take a Company Public; Government Regulations for Selling Stock to the Public; Executive Search Firms; Typical Financial Broker/Finder/Business Broker Forms and Agreements for Loans, Real Estate and Inventions; Lenders for Business and Real Estate; Directory of Small Business Investment Companies; 12 Speed-Read Books; 485 pages; $99.50.

REAL ESTATE BUSINESS SUCCESS KIT Contents: Mortgage Broker Guide; Mortgage Banker Guide; Income-Property Operation Data; Raw-Land Purchase and Sale; Industrial-Property Operation; Real-Estate Financing Methods; 2,500 Real-Estate Loan Sources; Sources of Distressed Properties; State Real-Estate Agencies and Administrations; Tax-Aspects of Real-Estate Operation and Ownership; Keeping Accurate Records of Real-Estate Operating Costs; Profit Aspects of Various Types of Real-Estate; 6 Speed-Read Books; 466 pages; $99.50.

BUSINESS BORROWERS BUSINESS SUCCESS KIT Contents: Reading Guide; How to Borrow Business Money; Glossary of Money Words and Terms; Business Methods for Money Borrowers; Selected Loan and Equity Capital Directory; How to Prepare Loan Applications; Directory of Selected Housing, Land, Farm and Business Programs in the Government; The Radical New Road to Wealth; Practice Forms for Loan Applications; Lenders of Funds for Business and Real Estate. 7 Speed Read Books; 596 pages; $99.50.

Credit Card Orders —Phone 1-516-766-5850

Please send me the BUSINESS INFORMATION KITS checked above. Enclosed is $__________ (Check or money order).

NAME

ADDRESS

CITY STATE ZIP

TO ORDER BY CREDIT CARD PLEASE INCLUDE THE FOLLOWING: Signature

Credit Card # Expiration Date Phone #

Send your order to IWS, Inc., 24 Canterbury Rd., Rockville Centre, NY 11570

Figure 2-2. A typical half-page ad.

or she buys what you offer. For example, with a weight-reduction program, show BEFORE *and* AFTER photos of a user of your method. For moneymaking programs, show a typical buyer in front of a luxury auto, at the wheel of a yacht, and so on. Such photos help your potential buyers put themselves in the same position by buying what you offer. Sales improve enormously when you include a suitable photo (or drawing) in your space ad.

• **Offer your buyers a bonus or bonuses.** Some buyers pay more attention to the bonus item(s) than they do to the main product or service they're buying. Thus, the bonuses in Figure 2-3 are mentioned in every letter and phone call we get ordering the item described in the ad. A suitable bonus can turn a losing ad into a winning one. And even a winning ad can be turned into a gushing money machine that delivers great bundles of money into your home mailbox every day of the week that mail is delivered. And, good friend, here's a Ty Hicks secret I never put into print before. *Use three bonus items—readers seem to go wild over three bonuses—as compared to one, two, or more than three!* Every ad of ours that has three bonus items in it has generated enormous amounts of money for us.

• **Ask for payment with the order.** Space ads that operate on the two-step basis—i.e., the buyer asks for information, (step 1), you send a flier or catalog in response to the request, the buyer reads what you send him or her and then orders, (step 2)—do not produce revenue as well as one-step ads. In the one-step ad, you ask for money and the buyer sends it, or calls you to order by credit card. And do you know what, good friend? In today's frenzied world, people don't want to wait for a two-step process. They want everything **NOW!** That's good for you because you get your money faster.

• **Include an ordering coupon in your ad.** In recent years some advertisers have eliminated the coupons from their ads. Why? Because it gave them more room for sales words. But this trend seems to have ended. Another Ty Hicks secret for you, my good friend, is this: *Buyers enjoy filling out coupons. It gives them a feeling of purpose, a sense of doing something worthwhile for their future!* So use a coupon for every space ad that's a half page or larger.

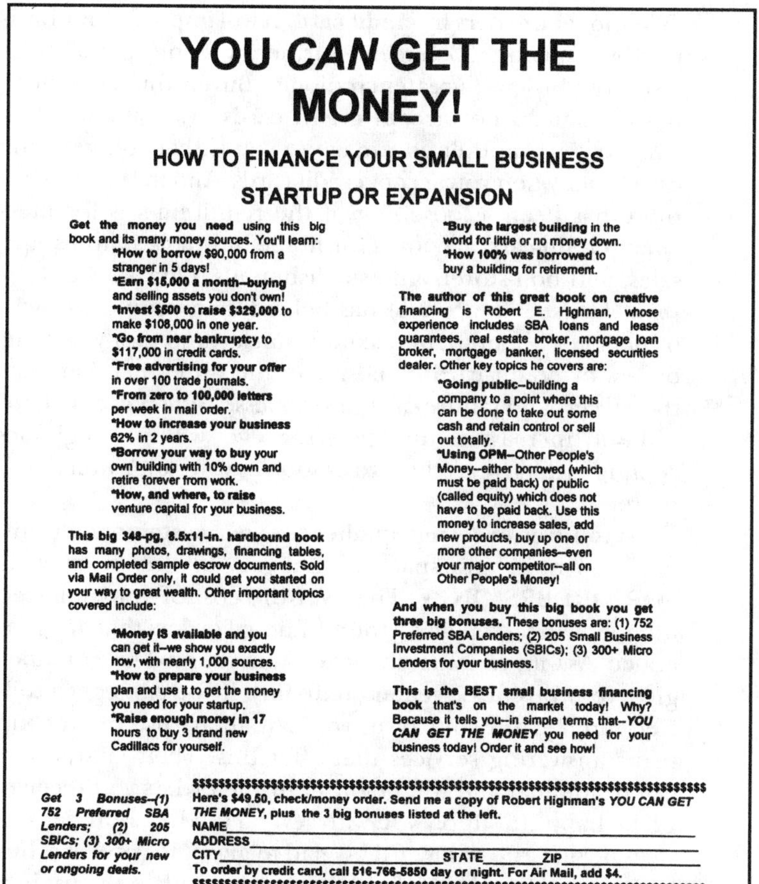

Figure 2-3. Offer bonuses for better response to your display ads.

- **Offer to take orders by credit card.** It will improve your business by as much as 33 percent. Further, accepting credit cards gives your business greater credibility. Buyers think that businesses that do not accept credit cards are somehow less trustworthy. Another advantage to you is that you get your cash faster when you accept credit cards. And in recent years there has been a loosening of the requirements for merchant credit-card accounts for home businesses, non-swipe sales, and non-storefront establishments. Our *Merchant Account Kit* (see Figure 2-4) has helped many home-business owners get a merchant account quickly and easily. Taking orders by credit card could mean the difference between the success and failure of your business. And credit card use will only increase as time passes. So get with it—begin accepting orders by credit card as soon as you can. You'll never regret it!
- **Use a toll-free ordering number for your customers.** Prominently print in your space ad that your toll-free number is **FOR ORDERS ONLY.** That way the cost of your toll-free number will be repaid by the additional orders that are generated. As with your merchant account, your toll-free number gives your business greater credibility. If you can't get a toll-free number on your own, you can always use one of the many answering services that offer this. Their charge per call is nominal and will be offset by the orders you receive. I'll be happy to supply you with several toll-free number services if you write to me. I'd be glad to give it to you here, but there is turnover in the field that might outdate the list in a short time. You can even get toll-free service for overseas customers—if you sell internationally. Such a number will really up your sales income from customers around the world who love to order by credit card over the telephone!

To show you how space ads can build any business, let me tell you about a Florida reader who gave me these details about his fortune-building activities during a recent telephone conversation:

"Your book *Mail-Order Success Secrets* gave me the idea for my mail-order business. I decided to sell name labels for overseas markets—especially the Latin American Hispanic areas.

HOW, AND WHERE, TO GET A

MERCHANT ACCOUNT
FOR YOUR BUSINESS

TO ACCEPT ALL MAJOR CREDIT CARDS FOR SALES

Do you want to make sales by credit card in your business? Are your customers offering to pay for your products or services by credit card?

If you answer YES to either question, then you need a MERCHANT ACCOUNT for your business so you can accept credit card payments.

Have you tried to get a MERCHANT ACCOUNT and been turned down? If you have, you know the feeling of rejection the turndown gave you. But don't worry, there's plenty of hope for you!

Ty Hicks, well-known business author, shows you exactly how, and where you can get a MERCHANT ACCOUNT TODAY. Better yet, you have unlimited free consulting time with Ty by phone or in person to answer any questions you may have about getting your MERCHANT ACCOUNT.

Here's what you get in this helpful, practical kit:

Why Get a Merchant Account?	Filled-Out Telephone Order Form for Credit Card Sales
How to Get a Merchant Account Today	Equipment Lease Agreement for Printer and Terminal
Getting a Merchant Account Directly from a Bank	Using an Independent Sales Organization (ISO)
Reasons Why Banks Reject Merchant Account Applications	Working with an ISO to Get Your Merchant Account
How to Get Your Merchant Account at a Smaller Bank	How to Protect Your ISO Dealings
What You'll Do to Get a Bank Merchant Account	How to Deal with a Typical ISO When Getting Your Account
Where to Apply for Your Merchant Account	Practical Tips on Working with ISOs Anywhere
Using Sample Applications to Improve Your Approval Chances	Typical ISO Agreements You'l Fill Out and Sign
Equipment You'll Use with Your Merchant Account Today	Appointment Agreement for an ISO
How to Key in a Card Charge on Your Merchant Account	ISO Agreement to Procure a Merchant Account
Telephone Procedures for Merchant Account Charges	Merchant Cover Sheet for an ISO
Saving Money on Your Terminal and Printer Equipment	Merchant Authorization for an ISO
Typical Merchant Account Application Used Today	ISO Client Application
Filled-Out Merchant Account Application	Equipment Sales Agreement for a Merchant Account
Resolutions to Open a Deposit Account for Your Merchant Status	Sample Bank Credit Card Service Rates
Equipment Purchase Agreement for Your Merchant Account	Equipment Purchase Agreement for a Merchant Account
Merchant Account Terminal of the Type Used Today	Use a Credit Card Processor to Handle Your Orders
Some of the Credit Cards You'll Be Accepting in Your Business	Use an Answering Service to Handle Your Credit Card Orders
Printer Used with Credit Card Sales-One of Many Types Available	Answering Service Application Form
Typical Credit Card Sales Slip You'll Use as a Merchant	Typical Answering Service Fees
Mail Order Coupon for Use with Credit Card Sales	Buy, or Merge, with a Firm Having a Merchant Account
Telephone Order Form for Credit Card Sales in any Business	

NOTE: Because you may get a Merchant Account from just one phone number in this kit, it is sold with the understanding that there will be no refunds made; each sale is final.

Enclosed is $100.00. Send me the *MERCHANT ACCOUNT KIT.*

NAME
ADDRESS
CITY   STATE   ZIP
To order by Credit Card please include: Credit Card #   Expiration Date
SIGNATURE   PHONE #

*(Send Check or Money Order or charge by phone—516-766-5850).
Send order to IWS., Inc., 24 Canterbury Rd., Rockville Centre, NY 11570.

Figure 2-4. Details about IWS, Inc.'s, Merchant Account Kit.

Checking other address labels, I found that none contained His-panic artwork—such as the flags of various South American nations, soccer-team emblems, national flowers, etc. I made some designs and had them printed. Showing them to Hispan-ics, I was amazed at their reaction. Every one of these people snapped up these address labels because they loved the colors and designs. So I launched my business by taking space ads in ethnic magazines and newspapers. The results were outstand-ing. I now sell 200 self-adhesive address labels for $15 via air mail. My business is booming because the space ads are pulling so strongly. And I have the whole world in front of me—because people everywhere love their nation's flag, their national flower, etc. Address labels may seem like a common product, but they're making me rich!"

Space ads are big in women's magazines where a variety of products are sold. Some of the biggest selling direct-mar-keted products for women are health-related. You can make a fortune in direct marketing to women items such as:

- **Vitamins** and other natural health-food products designed to improve and/or maintain women's health.
- **Exercise products** of many different types—from the small weights carried by joggers to full-size exercise machines for the home family room or basement.
- **Health publications** directed at women—especially newslet-ters presenting new ideas for healthier living in today's time-stressed world of working women.
- **Diet and personal health-oriented recipes** for women in-terested in controlling their weight and improving their physical performance at work and in their sports activities and hobbies.

Small one-inch space ads can bring you a fortune with any of the above products or services. Look in recent issues of women's magazines and you'll see many examples of BWBs who are earning a fortune from such direct marketing.

A BWB friend of mine in California told me he sells vitamins to women using small space ads. Some Monday mornings he re-ceives as many as 400 orders in the mail in amounts from $5 to

$89. His main job is to open the envelopes, endorse the checks, enter them on the bank deposit slip and go to the bank to deposit the day's receipts. After that he goes to the local race track and is always there in time for the first race. His direct-marketing income from space ads allowed him to retire three times!

Use Catalogs with Space Ads to Zoom Response and Sales

Catalogs are rarely thrown away until the next one comes along from the same company. So a catalog is like a book—it stays around longer than a newspaper or magazine. Our forty-eight-page IWS catalog, for example, which sells for $5, brings in thousands of dollars of business, year after year. Figures 2-4 and 2-5 show excerpt pages from this catalog.

You can get free four-color space-ad publicity for your catalog if you work with one of the catalog houses that does catalog promotions. Here's how it works:

1. **You send a copy of your catalog** to the promotion house for evaluation—many catalogs are accepted.
2. **You sign an agreement** with the catalog house allowing them to charge anywhere from $1 to $5 for a copy of your catalog.
3. **You allow the catalog house** to take four-color pictures of your catalog for use in their promotion.
4. **You send a copy of your catalog** to every name the catalog house sends you. Sometimes the number of names can be in the thousands; the catalog house keeps whatever money it receives for your catalog as payment for the ad it ran for your catalog.
5. **You fulfill all orders** received from your catalog. Sales can be in the many thousands of dollars from just one catalog—promoted by small space ads circulated by the catalog house!

A recent catalog startup is an excellent example of using space ads along with other direct marketing to produce large sales:

Do you need money for business or real estate?

If you do (and who doesn't?), you need:

SUCCESSFUL FINANCING TECHNIQUES FOR BUSINESS AND REAL ESTATE,

the newest book by Ty Hicks. A big 90 pages, 8.5 x 11 in., this new book covers Loans, Grants, Venture Capital, Going Public, 100% Financing for Real Estate, Mail-Order Success Secrets, and Using Borrowed Money to Make Money in Exporting. Look over the topics listed below. Then send a check or money order for $24.95 for First Class Mail delivery of your big book. Act now and get three big bonuses—(1) Business Lenders List—20 pages; (2) Real Estate Lenders List—14 pages; (3) How to Raise $300,000 to $50 Million by Going Public—10 pages. Here's what you get in this NEW book by Ty Hicks:

SECTION 1: How, and Where, to Get Loans for Any Business

Get Private Money for Your Business/Real Estate Needs
The Almost-Perfect Loan for You
Getting Loans the Easiest Ways Today
Using Credit Cards to Get Your Business Started
How to Raise Big Money Today
Get SBA Loans Faster, Easier
Help Banks Make Small Loans
Get SBIC Money for Businesses
Getting Loans in the United States from Overseas
Go Where You're Welcome and Get the Money You Need
Get Personal Loans for Clients
How to Get "Lo-Doc" Loans Today for Your Clients
Ty Hicks on Making Money as a Factor
Take People Out of Loans/Never Pay "Front Money" for a Loan

SECTION 2: Getting Venture Capital for a Business

Getting Venture Capital for Your Startup Business
Find Venture Capital Faster Today
Get Venture Capital and Grow Rich
Venture Capitalists Avidly Seeking Promising New Businesses
Go With the Flow for Venture-Capital Millions
How to Raise Big Money Today
Venture Capital is Booming for You—Again!
Find Venture Capital Sooner with These 7 Easy Steps
Easier, Faster Ways for Raising Venture Capital

SECTION 3: How, and Where, to Find Free Money Grants

How Almost Anyone Can Get a Free-Money Grant
Get Grants Easier Today This Way
Where to Get Large, and Small, Grants Today
Easiest Grants to Get Could Be For You
Get Grant Money Sooner, Easier
Find, and Get, Grants in Your Area Now
Getting a Grant for Doing Good for Others
Get Grants Easier Today Than Ever Before
Get the Easiest Kind of Grant Available Today

SECTION 4: Getting Public Money That Never Need Be Repaid

Raise Money with An IPO—Initial Public Offering
Get Public Money Using the New IPO Rules
An Easy Way to Raise Public Money
Get Public Money in the New IPO Rage
How To Raise a Quick Million Dollars
Get Public Money for Your Business Ideas
Getting Public Money is Easier Than Ever Today

SECTION 5: Making Big Money in Your Own Business

Get the Best Tax Shelter Ever Invented!
Fast Way to Start Making Money Now
Get Into Today's Most Needed Business
The Fastest Way to Your Own Business Success
Getting Started in Business is Easier Than Many People Think
Ideal Home Business for Married People
Get a Credit-Card Merchant Account Faster Today
How to Get Started in the Easiest Money Business
Using Credit Cards to Get Your Business Started
How to Have Fun While Making Big Money
Run Your Business from Home—and Grow Rich!

SECTION 6: Proven Money-Making Methods for Real-Estate Riches

5 Ways to Get 100% Financing of Real Estate
How, and Where, to Get Income Real Estate Down Payment Money
For Real-Estate Wealth, Get Assumable Mortgage Properties
"Paper Real Estate" Can Make You Rich
Use a "Sandwich Lease" for Paper Real Estate Profits
Make Big Money in "Paper" Real Estate
Real Estate Down-Payment Strategies That Work
Get Into "Paper" Real Estate Now/Secrets of Getting No-Cash Real Estate

SECTION 7: Mail Order Success Secrets for Beginning Wealth Builders

Make the Easiest Mail-Order Fortune Now
Secrets of Mail-Order Success for You
Seven Steps to Your Mail-Order Millions
How to Get Started in Mail Order for Almost Free
Use Catalogs to Make Your Mail Millions
How to Make Mail-Order Millions Today
Make Mailbox Millions Now
How to Become a Mailbox Millionaire
Mailbox Millions the Easy Way

SECTION 8: How to Make Riches in Exporting Using Borrowed Money

An Easy Way to Make Export Millions
Fast Export-Import Trade Leads & Finance
Good Ways to Make Your Export Fortune Now
Make Export Riches Today
Export Financing You Can Get Now
Easy Ways to Make Money in Exporting Today
How, and Where, to Get Export Financing
Seven Easy Steps to Get Started in Exporting
How, and Where, to Finance Your Exports
Start Exporting Your Way to Wealth in Just Hours
Export Financing Gets Better Worldwide
Exporting Can Be Your Way to Business Riches
Free Trade Assistance—Just a Phone Call Away
Get Your Export Financing Faster Today

ORDER NOW! Get your 3 BIG BONUS items: Business Lenders; Real Estate Lenders: Raise Public Money!

Send me Ty Hicks' SUCCESSFUL FINANCING TECHNIQUES FOR BUSINESS AND REAL ESTATE. My check/money order for $24.95 is enclosed. And be sure to send my 3 bonus items with my book via First Class Mail.

NAME_____

ADDRESS_____

CITY_____ STATE_____ ZIP_____

SEND ORDER TO: IWS, INC., POB 186, MERRICK, NY 11566-0186

Figure 2-5. A sample page from the IWS, Inc., catalog.

Two partners saw the need for a clothing and accessories catalog for young women, ages ten to twenty-four. This was a
neglected market because most catalog houses felt that women
in this age bracket didn't have enough money to generate large
sales. These two partners disagreed, and decided to start their
own catalog to serve the market they believed existed. They
started the catalog in the apartment of one of the partners.
Sales in the first year were $130,000. In its third year the cata-
log had sales of $30 million! This certainly shows that the other
catalog operators were wrong about the market. To achieve
such rapid success, the founders of this home-based catalog:
(1) Aimed their mailings at a neglected market; the young
women receiving the catalog were delighted to get it because
it enabled them to shop by mail for clothing and accessories
they needed; (2) Offered current "cool" fashions that appealed
to the age group at which their catalog was aimed; (3) Fea-
tured prices that were somewhat less than those of stores selling
the same or similar items. This made catalog buying more attractive to the young women who received it.

Now what does this real-life example show you—as a possible catalog operator working from your own home? Here
are three important pointers from this successful catalog:

1. **Find a niche market** for your catalog and it will prosper—
   and so will you.
2. **Select, and promote, unusual products** or services in your
   catalog.
3. **Give a price break** to your customers and they'll come
   back to buy—again and again!

Besides using space ads to promote their catalog, these
two partners came up with a great idea:

They paid students to give away their catalog free to other
students. These same student-distributors also placed free copies of the catalog in schools, colleges, and other areas where
school kids gather. The free catalogs got word-of-mouth advertising going—giving more free publicity and endorsements
to the catalog and its products. Result? Sales boomed, as detailed above.

A catalog promoted through space ads, free distribution, classified ads, on the Internet, and by telemarketing can make you rich in direct marketing! So if your product or service has catalog possibilities, draw up a short business plan (see Chapter 1) and send it to me. I'll be happy to review it completely free of charge—if you subscribe to one of my newsletters.

Get on the Air to Promote Your Products or Services

You can direct-market on the air via the radio in two ways:

1. During interviews conducted by the station host—you give information on your products or services that can be beneficial to listeners.
2. With 30-second, or longer, commercials that promote your product or service.

We've used both methods in our newsletter and publishing business. Of the two methods, interviews—which are free to you—produce faster results.

Getting on the radio interview or talk-show circuit is easy if you have a product or service that can help the listeners in your area. Typical products or services that pull talk-show interview requests include:

- **Advice or information on child care,** education, baby-sitting, and medical and dental treatment.
- **Advice on human relations**—with spouse, friends, business associates, and neighbors.
- **Advice on home-business** selection and startup, including financing.
- **Advice on vacation planning,** trips to take, what to look for in terms of cost, places to see, etc.

If you manufacture, print, or otherwise produce your product or service you are probably the best one to get yourself on the talk-show circuit. All you do is follow these easy steps:

1. **Locate the radio stations** in your area. Do this by checking in the yellow pages under "Radio Stations & Broadcasting Companies."
2. **Choose the stations** you think might be interested in interviewing you or one of your business associates.
3. **Call or write the radio stations,** telling about your product or service, and why it would interest their listeners. Agree to answer call-in questions from listeners. Most stations love this program format.
4. **Agree to whatever schedule the radio station offers** you for an interview. Most interviews can be done over the phone because it's not necessary for you to be in the studio. You can be at your home desk, answering the interviewer's questions. Call-in questions can be answered the same way.
5. **Subtly "push" your product or service** during the interview. If it's a book or course, refer to it during your answers to questions. Don't be afraid—your interviewer expects you to mention your product or service. And the interviewer may even help you by saying, "On page 123 you refer to Roy, who made a fortune in export mail order. How did he get started in that business?" This is your cue— you answer the question, referring to various incidents mentioned in the book. Result? People want to dash out and buy your book!
6. **Never be frightened by an interview!** You'll have fun answering questions while getting free advertising for your product or service. And when other stations hear about you, you'll get more requests for more interviews! Could anything be nicer than combining fun with free ads that bring in piles of cash to your bank account?

One of the best examples of selling books by radio interviews is that of a West Coast author. He sold some $256,000 in books during radio interviews. And these interviews cost him less than $100. His only cost was the postage and paper for the letter telling the stations he's available! Another author says that an interview a day could sell 9 million books in three years! If you earned just $1 per copy sold, your income would be $9 million in three years, or $3 million a year! Not bad for just talking!

In my book and newsletter publishing work I do hundreds of radio interviews all over the country. A station calls a week or so in advance, telling me the time and day they'd like to do the interview. I usually agree to their time slot. This makes it easier for the station to make plans. And do you know what? When you agree to the station's time frame, the interview usually goes longer! This means *you get more free time to push your item or service!*

These interviews sell thousands of newsletters and books. And they are fun to do—especially answering the call-in questions. They are my way of selling at no cost—other than time. You—too—can do the same and build great wealth in your own home-based business!

Sell Worldwide Using TV Infomercials

I'm sure you see dozens of TV infomercials—typically on late-night shows. These infomercials cover hundreds of different products and services—from auto windshield wiper blades to zebra-skin rugs. The infomercials are another great example of direct marketing. They sell directly to customers—you and me. All we need do is call an 800 or 888 number, place our order with our credit card, and—presto— the item is shipped to us.

And the beautiful aspect of infomercials is that they pull for years after the program ends. We get responses to our cable infomercials for as long as three years after the program is aired! All I can think is that some people take longer to react than others.

To sell your product or service using an infomercial, follow these easy steps, starting right now:

1. **Decide what you will sell** via your infomercial—pick a needed product or service so you get a big response.
2. **Choose a suitable price** for your product or service. We chose $99 for our "Mailbox Millionaire" course; we felt

that a price under $100 would be attractive to most buyers. Sales have proven it.

3. **Get a producer for your infomercial.** You can get a competent producer at a local school that teaches TV production. Such producers will often work for you free of charge, just to get the credit line on your show.

4. **Select an actor or actress for your infomercial.** This could be you—if you like performing. Or, if you dislike acting, contact a local acting school and ask them to send you a few candidates for the part. You'll get more volunteers than you need! Again—many will work free of charge just to get the credit line on screen.

5. **Produce the infomercial.** This can be done right in your own home using a video camera, saving the cost of a set. Your only cost will be for the videotape, plus a few cents for electricity.

6. **Use the interview technique** to present your first show. All you need is a person to ask you or your stand-in actor or actress questions about your product or service. The questions are answered in a way that shows the product's features and selling points. With a series of well-planned questions you can have an interesting show that will pour dollars into your bank account every time it airs.

7. **Negotiate for airtime for your infomercial.** Most producers of infomercials do not pay for airtime. Instead, the station agrees to run the infomercial free and shares in the sales income. Typically, the station receives 50 percent of the money that comes in, which pays for the airtime. So if your infomercial brings in $25,000 in sales during, and after, its airing, you keep half, or $12,500, and the station keeps the other half. So your only cost will be the videotape and the making of three copies of the original!

As you can see, you can get started direct-marketing via infomercials produced at home at low cost.

Now I'd like to let you in on one of the best-kept secrets in mail order and direct marketing today. This secret is almost a guaranteed way for you to get rich in mail order—sooner than you think.

Go International to Build Your Home-Based Mail-Order Riches

When I talk to Beginning Wealth Builders around the world, I like to tell them to use my *Triple-M* formula for getting rich, namely *Make Mail Millions*. For truly, good friend, *you can make your fortune in international mail selling today easier, sooner, and better than in almost any other business!* In this book I give you the approach that works for thousands of successful, happy BWBs everywhere.

No matter where you live you can sell the products of your country in another country by putting the power of the mails to work alongside carefully chosen classified or space ads, and—possibly—telemarketing and video infomercials. How can I say this? Because—friend—I operate an international mail sales business that for years has sold products throughout the world. Also, a number of my friends make big money the same way.

"But what about postage?" you ask. "The postage bill will kill me!" Not if you figure your postage as part of the cost of doing business. Where postage costs seem excessively high (they really are not) in relation to your product cost, you can:

1. **Add postage costs** to the product cost.
2. **Show the postage cost separately** and have your customer pay the postage.
3. **Ship the item by surface mail** (sea mail) at the lowest possible cost.

Now, let's say I've convinced you that international mail-order sales might be for you. How can *you* get started? Here's how—in eight easy, fast steps.

STEP 1: PICK YOUR OVERSEAS MAIL-SALES PRODUCT OR SERVICE

In many cases, people overseas need different products than customers in domestic markets do. For example, a good friend of mine has a highly profitable and fast-growing business selling thousands of technical books that he markets by overseas mail sales. Are these the recently published or newer books? No! They are *old* books that were published twenty-five to fifty years ago.

"How can he sell such old stuff?" you ask. "Very easily," I reply. Many overseas countries—such as the developing nations—are so far behind in their technology that a twenty-five-year-old book seems brand new to them! These "old" books are in such great demand that my friend pays finders' fees to people who find copies of old engineering books in good condition. If he can't find enough copies of a good book, he pays to have it reprinted, after getting permission in writing from the publisher of the book.

When picking your overseas product or service, keep these important ideas in mind. Overseas people:

- **Seek** and need *lower-cost* products and services
- **Prefer** *simpler* products and services
- **Will read** *long ads* and advertising copy
- **Are willing** to *wait* during a long delivery period
- **Often pay** by *credit card*, giving you instant cash

STEP 2: USE IDEAS AS GUIDES

Using the above ideas as guides, you can start to explore—that is, test—your product choice on a dry-run basis. For instance, let's say that you see an ad for the auction of several different types of can openers, both manual and electric. Right away you decide that one of these might be a good product for overseas mail-order sales. So you start to explore the profit potential for yourself.

You go to your local library and get several books on the countries in which you think you can sell can openers. From a careful reading of these books you quickly learn that:

- The people in the countries you've been considering *don't* use canned foods because they can't afford them.
- No other canned goods are used in these countries.
- Electric can openers wouldn't sell because very few homes have electricity.

But your research isn't wasted. You learn that the people in the countries you have in mind are wild for:

- Fancy combs
- Pocket knives
- Cheap wristwatches
- Low-cost bicycles
- Small solid-state hand-charged radios

With this information in hand, you dry-run your market more completely. To do this, you more accurately select the countries in which you'll do overseas mail sales. Let's see how you'll do that.

STEP 3: INVESTIGATE YOUR OVERSEAS MAIL-SALES MARKETS

To be a mail-order sales market, an overseas country must have:

- **Enough people**—say 100,000 or more—to support sales
- **Demand** for a product based on: (1) contact with the outside world, (2) local customs, or (3) personal habits
- **Access** to publications that carry mail-order ads
- **Dealers** interested in handling mail-order type products

To find out if the countries that interest you can meet these requirements:

1. **Check population statistics** using *The World Almanac*, the United Nations *Demographic Yearbook*, and similar publications available in your local library.
2. **Use geography** and similar books, also available in most libraries, to learn how much the people know about external products, and what local or personal customs might lead to sales of the products you're promoting.
3. **Next check the international distribution** of the publications in which you might advertise. You can do this by glancing at the circulation statement given in *Standard Rate and Data*, available in any large public library. If the overseas circulation is small—say only a few hundred copies—then you might want to consider using local publications published in each country instead of large

international publications. This approach can considerably reduce your ad cost because ad rates in local publications are lower than in international ones.

4. **Obtain a copy** of Volumes 1 and 2 of *Worldwide Riches Opportunities: 2,500 Great Leads for Getting Rich in Overseas Trade Without Leaving Home*, $25 per volume, from IWS, Inc., P.O. Box 186, Merrick, NY 11566. Check in each volume the listing of dealers, importers, wholesalers, and the like who might handle your product in the countries that interest you. If you find several importers seeking your product, you can assume that it is worth sending letters or faxing each importer to find out the quantities, delivery dates, and prices that interest him or her.

Once you have the information listed above, you can make a definite decision about each country you've considered. To show you how to do this, let me give you two examples of people who've hit it big in international mail sales.

STEP 4: MAKE YOUR PROMOTION CHOICES PROFITABLE

Ted C. wanted to go into international mail sales because he felt he had three great products—ladies' synthetic dresses, synthetic bed sheets, and men's synthetic shirts. Ted believed these products were great because he:

- Could buy rejects from a local mill
- Could repair the products easily—if needed
- Could undersell anyone in the world
- Had the latest fashions and designs

With his products tentatively chosen, Ted decided to study his markets. He chose three markets to study: Europe, Japan, and South America.

Using books at his local library, Ted found, at no expense other than his time and energy, that:

- **European markets** were flooded with cheap imitations of American products; these imitations were priced lower than he could price his products.

- **Japan** had strict import regulations that would severely limit the number of items that he could sell, thereby making his profit potential extremely small.
- **South America** was a booming, teeming market, hungry for synthetic-material products that were well-designed and stylish.

With this information in hand, Ted turned to *Worldwide Riches Opportunities,* mentioned above. He was delighted to find lists of a number of importers seeking the products—and similar items—that he had available. And, of course, price was an important factor in the selection of these products by the overseas importers.

Next Ted investigated the number of publications—newspapers and magazines—serving the South American market. He was pleased to find that next to the United States and Europe, South America probably has more newspapers and magazines than any other area in the world. And the rates charged for advertising in these magazines and newspapers are low compared with the ad rates in similar publications in other populated areas.

Using this information, Ted took three quick steps:

1. **He contacted the importers** listed in *Worldwide Riches Opportunities,* asking about their interest in his products.
2. **He ran a small ad** in a well-known South American women's magazine, telling about his products and their prices.
3. **He ran a free ad** in *International Wealth Success,* the monthly newsletter for beginning and experienced wealth builders, to which Ted was a regular (one year, or longer) subscriber.

To Ted's delight he was quickly flooded with mail and fax orders from both importers and mail-order buyers. Today, less than a year later, Ted is shipping more than $70,000 per month worth of products to South America importers and mail-order buyers. Since Ted's synthetic products are light in weight they are easily shipped by air. This means he gives fast, efficient service, which keeps his buyers coming back again and again.

STEP 5: EARN HIGH PROFITS IN YOUR BUSINESS

To those people who ask him about his profits, Ted replies: "My rate of profit is the highest in the mail-order sales business—25 percent before taxes." On a volume of $70,000 per month this means that Ted's profit is $17,500 per month, or $210,000 per year. That's not bad, particularly since Ted spends only two days a week on his international mail-order sales business. For the fun of it, figure his hourly before-tax profit, assuming that Ted puts in fifteen hours per week on his business and works fifty weeks per year.*

STEP 6: START SMALL—GROW BIG, FAST

Roberta L. went into international mail-order sales to finance her vacation trips to foreign lands. When she started, Roberta hoped to earn about $50 per week from her business. Today, two years later, Roberta often has a $5,000 week. "It's almost unbelievable," Roberta laughs. "Sometimes I try to 'run away' from the money."

Since she wants to use the **KISS** principle—Keep It Simple and Safe—in her business, Roberta chose to market baby toys by mail-order sales.

What Roberta likes about baby toys is that they are:

- **Easy** to ship
- **Safe** when properly chosen
- **Simple** to price
- **Readily** obtainable

"With such features," you ask, "why aren't more people in the business of international baby-toy mail-order sales?"

---

*The answer is $250 per hour.

For the simple reason that *other people don't understand the market for baby toys the way Roberta does.* Why? Because before going into the baby-toy business, Roberta did what every BWB should do, namely:

- **Studied** the *markets*
- **Analyzed** *which* toys would be popular
- **Determined** the acceptable *prices*
- **Found** low-cost *suppliers*
- **Picked** a profitable *marketing* strategy

Roberta's marketing strategy will interest you. Why? Because selling baby toys to *individual* overseas families by mail order and direct mail is a loss-type business. But you can make money selling this way to overseas:

- Department stores
- Military PXs
- Importers and agents
- Schools
- Libraries
- Hospitals

Using these markets and soft, safe toys, Roberta has a $500,000-per-year business going for herself, using international mail-order sales. Although she doesn't have to leave home to conduct this simple business, Roberta enjoys taking her vacations in the areas where her customers are located. Such vacations allow her to check up on the type of service her customers are receiving. This makes for repeat orders and higher profits. And the vacations are more enjoyable! Using these methods, you too can build a quick fortune in international mail-order sales.

STEP 7: GET TO KNOW INTERNATIONAL MAIL ORDER

Some of the friendliest people in this world work in the post office—here in the United States, overseas in England,

France, Germany, and elsewhere. How do I know? Because I've worked with many of these fine men and women in my own international mail-sales businesses. I've always found these people to be willing, interested, and helpful when approached in a polite and businesslike way.

Every post office in the world has an enormous amount of *free*, valuable information available to the international mail-sales BWB. To get this information all you need do is ask the post office for it! This information covers:

- **Lowest cost** mailing rates
- **Fastest methods** of delivery
- **Correct wrapping** procedures
- **Simple addressing** methods

For instance, you can send packages of books to Canada and Mexico via fast, first-class delivery for little more than the low-cost special standard-mail book rate. There are plenty of other valuable money-saving ideas waiting for you in your post office.

An interesting leaflet, "International Mail," is available free from the U.S. Postal Service. You should have it on hand if you plan to make international mailings. In it you can find almost anything you want to know about overseas mail.

One last point to remember for any mail-order sales operation: Always get a receipt for the postage you buy. Your mailing costs for business purposes are, in general, completely deductible as a business expense on your income-tax return.

STEP 8: KNOW YOUR OVERSEAS PUBLICATIONS

In international mail-order sales you will, in general:

- **Advertise** less
- **Spend** less for ads
- **Sell** more to dealers than in domestic mail-order sales

There are many reasons for this, including:

- **Overseas customers** buy more from dealers or shops, though this is gradually changing in many countries.
- **Money** isn't as readily available.
- **Mail order** isn't as well-known.
- **Sending overseas** for a product takes energy.

But don't let these facts discourage you. Recognize them and plan to earn a profit. And remember, friend, *mail order is rapidly growing in importance throughout the world!*

Get to know the publications in each country in which you plan to promote your products by mail-order sales. Most of the large publications:

- **Have** advertising offices in foreign countries
- **Publish** English-language data in their ad rates
- **Will translate** your ads free of charge
- **Are ready** to help you in many ways
- **Will send** you free copies of back issues

Study the back issues of the publications you're considering. (You can get free copies of any magazine by writing to the ad manager and telling him or her you're thinking of advertising in it.)

Note these facts during your study:

- **Types** of items advertised
- **Typical size** of mail-order ads
- **Location** of the mail-order companies
- **Average price** of the mail-order products

See if your planned product or service offering falls within the ranges shown by the above study. If your product or service is priced about right, can be advertised in the space available, and is similar to other products being sold by mail order, then you can feel safe in running some test ads.

But if your product seems to fall short in one or more ways, you should investigate further before moving ahead. You can get a lot of helpful moneymaking information from:

- **Ad departments** of overseas magazines and newspapers
- **Importers** in the countries you're considering
- **People** familiar with the countries

Only if the opinions given by these people seem hopeful—and profitable—should you consider going ahead. Then rely on your own business sense. If your "gut feeling," as they say, tells you to go ahead, then do so. But if this same feeling warns you off, then turn to another product or market. But above all, don't give up!

And why do I say "Don't give up"? Because:

> This is a big world we live in. If you take the time to study a market carefully after finding the right product or service for it, you're certain to make money from your sales.

Believe me when I tell you this. I have nothing to sell you except *your* success. You can make big money in international mail sales—if you carefully follow the general guidelines I've given you in this chapter!

Follow the Direct-Marketing Road to Your Home-Based Wealth

Direct marketing from home is probably the best opportunity for many BWBs to get started earning a fortune in their own business. With the mail services and fax machines you never have to meet your customers, never have to talk to your customers, and never have to meet a customer face-to-face—unless you want to. So you can be as private as you wish.

Or if you are a people person who loves meeting new customers, you can have your customers call you to order what you offer. And—if you want—you can have them drop by your home to pick up their order. You get to meet new people while they pay you money! Could you ask for a better deal?

Most BWBs start their home-based direct-marketing career using the mail. Marketing by mail is simple, quick, and low-cost. And, as the United States Postal Service points out:

1. **Direct mail improves your return** on investment. Why? Because direct mail lets you know precisely how many responses or sales you get for every dollar you spend.
2. **Direct mail cultivates relationships.** Because direct mail can be tailored for individual audiences, it lets you talk to your loyal customers about what's most relevant to them.
3. **Direct mail builds brands.** It gives you the time and space you need to get your message across. And it can allow for a direct response to your message.
4. **Direct mail targets customers.** Why advertise to everyone when you can use direct mail to speak directly to the people you want to reach?

There you have your reasons for starting—today. And I'll help you every step of the way. Just contact me to get whatever help you need—including financing of promising projects that are not in the financial publishing field (this avoids any possible conflicts of interest). So get started—today. You have a willing helper as close as your phone, fax, or mailbox!

CHAPTER 3

EXPORT YOUR WAY
TO GREAT WEALTH

ONE OF THE fastest, and best, ways to get rich in a home-based business today is by exporting your way to great wealth. Why do I say this? And how can I say this? Let's answer these two questions in order.

Exporting is a fast way to build riches in a home-based business because:

1. **Your customers want what you export** because they sell the item in their own country and make money from it. So they have a *business* need for your product or service—it's not an emotional or spur-of-the-moment buy.
2. **Businesses pay with checks or letters of credit** that don't bounce—you can trust their payments to clear so you get your money in *good funds*, as they say!
3. **Repeat orders can go on for years** from satisfied customers who often buy in larger and larger quantities—again and again. Your cash flow income just continues to grow.
4. **You never see your customer**—unless you want to. All your business can be done directly from your home. Your customer doesn't care where the item comes from, as long as it is a good value for the money, and is delivered on time in acceptable condition!

Don't become nervous when you think of exporting! Why? Because exporting has been around for centuries. Fortunes have been built by exporters all over the world.

They live the good life, some of them running their businesses out of small cubicles at home, with almost no overhead. You—too—can do the same. Let's see how *you* can do the same—right out of your own home, no matter how big or small! Then you might write a letter like this one from a reader in Guam:

> "About three weeks ago, I sent out twenty letters to Asian buyers from *Worldwide Riches Opportunities.* Ten days later I got a request from a Hong Kong company to give quotes on aluminum scrap. It feels great to get the business going. I am now applying to get into the China market, as you suggested." (Turn to the back of this book for a listing and description of *Worldwide Riches Opportunities.*)

How to Get Started Building Export Riches from Home

To be successful in exporting you should handle a product or service that you like and about which you know something. Why do I say this? Because:

1. **If you like what you're exporting** you do a better job in your business. This shows through to your customers and they return to order again and again, giving you a steady cash flow. And—by the way—you have more fun in your business because you like the item or service you're handling. Result? Your business grows steadily.
2. **If you know something about the product or service** you're exporting you can be more helpful to your customers. They'll welcome your help and know-how. And they'll show their appreciation by ordering more from you— sending you money to show their thanks. Could you ask for a better way of being appreciated?

People often call me (at the number listed in the last line of the text of this book) and say: "I want to get into exporting. What product should I start with?"

My answer is: "Start with a product or service you like and about which you know something."

A frequent response is: "But I don't know what I like; and I don't know much about anything."

My suggestion is: "Sit down with pencil and paper and list the sports, hobbies, businesses, and activities you *do* like. Then see if these can be converted into an exporting business."

Plenty of readers apply pencil to paper and come up with products they like and about which they know something. Popular exports today include:

- **Medical equipment and supplies** for developed and developing nations.
- **Food of all kinds**—especially wheat, beans, meat, fish, poultry, salad and cooking oils, fruits, shellfish, etc.
- **Computers and software**—both new and used—for education, business, and home use.
- **Clothing**—both new and used—especially jeans, cowboy jackets, children's and women's garments, etc. Work clothes of various types are also popular exports.
- **Books, courses, and instructional materials** for adults seeking self-improvement in a career, or to change their present career to a new one that offers greater opportunities.

Now that you know what's popular and selling well, let's set the scene and then put you into this great business—easily, and at low cost. But before we get you into this great business, take time to recall that:

Your world today is teeming with more than 5 billion people. And almost every one of these people needs certain basic items—a bed, clothing, grooming products, tools, toys, medicines, etc. You can supply many of these products from your own home while you export your way to great riches. And, as your exports gain wide acceptance, your wealth will grow because population experts are predicting that within a few years there will be more than 7 billion people in this world of ours.

Take Eleven Lucky Steps to Export Riches

There are eleven simple, fast, and luck-laden steps you can follow to build export riches—no matter where you live. To take these lucky eleven steps, you DO NOT need:

- A high-cost business address
- A fancy office
- A factory
- A warehouse
- A big payroll
- Expensive machinery
- Patents or licenses
- A college education

You do, however, need a few simple items:

- **A typewriter**, word processor, or computer (you can rent one)
- **Letterheads** (i.e., *printed* letter paper and envelopes)
- **A mailing address** (your home address is suitable)
- **A pen** to sign your name
- **A few reference books** (which are listed below)
- **A telephone** (though you can get by for a while without one)

Now here are the eleven lucky steps I recommend that you consider taking to make BIG export riches yours quickly and easily, from your own home. *You* can take these steps *now* because I've watched as hundreds of people everywhere have done just that. It makes no difference how small you are today. You can easily be *big* tomorrow if you take these eleven steps:

1. **Choose** the types of products you'd like to export.
2. **Determine** which overseas firms seek these types of products.
3. **Find** those firms in your country that carry the products you've chosen to export.

4. **Write** or fax the overseas firms you found in step 2 to tell them you can supply the products they need; ask them to tell you the quantities required.
5. **Ask** for price quotes from the suppliers in your country once you know the quantities the overseas firms need.
6. **Send** the price quotes to the overseas firm without identifying your supplier, unless you have the written Supplier Agreement mentioned later in this chapter; ask for a firm purchase order.
7. **Order** the items from your supplier *after* you receive a firm purchase order and guarantee of payment.
8. **Obtain** any supplier-required cash down payment from your overseas customer.
9. **Add** a suitable fee for your services.
10. **Arrange** the shipment to the overseas purchaser, or have a freight forwarder do so for a small fee, which your customer pays.
11. **Collect** the money due you, deduct your fee, and send the balance of the payment to your supplier.

It's Easy to Start Exporting Now

Before we explore each of the eleven easy steps to export wealth, let's look at how *you* can get started in exporting your way to great wealth from your own home. In doing this, we'll use the eleven lucky steps you will take—one at a time.

To show you how *you* can take these steps, I'll put you into the business of exporting a certain product. Just keep in mind as you read about the steps that you're taking that these steps apply to *any* product you might select except, perhaps, guns, bombs, warships, and other arms products. However, I'm assuming that exporting such products does not interest you. By that I mean that I think you're probably more interested in products that *help* people (i.e., that are *constructive*), as opposed to *destructive* products. Now let's put *you* in the business of making your fortune in exporting. We'll begin with some definitions.

How Exporting Can Work for You

A firm or individual handling the export of items for other firms or individuals is called an *export management company (EMC)*, when operating as a company, or an *export management agent (EMA)*, when operating in the name of an individual. Since some Beginning Wealth Builders hesitate to spend the $25 most states require for the registration of a company, we'll assume that you plan to do business as an export management agent. Why? Because in many states you need not register your business when you operate it in your own name, for example:

John/Jane A. Doe
Export Management Agent
123 Any Street
Anytown, U.S.A. 00000

The above arrangement of your name and address might be useful to you when you have your letterhead printed. Or you can use other layouts your printer might suggest.

Tips for Building Your Export Income

As an EMA you can work in two ways, or in a combination of these ways:

1. Buy–sell
2. Commission on each sale

In the buy–sell arrangement you *buy* items from a domestic producer *after* you get orders from your overseas customers. The usual price you'll pay for items you export on a buy–sell basis is about 45 percent of the price you charge your overseas customer. Thus, on an item you sell to your overseas customer for $100 you'll pay the domestic manufacturer $45 for it. This means that your gross profit is $100 - 45 = $55 per item sold.

When you work on a commission basis, you will usually receive a commission of 5 to 20 percent of the price at which you sell the item to your overseas customer. Thus, on the above item, with a 20 percent sales commission, you would receive 0.20 × $100 = $20 per item sold. This is also your gross profit on the sale.

Learn the Numbers of Export

"Ty," you say, "any fool would rather work on a buy–sell basis than on a commission basis for this item. He or she would make more than twice as much on the buy–sell basis."

This is true, and it shows that you're thinking. But let's compare the two arrangements and see what *you* have to put up. On a buy–sell deal you must:

- *Buy* the item—that is, put up *cash* for it
- Take *all* the credit *risk* (or buy insurance to protect yourself from bad credit)
- **Probably have to pay** an overseas representative a commission to help you handle the sale
- **Wait to be paid** by an overseas firm instead of by a firm in your own country

So you see, buy–sell may *appear* to pay you a high profit. But like everything else in life, you must:

- **Risk more**
- **Wait longer**
- **Work harder**
- **Or take on** all of these burdens to earn the large profit

Start Right, Build Fast

Probably the easiest way to start in the export–import business is as an export management agent, working on a commission basis. Why do I say this? Because as a commission export management agent you:

- **Need** *no* **capital** (you don't *buy* anything)
- **Can start** *without* an office
- **Don't need** a payroll
- **Can exist** on plain paper, stamps, and a fax send/receive facility—such as a quick-copy shop

Once you make a few big commissions (some agents can earn as much as $1 million on *one* sale!), you can easily begin to work a few deals on a buy–sell basis. So don't knock commission sales—they can easily lead to greater income later on, after you've built some capital and experience. Or, if you want, you can make all your sales on a commission basis. Plenty of export management agents do, and get rich just as fast as the folks who work on a buy–sell basis!

The main point for you to keep in mind here is that you must be careful to:

- **Start right**
- **Work hard**
- **Build fast**

So if you have money, consider starting on a buy–sell basis. But if you're out of money, start as an export management agent working on commission. Either way, you'll eventually hit the *big* money. Now let's get you started today taking the eleven easy steps to building *your* export wealth!

STEP 1: CHOOSE THE TYPES OF PRODUCTS YOU'D LIKE TO EXPORT

You can export almost any type of product, from aardvarks to Zulu headdresses. The products or items you export can be:

- Manufactured
- Untreated raw materials
- Partially finished parts
- Fully packaged items
- Live animals or food—fish and the like
- Growing plants, trees, or vegetables

As a general concept, you can say that:

If people need an item or product for any legitimate purpose, this item can be exported, unless there are government rules against its exportation.

But allow me a word of warning: Don't go into the business of exporting a certain item just because you *like* the product. Remember this key idea about any business, including exporting:

Your liking of, or attraction to, a product does not necessarily make a profitable market for that product!

In general, the best products to start exporting are:

- **Manufactured** industrial products
- **Industrial** raw materials
- **Commercial products** (personal computers, software, office supplies, school furniture, and similar items)
- **Consumer products** (books, clothes, novelties, and so on)

So pick the general type of product you think you might export. In making your choice, these factors can help you:

- **Knowledge** of the product or business
- **Special contacts** in the supply or source end of the product or business
- **Known large demand** for the item, as determined in this next step

STEP 2: DETERMINE WHO WANTS WHAT

Your export business will earn you profits because you serve a need—the need that overseas firms have for the products you offer to export. But before you can offer to export a product you must know who wants what.

The best way to learn who wants what is to read the various publications that list the product needs of numerous firms overseas. Such publications are available from the U.S.

Department of Commerce (on a fax–download basis), international airlines, your state export department, overseas ocean shipping companies, and some trucking firms. Just look in your yellow pages and call or write local firms. Ask for any free information they have on export leads. You can contact the Department of Commerce by calling (202) 482-1986. Ask for free data on their STAT-USA/FAX. We at IWS use this excellent service.

Another way to learn who wants what is to use copies of *Worldwide Riches Opportunities: 2,500 Great Leads to Becoming Rich Without Leaving Your Own Home,* Volumes 1 and 2, available for $25 each from IWS, Inc., P.O. Box 186, Merrick, NY 11566. The leads in each volume *do not* duplicate one another.

With these big books on your desk, you can easily find which overseas firms want what products. The books list:

- Products and services sought
- Type of price quotation wanted
- Name of individual to contact
- Name of firm
- Complete address of firm, telephone number, and fax number (if available)
- Overseas lenders who may finance your exports (Volume 2)

To use these handy books, all you need do is:

1. **Look for listings** in *Worldwide Riches Opportunities* of firms that seek the product or products you've decided to export.
2. **Study each listing** to determine if the items sought are the ones you really want to export.
3. **Make a list** of the firms you believe will buy your exports, using *Worldwide Riches Opportunities* as your guide.

STEP 3: FIND SUPPLIERS FOR YOUR EXPORTS

You now know *who wants what.* Your next step is:

Find out which firms will supply the items you plan to export; try to find as many suppliers as possible.

To find the suppliers you seek, go to your public library and:

1. **Refer to** a copy of *Thomas Register of American Manufacturers* and study its listings thoroughly. (If your library doesn't have a copy of this excellent thirty-four-volume reference, you can get details on ordering a set by writing to Thomas Publishing Co., 5 Penn Plaza, New York, NY 10001.
2. **Obtain copies,** at your library, of directories of manufacturers and suppliers in various states. Study them for suitable sources of exports.
3. **Look** on the Internet for manufacturers' Web sites.
4. **Do the same** with trade associations' membership lists.
5. **Don't overlook** annual issues of industrial magazines, which often list manufacturers and product data. These issues are called by various names, including: *Buyer's Guide, Product Directory, Industry Survey,* and so forth.
6. **Prepare a list** of the suppliers you think could meet your export needs.

STEP 4: WRITE OR FAX OVERSEAS FIRMS

Send an air mail letter, or a fax, to your overseas potential customer that states:

Your Letterhead
Company Name
Address
Telephone/Fax

Mr./Ms. [Insert Name]
[Insert Company Name]
[Insert Address]

Dear Mr./Ms. [Insert Name]:

We can supply the [Insert Name of Item(s)] you are seeking in any quantity you need. Shipping can be by any method you choose.

Kindly inform us as soon as it is convenient what quantities and delivery schedule you seek. Once we have this information, we will quote prices on a CIF basis.

Very truly yours,

[Your Name]

STEP 5: ASK FOR AND OBTAIN PRICE QUOTES FROM YOUR SUPPLIER

Your copy of *Worldwide Riches Opportunities* will generally tell you the basis of the price quotation your overseas customer wants from you. Further, your customer will tell you, in Step 4, the quantities needed. With these facts in hand, you can easily obtain price and delivery schedule quotations from your prospective suppliers.

The best way to obtain valid price and delivery quotations from a supplier is to request the quotes using a *printed* letterhead. Handwritten requests for quotations will usually fail to bring any response—not even an acknowledgment. So resolve today to begin acting in a completely professional way—if you've been trying to get along without letterhead. Make every quotation request on your printed letterhead!

Get the Highest Discount Possible

Now here's a valuable pointer that many beginners overlook.

> Many suppliers give a larger discount on items purchased for export. So be sure to state on your quotation request that the item is for export only.

By using this pointer you can save your overseas buyer as much as 20 percent. Having the extra discount to work with may allow you to underbid another exporter who's trying to sell the same product to the same overseas buyer.

If you can locate more than one supplier, get at least two or more price and delivery quotes on the item you plan to export. With several quotes on hand, you:

- Can compare prices
- Can compare delivery schedules
- Can give your overseas customer the best deal
- Can give your overseas customer alternatives on price and delivery schedules when such alternatives exist

Next make a list of the prices and delivery schedules you've received. Keep all the data related to each overseas customer in a single file folder. This will help you work more efficiently and more rapidly. Why waste time when saving it can put more money into your pocket?

Work Fast to Save Time

Here's another set of moneymaking tips you can put to work instantly in your home-based export–import activities:

- **When you're in a hurry,** *telephone or fax your suppliers* for a price and delivery schedule quotation.
- **Follow up** your telephone or fax request with a written request on your printed letterhead.
- **Never quote** a price to your overseas customer until *after* you have a *written* price and delivery quotation from your supplier.
- **To get the most** out of your letterhead, use a company name that will be suitable for both domestic and foreign operations. Then identify your group, for the purposes of the quote, as the *Export Division.* This will help establish the fact that you seek an export discount.

Protect Your Time and Energy Investment

When you expect to specialize in exporting one type of product, it might pay you to prepare, and have signed by each of your suppliers, a Supplier Agreement, mentioned earlier in this chapter. The usual Supplier Agreement is a letter that you send to one or more of your suppliers confirming several facts, namely:

1. **You discussed** (usually on the phone or by fax) your finding of overseas customers for the supplier.
2. **Your supplier** agreed to your finding such customers.

3. **He or she agreed** to sell to you, for export resale, certain types of products, materials, or services.
4. **A specific discount,** or class of discount, was agreed upon by the supplier and you.
5. **All future sales** of the specific item to the company or country mentioned in the agreement will earn a commission for you of a stated amount or percentage, whenever you negotiate the sale.

Here's a typical example of one form of the Supplier Agreement letter.

Warning: DO NOT USE THIS LETTER IN THE FORM GIVEN HERE UNTIL IT IS APPROVED BY YOUR LAWYER.

Your Letterhead
Company Name
Address
Telephone/Fax

Mr./Ms. [Insert Name]
[Insert Company Name]
[Insert Address]

Dear Mr./Ms.[Insert Name]:

This letter confirms our recent conversation concerning the export of certain items available from [Insert Name] Corporation. In these conversations we mutually agreed that:

1. [Insert Name]Corporation is interested in having me find, and sell to, overseas customers throughout the world (or in the following countries:[Insert Names]), the following products, materials, or services: [Insert Names].
2. [Insert Name]Corporation will sell to my firm, named above on this letterhead, the following: [Insert Names] at an export discount of [Insert Amount] percent, or [Insert Amount] percent off the overseas list price.
3. All future sales of the products, materials, or services mentioned in paragraph 2 in the geographic areas mentioned in paragraph 1 will be credited to my firm, whenever my firm negotiates the sale or there is a repeat order by an organization or individual whose first order we negotiated. For each such repeat sale a commission of [Insert Amount] percent of the selling price will be paid to my firm.

4. Please indicate your agreement to the above terms by signing in the space provided below and returning one copy of this letter to me for our files. The other copy is for your file.

Very truly yours,
[Insert Name]
Agreed: [Insert Name and Title] Date [Insert Date]
[Signature]

STEP 6: SEND THE PRICE QUOTES TO YOUR OVERSEAS CUSTOMERS

With your price and schedule quotes in hand, you are ready to contact your overseas customers. You can do this in three ways:

1. Telephone
2. Fax or cable
3. Air mail

Air mail is the cheapest. However, you can often get faster action using fax, telephone, or cable. If you're in a hurry to make money in exporting, consider the possibility of using the telephone. But before you make an overseas phone call:

1. **Check out** the phone rates with your operator.
2. **Ask the operator** what are the *cheapest* times for you to call.
3. **Determine**, from *Worldwide Riches Opportunities*, if the overseas customer speaks English. (This is not always given, but if a firm asks for quotes in the native language, you can assume they *do not* speak English fluently.)
4. **Try to obtain** a person fluent in the language to talk for you, if you can't speak the language.
5. **Prepare** a list of what you'll tell your overseas customer.
6. **Convert** the prices you'll quote into marks, francs, pounds, or whatever other monetary units your customer might use.
7. **Prepare** another list that details what information *you* want from your overseas customer.

If you follow these hints you won't lose time or money while making your overseas call. To keep track of how long you talk, buy one of those three-minute timing glasses and keep it alongside your phone.

Instead of calling, you can fax your overseas customer if he or she has a fax number. (At this writing, about 40 percent of overseas firms do have a fax number.) Summarize the above information on one page to save fax time. Put the usual cover-sheet information at the top of the page. Ask your overseas customer to reply by fax. This will save time.

Make Your Communications Pay Off

Profit-making pointers that I've found useful in my home-based overseas export communications and correspondence—such as letters, faxes, memos, cables, e-mail, and so forth—are:

- **Always use air mail or fax** when writing—never send a quotation letter by surface mail.
- **Use two languages** (if possible) in your letter—English and the language of your overseas customer.
- **Quote prices** in both dollars and the local currency of your customer.
- **Where quotes are requested on a CIF basis** (i.e., C = cost, I = insurance, F = freight), get the necessary figures *before* you write.
- **Provide a return-addressed** (but not stamped) air-mail envelope and fax and phone numbers for your customer to use. This prevents mistakes in your address and speeds the reply.
- **Consider using a form letter** (available free from IWS) which your overseas customer can use to answer you quickly and effortlessly.

Remember this important fact about exporting products to overseas customers and you'll never go wrong.

Successful exporting resembles highly specialized direct-marketing mail order and direct mail. Make it easier for your customers to order and you'll earn higher profits sooner!

Now, for your final correspondence (phone, fax, cable, or mail) export wealth-building strategies, keep these pointers in mind:

- **Never** identify the source of your export items unless your overseas customer asks you to do so, and you have the written Supplier Agreement, mentioned above.
- **Be ready** to reduce your commission if by doing so you sell the items at a profit.
- **Never** reveal your commission percentage or amount to your overseas customer. Your income for arranging the deal is none of his or her business!

STEP 7: ORDER THE ITEMS YOU PLAN TO EXPORT

As soon as you have a valid written purchase order from your overseas customer you can order the items from your suppliers. To prevent loss of your time and energy:

Never order an item from your supplier until after you have a valid written, and signed, purchase order from your overseas customer.

This cautionary warning means that you must:

1. **Never** order items from your supplier on speculation.
2. **Never** lay out cash on a verbal order.
3. **Accept** only *written* purchase orders.
4. **Use** a *printed purchase order*, sold in stationery stores, to order your export items. (Purchase orders of this type are also easily obtained from business printers.)

STEP 8: OBTAIN THE SUPPLIER-REQUIRED
CASH FROM OVERSEAS CUSTOMERS

Where you must make a cash down payment for the items you are exporting, insist that your overseas customer advance the needed amount to you. As a profit-making guide:

Never lay out any of your own cash for an overseas customer. You are better off losing the sale than putting up your own cash.

Follow this rule inflexibly until your export business becomes so large, and you know an overseas customer so well, that you can afford to take the risk of putting up the cash. But at the start you probably won't be able to afford the risk. Therefore:

1. **You must** be businesslike at all times—this means getting the needed cash in *advance.*
2. **Overseas customers** will respect you more when you insist on your rights.
3. **Getting** the necessary cash in advance will allow you to start your export business for just the cost of printing and correspondence. This means you will need less than $100, if you buy wisely.

Step 9: Add a Suitable Fee for Your Services

Now here's a key pointer you should follow in *every* export deal:

> Never contact an overseas customer to give him or her a price quotation until after you've applied your export commission to the price of the item you're exporting.

The usual commission you'll earn on an export deal when acting as an export commission agent is 5 to 20 percent of the amount you charge your overseas customers for the items you export. The lower commission applies to higher-priced items. A higher commission applies to lower-priced items.

If you fax, cable, or write your quote and you wish to use a foreign language that you do not speak, obtain or refer to a copy of *Commercial Correspondence in Four Languages,* IWS, Inc., P.O. Box 186, Merrick, NY 11566, which costs $25. This handy book allows you to translate or write overseas letters in a foreign language quickly and easily in four languages— English, Spanish, French, and German.

Use a Letter of Credit

The safest way for you to get your money from your overseas buyer is for him or her to use a *letter of credit.* This is a letter that his or her bank sends to your bank guaranteeing that the purchase price of the goods will be paid to you when the goods are either:

- Shipped by you
- Received by the customer

Any shipping deal you work out with your customer should be mutually convenient.

You might also work out an in-between payment deal, such as half payment on shipment, the balance on receipt of the shipment. Since your shipment will almost always be protected by insurance, you need not worry about the loss of the other half of your money in the event the airplane crashes or the ship carrying your goods sinks.

Consider Using Your Bank Export Agents

Another approach to getting your money from your overseas customers is to use your bank's export agent. The bank's export agent does several jobs for you, including:

- **Checking** out your overseas customer
- **Arranging** for letters of credit
- **Processing** export documents
- **Collecting** your money

"Why should I use a bank export agent when I can do all the work myself?" you ask. True, you can do *all* this work by yourself. And plenty of beginning exporters do. But while you're doing *this* work, you can't be looking for new business or new customers. So you just have to make a business decision. You either:

- **Spend** your time on detailed paperwork
- **Or pay** someone else to do the paperwork

Now there is really nothing difficult about doing export–import paperwork. The book *How to Prepare and Process*

Export–Import Documents: A Completely Illustrated Guide, available for $25 from IWS, Inc., tells you exactly how to handle the paperwork in exporting. But it *does* take time to do this paperwork. A bank export agent can save you this time because his or her staff will do the work for you. But you will have to pay the bank a small fee, which will reduce your profit a trifle.

Use Smart-Money Export Methods

Two other ways to save time and effort in exporting are:

1. **Sell** to local representatives
2. **Sell** to import agents

In the United States today, there are thousands of local representatives of overseas governments and firms. They act for:

- **Civilian** buying groups
- **Industrial** firms
- **Special** projects of various kinds
- **Military** buying groups

You can sell directly to many of these groups and bypass the filling out of export documents and long waits for your money. A comprehensive list of these reps, *Industrial Reps of Overseas Countries,* is available from IWS, Inc., for $15. These reps fill out all papers for you and pay fast.

Overseas *import* agents will often handle your *exports.* Thus, an import–export agent in England will be glad to handle your exports for a small fee. Since the agent is dealing with the documents every day of the year, and has them on a computer, he or she can fill them out for you faster. Also, he or she can help speed up the payment to you from the overseas buyer. A number of these import agents are also listed in the book mentioned above.

STEP 10: ARRANGE SHIPMENT OF THE ITEMS ORDERED BY YOUR CUSTOMERS

By working carefully, you can get your supplier to ship the item(s) to your customer. This is called *drop-shipment,* and it will:

- **Save** you time
- **Save** you money
- **Get** items to your customer faster
- **Make** your life less complicated

Now I want you to understand one fact clearly. That is:

Not every supplier will drop-ship for you. But you can get more suppliers to drop-ship if you try to sell them on the idea.

So you see—even in mail-order export—you still have to be a salesperson. As one top wealth builder recently said: "Everyone in the world is selling something."

Now I'll admit to you that the papers and documents that have to be prepared for overseas shipment of items can be frightening the first time you see them. But you can do the work yourself if you follow a few simple directions. For a complete guide to preparing the needed documents, buy a copy of the book mentioned above—*How to Prepare and Process Export and Import Documents: A Fully Illustrated Guide,* from IWS, Inc., P.O. Box 186, Merrick, NY 11566. The price of this guide is $25. Having a copy of it on hand can easily save you thousands of dollars in time and mistakes.

You can save time and money in your export activities in other ways, including:

- **Requiring your suppliers** to prepare shipping documents, where doing so would not reveal any of your business secrets.
- **Requiring customers** to supply you with filled-in import documents where they are required. This reduces the time you must spend on them.

- **Using freight and insurance specialists** on a free basis to assist you in figuring the costs and best way to handle the items you export.
- **Using the free services and advice** offered by airlines and shipping firms on the best and cheapest way to ship a given export item.

STEP 11: COLLECT YOUR MONEY FROM YOUR CUSTOMERS

Basically, there are three ways to collect payments for overseas sales:

1. Cash with order
2. Cash on delivery
3. Staggered payments

Cash with order is the safest way to be paid for overseas sales. But it's also the most difficult arrangement to negotiate, particularly when you're just starting. However, I personally prefer this way of being paid, even though I recognize that it:

- **Can** cause loss of orders
- **Makes** you look "hungry"
- **Reduces** the speed of making business friends
- **Can** limit the rate of growth of your business

But cash with order is not all bad. Why? Because:

- **You get** your money *before* you ship.
- **There's usually** enough time for the check to clear.
- **You don't** spend money and time on unnecessary bill collections.

Cash on delivery seems like a perfect way to handle exports because you deliver your product and collect your money in one swift step. But life doesn't always work that way because:

- **Your shipment** may be refused for any number of reasons.
- **You will** have to pay warehouse charges until the goods are delivered if your shipment is refused.
- **Your exports** may be damaged in the warehouse, leading to more problems.
- **Predictions** of the actions of overseas buyers are difficult to make—and the best way to reduce or eliminate this problem is to make no predictions at all!

So you see that C.O.D. can be a problem-maker for you, unless you know your customer. Of course, once you get on a cordial basis with your customers, you can select those with whom you'll work via C.O.D. But as a start, work on the basis of cash with the order. Then you'll have few problems collecting your money.

Staggered payments are the next best thing to cash with order. When you receive staggered payments you are paid in this way:

1. **A portion** of the total purchase price—say 25 or 33 percent—with the purchase order.
2. **An equal** payment at an agreed upon later date, prior to the final delivery of the items ordered.
3. **A final** payment on delivery of the items ordered.

Why is the staggered payment arrangement a good one for you when you're just starting in export–import?

- **There's less** danger of a refused C.O.D.
- **You're paid** as the deal progresses.
- **Your only** investment is in shipping.
- **You can't** be hurt badly.

Get Your Bank to Work for You

Many big banks have large, expert staffs who'll work for you *free* of any charge when you deal in export–import items of many kinds and have an account in the bank. "Why will these banks work for me free?" you ask. There are many reasons, including:

- Banks want *all* the business they can get.
- Foreign exchange business is *profitable.*
- Doing business overseas helps banks *expand.*
- Export business is a *paper business*—which all banks love.
- Doing business with a domestic exporter can *attract* an overseas customer.

"Now how can a bank help me in my export business?" you ask next. Domestic banks can help you in many ways, including:

- **Processing** letters of credit
- **Financing** your exports (partially or completely) when necessary
- **Preparing** export–import documents
- **Checking** out overseas customers
- **Providing** up-to-date data on foreign markets
- **Giving** you the best exchange rate
- **Corresponding** with overseas customers
- **Plus** many other services

You may not (and need not) believe what I tell you about the help big banks can offer you in exporting. To verify what I say, just call, fax, or write the International Department of any of the following randomly selected banks whose local address you'll find in a large-city telephone book where the bank has a branch:

Bank of America
Citibank
Chase Bank
Bank of New York
Bankers Trust

When you call, ask for an export officer. As soon as he or she comes on the line, ask what services the bank can offer an export firm or agent such as you. You'll be both surprised and delighted by what you hear. For instance, at the time of this writing, the Bank of America had some 700 import–export experts on its staff! And all the other banks listed above also have large staffs.

Know What Your Bank Can Do

Having a bank that can work internationally is your first step in getting free help. To make the best use of your bank's facilities, you must know what your bank can do. As an example of what a bank can do for firms in international business, in addition to other services, one bank:

- **Will transfer** money from one country to another in twenty-four hours.
- **Offers** import–export credits to help you finance your exports.
- **Helps** you prepare the export documents you need to export specific items.
- **Will act** as the opening and paying bank for you.
- **Can help you collect** the money owed you by your overseas customer.
- **Supplies** "clean" letters of credit for you, reducing the amount of supporting paperwork you need.

Not every bank will offer you *all* these services. So don't expect to get every service you need from *every* bank. Yet some banks may offer you *more* services. The only way to find out is to ask the bank of your choice.

Note that the banks listed above are certainly *not* the only ones that can give you export–import help. There are hundreds of others around the United States. All you have to do to check your local bank is to make a quick phone call and ask: "Do you help with export–import business?"

At the time of the writing of this chapter, U.S. banks had some 1,500 overseas branches all over the world. Within a few years, there will be 2,000 or more branches. Can you think of any better way to be represented locally than by a big-name bank?

And now that I've told you how to work with a good bank that has widespread overseas offices, take the first step and open a business account at the bank of your choice. You'll be repaid over and over by the many free services you receive.

Get Rich Doing Things the Right Way

The eleven steps given you in this chapter aren't the only way to export items to overseas buyers. But these steps are and have been:

- **Proven** by actual use
- **Practical** for you
- **Profitable** to you

I'm sure that as you gain experience in export–import you will vary some of these steps slightly. Great! Write me a letter telling me how you changed a given step and what results you obtained. If you give me permission, I'll pass your hints along to other export–import operators.

The main intent of the lucky eleven steps listed above is to help you do things the *right* way. Once you start doing things the right way, you earn more from your efforts *sooner*, and with *less* work. Could anything be better for you?

Now I want to give you some interesting real-life examples of how home-based BWBs are building wealth in their own export businesses today. As part of these examples we'll give you many valuable pointers on successfully running *your* home-based export business.

Move into Export Riches Today

Sixty-five percent of the more than 5 billion people in the world today haven't yet reached the bicycle-owning stage in life. Yes, the world's people hunger for the raw materials and manufactured products that can give them a better life. And you can help give them this better life by exporting the items they need. Further, as the income and wealth of over-seas people increase, the demand for your exports will grow.

And don't worry about competition. With a market of more than 5 billion people—and predictions of a market of more than 7 billion people in the relatively near future—there aren't enough ambitious and capable business people like you to fill the need. So welcome competition. The more overseas people see your exports, the more they'll want.

Now let's look at some real-life BWBs who are building wealth in their own home-based export business. You'll see how you—too—can get started in this great business serving the needs of the world.

Is Exporting Mail Order?

No; the export business isn't the same as the direct-mail or mail-order business, even though the usual export business is carried on almost entirely by mail or fax. Now figure that one out.

That's what Carl L. tried to figure out after making an $80,000 profit during his first year in exporting. Here's how Carl built his profits.

For years Carl L. had idly dreamed about working in his own home at a mail-order business. Why? Because Carl hated to travel any further than to the local golf course. Since the mailbox was nearer than the golf course. Carl thought that mail order was his dream business. Further, the sale of products by mail order had a basic appeal to Carl.

Because he disliked all forms of travel, Carl ignored export–import, thinking that this business required worldwide travel. Actually, the only required travel is between your home and the corner mailbox or your fax machine.

Get the Data You Need

One evening, while visiting a friend's home, Carl chanced on a copy of *Worldwide Riches Opportunities*. Flipping through this book, he was amazed to see the thousands of overseas firms seeking exported products and raw materials. The instructions included in the book were clear and easy to follow. Carl decided to order a copy of the book for his own use. So he sent $25 to IWS, Inc., P.O. Box 186, Merrick, NY 11566, for a copy of Volume 1. Later he ordered a copy of Volume 2 for $25 and subscribed to the Department of Commerce STAT-USA/FAX.

When his copy of the book arrived, Carl sat down and studied it in greater detail. He soon learned that exporting *isn't* mail order. But you can hardly get anywhere in exporting without using the mails or a fax machine.

Make Exporting a Painless Business

Carl was interested in electronics. So he decided to see if this interest could be matched with overseas product and equipment needs. To do this, Carl:

1. **Studied** the list of export needs in the book he purchased and faxes he gathered.
2. **Listed** the needs in the product area that interested him.
3. **Counted** the needs in that area of interest.

To his delight, Carl found more than 200 firms listed in *Worldwide Riches Opportunities* and the faxes that sought electronic products or equipment. This number of potential customers, Carl reasoned, was an excellent starting base for his business.

Learn from Past Experience

Having been in another business several years earlier, Carl decided that the lessons he'd learned in that business would not be wasted. Those lessons were:

- **Avoid** every possible business problem.
- **Make** the smallest possible money investment in a business.
- **Invest** plenty of time, energy, and skill in the business.
- **Try to work** just with computer, fax, paper, typewriter, envelopes, and stamps.
- **Sell to** companies instead of individuals wherever possible.
- **Collect** as much money in advance as you can.
- **Try to** develop repeat sales instead of one-shot sales, but stay flexible at all times.
- **Make profit** your major objective because without a profit a business is just a drain on your energy.

Starting with these concepts, Carl soon built a highly successful, problem-free export business. Here's how he did it.

Help Your Customers Place Orders

Overseas customers usually have specific product needs, such as:

- Manufactured items
- Raw materials
- Semi-finished products
- How-to publications of all kinds
- Plants, factories, and other large facilities
- Both high- and low-technology items
- Computer hardware and software

Carl isolated "multiple needs" listed in *Worldwide Riches Opportunities* and his faxes. These were duplicate needs expressed by two or more overseas firms. It would be easier, Carl thought, to sell items wanted or needed by more than one buyer.

With this as his guiding idea, Carl prepared a list of electronic components and equipment that he found were needed by overseas buyers. Then he checked a number of electronics catalogs, seeking price data on the items on his list. As a check on the catalogs, he called the firms that had published them and obtained data on discounts and deliveries. With this information in hand, Carl prepared his own four-page catalog. To help his customers order his products, he attached a fifth page containing an easy-to-use order coupon.

Get Your Data to Your Customers

With his catalog ready, Carl went to a local offset printer and had 100 copies of each page printed at a cost of 10 cents per page, for a total cost of $50. Carl collated the pages himself on the kitchen table and then stapled each catalog.

With his catalog ready, Carl addressed 100 air-mail envelopes, using the company names and addresses obtained from *Worldwide Riches Opportunities* and his faxes. He also addressed 100 air-mail return envelopes to help his customers order more easily. His total cost for the envelopes was $20.

Get Your Message Out to Buyers

Next, Carl mailed his catalog to his overseas prospects at a total cost of about $100 for outgoing postage. But instead of sitting back and doing nothing while he waited for orders to roll in, Carl turned to his copy of *Worldwide Riches Opportunities*, Volume 2, and to additional faxes to isolate other multiple needs. Within a few days, he had multiple listings of overseas firms that needed three other items that he knew he could supply.

Build Your Business Fast

Carl's work paid off quickly. Within a week of his first mailing, he received his first order for electronic components. And, good news, the order was accompanied by a check for $2,750. This first check more than paid for:

- Department of Commerce faxes
- *Worldwide Riches Opportunities,* Volumes 1 and 2
- Printing of product data
- Overseas mailings
- Printing of return envelopes

Carl's profit on his first order was $268—a little less than 10 percent. This is excellent, when you stop to think that most new businesses lose money during their first year. Carl—by following the Hicks recommendations in this and previous chapters—made a profit during his first month.

Carl's first order was followed by fourteen other orders during the following ten days. Some orders were larger than the first; some smaller. But Carl's total profit during his first month in business was $3,874. Not bad on an investment of less than $300.

When Carl analyzed his investment in his new business, he found that his biggest outlays were:

- **Time** (which costs nothing when you're poor)
- **Energy** (which most people have)
- **Paper** (costs little)
- **Postage** (the world's best bargain)
- **Faxes**

This brings us to an important moneymaking principle for you:

> The fewer the items (raw materials, machinery, personnel, and so forth) you need for your business, the sooner you can show a profit.

Grow Rich on Paper

Thousands of Beginning Wealth Builders consult me in person and as subscribers to my monthly newsletter *International Wealth Success* about going into business for themselves. When they are interested in mail-order type businesses I tell them:

Build a fortune out of paper. All you need is a letterhead and some stamps and you can become an instant millionaire.

Thousands of people become rich this way every year without:

- **Ever seeing** the product they sell
- **Even touching** the product
- **Ever doing** hard physical work

Carl built, and runs, a paper empire that delivers more than $100,000 a year in profits to him in his home. You can do the same if you just keep in mind this important principle:

"Paper" businesses can be just as profitable as any other business, and can be started for a much smaller investment on your part.

But let's say that you want to avoid the fuss and bother of export forms and similar documents. Is there any route you can take to export riches? Yes, there is.

Export the Painless Way

Some of my friends hate paperwork of all kinds. They much prefer face-to-face dealings with prospective buyers. Yet these same BWBs want to get into the export business. How can they? Here's how.

Paul P. is a man I describe as a paper-hater. He

- **Abhors** paperwork
- **Loves** on-the-spot selling
- **Is an** excellent talker
- **Dresses** well
- **Likes** the idea of exporting

"Paul," I said during his first talk with me, "you're a capable guy, and I want to see you make it big in exporting without getting involved in a yard of paperwork on each deal!"

"Ty," he answered, "now you're talking my language. But how can I get around having to fill out those reams and reams of computer-based customs documents?"

"There really aren't reams of documents, Paul," I said. "It just seems that there are!" Then I told Paul how to export "without papers." You can do the same. Here's how.

Use Your Head to Build Export Riches

In nearly every country of the world, there are industrial representatives on embassy staffs sent overseas to represent one country in another country. These reps can act for:

- Their government
- Firms in their country
- Individuals in their country

Now let's say that a large firm overseas seeks the product you export. But you would prefer to avoid all the paperwork. What can you do? Here are five lucky steps you can take to build great wealth by exporting without large amounts of paperwork:

1. **Contact** by air mail, phone, fax, or in person, the industrial rep at the embassy in the country to which you plan to export—for example, France.
2. **Tell the rep** the name of the firm in his or her country (France, in this case) to which you plan to export.
3. **Explain to** the rep that you would like to have him or her, or his or her agency, handle the export of the items sought by the firm in his or her country. (To arrange such a deal you may have to take the rep to lunch or dinner once or twice because such deals are often put together outside the office.)
4. **Have the rep** contact the firm in his or her country; have him or her ask if his or her handling of the export details (*not* the financing) will be acceptable to your customer. (It usually will be.)

5. **Go ahead** with the deal after you obtain written or verbal notice from the rep that your customer will let him or her (or his or her embassy) handle the export arrangements.

Returning to Paul's case, we can see how such an arrangement with a rep can work out. Here are the details.

Sell Here for Profits There

Paul's a born salesman. He loves to talk to people, to sell them his product. But first Paul had to learn whom he should be talking to in the various embassies. To get the reps' names, Paul obtained a copy of *Industrial Reps of Overseas Countries* ($15 from IWS).

With this list in hand, Paul called embassies to get the name of the industrial reps. To save money, Paul called after 6 P.M., knowing that most embassies have one or more people on duty until midnight. This worked well at ten of the embassies and Paul spent only $9.20 on calls to get the names of the ten reps. (He could have spent about half this much to obtain the same information by mail, but much more time would have been required.) Another reason for calling on the phone is that you get the name of the current rep. With a high turnover rate the reps may change quickly.

Next, Paul arranged sales of items to overseas firms in the ten countries whose reps' names he obtained. To make these sales, Paul used the Department of Commerce's STAT-USA/FAX, copies of the monthly newsletter *International Wealth Success*, and the IWS publication *Worldwide Riches Opportunities*.

Once the deals were arranged, Paul contacted the industrial reps whose names he had obtained earlier. Most of the reps were delighted to handle the export papers. Why? Because it helps the rep show his or her boss how efficient the rep is! What was Paul's profit on these transactions? It was $72,814 in three months. Not bad for a beginner who hates paperwork.

Mail Your Way to Export Riches

Up to now we've been talking about exporting items that fill the specific needs listed in *Worldwide Riches Opportunities* and Department of Commerce faxes. Another approach to making millions in exporting is to use overseas direct mail or faxes. But instead of mailing or faxing to overseas consumers, you mail or fax to overseas industrial firms. Why? Because:

- **Sales** are easier.
- **You're paid** faster.
- **You have** fewer complaints.
- **Repeat sales** are often possible.

I call this method overseas industrial direct mail/fax.

How do you mail or fax your overseas industrial ads? There are three ways:

1. Surface mail
2. Air mail
3. Telephone fax lines

Use surface mail when: (1) You have the time to wait four weeks for your mail to arrive at its overseas destination; (2) You are trying to save money on postage; (3) You have large, bulky items, such as catalogs, to send to your overseas prospects.

Use air mail or fax for your overseas direct ads when: (1) Time is important in the delivery of your ad; (2) You want to impress your overseas prospects with the efficiency of your service; (3) Your mailing material is so light or short that the extra cost for air mail or faxing is not excessive.

Where can you obtain the names of firms for your direct mail and fax ads? Use your copies of *Worldwide Riches Opportunities* and *International Wealth Success*. These handy publications give you the complete firm name, address, products sought, and, in many cases, the name of the individual to whom you should send your direct-mail ads.

Note: You are allowed to fax ads to overseas potential customers because they have expressed a need for information on the types of products you are advertising. This expression of need for information makes it permissible for you to send the data about your products or services.

Follow Up with Easier Sales

Once you make an industrial sale using overseas direct-mail or faxed ads, arrange to have your supplier drop-ship the item, if possible. (In drop-shipping your supplier ships the item directly to your customer for you.) This reduces your export paperwork. And it is one way to achieve easier sales in overseas industrial mail order.

Another technique for obtaining easier sales is to include a lightweight or condensed copy of your catalog with every mailing or fax you make to any overseas contact. This simple method can generate sales for years to come. When thinking of advertising, remember this key fact:

> The cost of printing and mailing a catalog is small, compared to the potential profit you can earn from a big overseas sale.

Build Your Wealth Everywhere

Now before I close this chapter I'd like to tell you about one other Beginning Wealth Builder, who's hitting it big in exporting and related deals. This BWB—Ray, by name—used a lead in *International Wealth Success* to negotiate a contract to sell 3,000 bushels a month of alfalfa seed to a South American country. All Ray had to do was get a seed seller together with a seed buyer. For arranging the deal, Ray receives a certain monthly commission. The contract is guaranteed by a bank in the seed grower's town.

Shortly after swinging the seed deal, Ray came across an attractive and profitable apartment house costing $87,500 that he wanted to buy. The down payment was 20 percent or $17,500. But, like many other BWBs, Ray didn't have the required down payment. Even though he didn't have the money he needed to take over the building, Ray decided to talk it over with his bank.

During the conversation, Ray casually mentioned that he had a contract to supply 3,000 bushels a month of alfalfa seed to a South American country. The banker's ears immediately perked up. He asked a few questions and then told Ray:

"You can use your seed contract as down payment on this income-producing apartment house and we'll finance the first mortgage—$70,000—for you also!"

Ray was delighted. Why? Because by just investing a few pennies in stamps and paper, he was able to:

- **Develop** a steady, monthly income from exporting.
- **Use** his export income as collateral for another income producer for himself.
- **Shelter** from income taxes some of his export income with the allowable depreciation on the real estate.

Since Ray needed only about 95 percent of his monthly export payment to cover the repayment of the down payment loan, he's receiving 5 percent for himself. Further, he has an excellent monthly income from the rental apartment house taken over by using the bank-guaranteed seed contact! So you see, exporting can make *you* rich.

You Can Make It Big in Exporting

Only about 8 percent of the firms in the United States are exporting at the time of this writing. With such a small number selling items overseas, there is an enormous opportunity for you to strike it rich on a very small start—less than $100. Just use the hints, books, and newsletter listed in this chapter and you'll soon be on your way to the wealth you seek. Then you may call me, as this reader did, to say:

"It has taken us two months to put a $925,000 sale together to ship fifty containers of food—red kidney beans, green peas, etc.—to Panama. But our commission will be in the $75,000 range. The entire sale is covered by a letter of credit. Thanks for the lead from your newsletter, and the advice."

CHAPTER 4

Import Riches Can Be Yours

Importing is the opposite of exporting. When we *import* in our home-based business, we buy products from overseas firms and sell these products in our own country. As a home-based importer, you hope to find a unique product that will have large-volume sales in your own country.

Beware of Import Traps

Many beginners think that importing is the simplest way to riches known to man or woman. "All you have to do is find a good product and then sell it," they say. That's basically true. But take it from me, Ty Hicks, who has done plenty of importing from throughout the world that:

- **Finding** a good product isn't always easy.
- **Controlling** product quality can be a real problem.
- **Import regulations**—for certain items—can be troublesome.
- **Selling** the product in your own country can be the biggest problem of all.

Now, good friend, don't call me a negative thinker. That I'm not! But I *do* want to warn you of the day-to-day problems associated with importing *before* you rush out to buy some foreign products. If you listen to me and follow my advice, you may be able to beat my present record with imports. What's more, it won't cost you anything to listen!

"And what's your record?" you ask. *Just this: Working less than three hours a week on the import business, I've been able to find, and import, products that are currently achieving sales of more than $250,000 per year—$254,336 during the year of this writing.* Now if I can do that in less than three hours a week, think of what you can do in forty hours a week!

Anybody Can Make Money in Importing

"Sure, Ty," you say. "*You* can make sales of a quarter of a million dollars per year in importing. But can *everyone* do the same?" Positively—I reply—if they try. However, you can't just sit back in your home and expect profits to fall from the sky. But I can guarantee you this:

> If you follow my suggestions (altering them to suit local conditions), read, and use books, the Internet, and other guides I recommend, you can hit the big money in your home-based importing business.

To show you that you can easily hit the big money in home-based importing, I'd like to give you a few quick examples of real people, just like you, who hit the big money in home-based importing without:

- **Investing** large sums of money
- **Working** long hours
- **Selling** door-to-door
- **Having** any special skills or training

Seeing how these "people in the street" made the big time will, I hope, encourage you to do more to build your own success.

Disabled Man Works at Home and Prospers

Sam T. was injured and disabled by an industrial accident and confined to his home. Time hung heavily on his hands because, before his accident, Sam had been a busy and active person. So he began to look around for something to do at home that would keep him busy, and possibly increase his income, because his disability payments were small.

Sam is a tropical fish hobbyist. One day a friend asked Sam if he knew where a rare South American fish could be obtained. Sam didn't know, but he promised to find out. This promise led Sam on a two-month mail, fax, Internet, and phone hunt without turning up one source. "I'd pay anything for such a fish," the friend said when Sam told him of the blanks he'd drawn.

This remark set Sam to thinking. If his friend would pay "anything" (i.e., a high price) for such a fish, would other tropical fish hobbyists do the same? Sam did some quick market research by calling several fish hobbyists on the phone. To his surprise, eight out of ten, or 80 percent, said they'd be delighted to pay whatever the going price was, just to be able to get such a rare fish. And several suggested other species of fish they'd gladly pay high prices for. The combination of the remark and his research put Sam into the home-based imported-fish business.

It didn't Sam long to take the action needed to convert his market information into money, namely:

1. **Making** a list of the fish people wanted.
2. **Contacting** by mail, fax, Internet, and phone overseas suppliers of live tropical fish.
3. **Obtaining** by mail, fax, Internet, and phone price lists of the fish his potential customers wanted.
4. **Negotiating** by mail, fax, Internet, and phone prices on quantity purchases of tropical fish.
5. **Working** out by mail, fax, and phone suitable ways to ship live fish by air freight (the fish are sealed in plastic bags of fresh or seawater).

6. **Advertising** his import services in suitable tropical fish
    hobby magazines, on the Internet, and in marine news-
    papers that have fish hobbyist columns.

Sam's home-based importing business expanded from
zero to $5,000 a month in a few months. Fish hobbyists, he
finds, want rare fish of all kinds and are willing to pay high
prices to get what they want. Since the fish are lightweight
and easy to handle, Sam has no shipping problems. Not one
fish has failed to reach its buyer in healthy condition.

Today, Sam has a prosperous home-based import business booming for him. Because he is confined to his home,
he is delighted he can conduct his entire business from there,
using the mail, fax, Internet, and phone. Sam never has to
leave his home to do a single chore for a customer!

Divorcée Makes Big Import Profits

When Beverly L.'s husband divorced her, he left her with
only a few hundred dollars. Beverly was shocked by the bit-
ter divorce and frightened by the prospect of supporting
herself. But Beverly, like most people, has more courage,
creativity, and energy than she either realizes or gives herself credit for.

A chance remark by a friend got Bev to thinking. "If I
were you, Bev," this friend said, "I'd take this chance to go
into business for myself, instead of looking for a job working for someone else." But, like most of us, Bev couldn't
take action on her dreams of a home-based business immediately. So she took a temporary job in a greeting-card store
to earn a few dollars to tide her over. Taking this temporary
job was the best decision Bev ever made, because it put her
in the home-based importing business.

At the store, Bev soon noticed that big, expensive greeting and condolence cards of all types were "in." Since there's
an enormous profit on a single sheet of paper printed on

two sides and folded only twice, and sold at $5 or more, Bev decided to investigate such cards further.

What Bev quickly learned was that fancy, expensive greeting cards:

- Could be printed cheaply overseas
- Were easy to import by air freight
- Are fast becoming status symbols
- Move quickly in the right stores

With these facts in hand, Bev checked out several European printers that had offices in the United States. Within a few days, she was given cost estimates by the printers for different numbers of cards.

Using her card-shop experience, Bev made some sales estimates of the number of cards that could be sold by the store in which she worked. She also made some estimates of the number of cards she could sell by home-based mail order to greeting-card stores throughout the United States.

Using these estimates as a guide, Bev placed her first card order using $300 she had borrowed from a friend. Within a few weeks of receiving the cards, Bev sold them out for a total of $2,750, more than nine times the cost. She promptly quit her temporary job and started working full time at home.

Today, Bev's home-based imported greeting cards are selling at a rate of more than $3 million per year. Besides importing and selling these cards, Bev:

- Opened her own greeting-card store.
- Plans to franchise thirty-six other card stores.
- Went into manufacturing her own "imports" using printing plates from overseas.
- Expanded her imports to include books, paintings, china, and other items.

Truly, Bev is living a wonderful life off well-chosen imported products. This includes:

1. **A high income**—more than $100,000 a year—from her business.
2. **Worldwide travel** at no expense to her.
3. **Mini vacations** wherever and whenever she wants them.
4. **A safe, secure future** with a big pension when she wants to retire.

Make Your Life a Big Success

You can have the same sort of profitable home-based income in importing as Sam and Bev. All you have to do is seek out the right import, find a market for it, and then sell, sell, sell! This chapter shows you exactly how to take these important steps. Taking these steps will, hopefully, put you in the big-money chips the same way that the following BWBs were put on wealth-studded roads to success:

- **A radio personality** built a $4 million fortune in four years importing electonic stereo and computer equipment from home starting on $100 borrowed from his brother.
- **A housewife** is earning a $27,000 a year profit at home importing wax flowers for resale to florists. Her starting capital was just a few postage stamps.
- **A farmer** is earning $180,000 a year at home importing exotic foods for restaurants and taverns. He obtained his startup capital by putting part of his land up for a crop subsidy of $95,000 in one year.
- **A real estate agent** is earning $110,000 a year at home importing copper bracelets and necklaces. He got some of his financing and product-source leads from the monthly newsletter *International Wealth Success*.
- **An auto mechanic** is earning $18,000 at home a year in his spare time importing foreign auto parts. His starting capital was $56 he saved from his regular pay.
- **An accountant** is earning $57,000 a year in his spare time at home selling personal-product imports by mail order. His starting capital was $750, which he borrowed.

Yes, you *can* build fast import wealth in a variety of fields. Now let's see what other features and techniques will be helpful to you in your search for import wealth enthusiasm and results.

But before we move to these features and techniques, let me say one more thing about my own importing activities that will encourage you. When I started my importing activities, I knew nothing about imports, such as:

- **Where** to find overseas products
- **How** to process import documents
- **When** to order products
- **What** to do about shipping strikes
- **Why** importing could be enormously profitable

You're about to obtain all these—and many more—facts in this chapter. So you should easily exceed my record in just a few months. Let's get *you* started doing that right now!

Why Importing Can Be So Profitable

Any business has two basic types of costs in its operation— fixed and variable. A *fixed cost*, also called an *overhead cost*, is a cost that goes on and on, for one year or longer, whether you sell a penny's worth of product or not. Typical fixed costs are:

Rent for office, factory, or other quarters
Insurance for the firm
Management salaries
Part of the firm's electric and telephone bills

The other type of cost, the *variable cost*, is sometimes also called an *out-of-pocket*, or *OOP*, cost. The main feature of a variable cost is that you pay it only when you make, or buy, a product or service you sell. Typical OOP costs include:

Materials
Freight
Production labor
Packing
Postage

"Now why are we looking at these costs?" you ask. Because they contain the key to why importing can be so profitable. This key is:

The lower the fixed costs (or overhead) in any business, the higher (in general) the profit the business can earn.

In importing, if you can operate from your own home as many BWBs do, your fixed costs (rent, light, heat, etc.) are essentially zero. Hence, all your costs are variable—*you don't spend until you're ready to sell!* So your profit on each sale can be enormous because you don't have any:

Factory
Large machines
Big production payroll
Interest payments on mortgages

Know the Numbers in Import Profits

"What kind of profit are you talking about?" you ask. I'm talking about a profit of 65 cents on $1, or 65 percent, before taxes in your home-based business. Compare that with the usual profit of 10 cents on $1, 10 percent, before taxes— which is what the typical manufacturing firm earns. Now you see what I mean about the high profits you can earn in home-based importing. These high profits mean:

- **You'll get** a bigger return for your time.
- **You can start** with an investment of less than $100.
- **You can run** the business right out of your home.
- **Your wealth** will grow faster than in almost any other business.

And if you should make a mistake, which I certainly hope you do not, the amount of money you could lose is small. This is particularly true when you compare the potential losses in importing with the potential losses in almost any other business, such as manufacturing.

So you see, importing *can be highly profitable*, provided you know what you're doing. And the key to knowing what you're doing is your next step toward wealth.

Have a Market Before You Buy

Importing consists of three basic steps:

1. **Finding** your product or service
2. **Getting** your product or service
3. **Selling** your product or service

The first two steps are relatively easy. You don't have to look too far to find your product. Today, you can often find suitable products to import by searching for them on the Internet. You can get lots of free help from the International Trade Administration at *http://www.ita.gov*.

Selling Your Product

You can import the most beautiful items in the world. But if you can't sell them, you've wasted your time and your money. So that's why I say:

Have a market for every import BEFORE you buy it. Never order an import until you know how many units you can sell, and at what price.

To find out how many units of a given product you can sell in your home-based business, you'll have to do some market research. Though this may frighten you, market research is really easy to do—especially if you plan to sell a small number of higher-priced items, such as 1,000 units at $150 each. But if you're planning to try to sell 1 million items at $2 each, your market survey and research work can be a big job. To take the scare out of market research, just think of it as finding out how many people might buy a certain item at a stated price.

Quick Market Survey Techniques

To research the market for higher-priced items you plan to import, you can make a quick market survey in your home-based import business by:

1. **Determining** how many units other firms are selling. Look at the most recent *Statistical Abstract of the United States*, available from the U.S. Government Printing Office, Washington, D.C. 20402, for a full rundown on unit and dollar sales of various products.
2. **Studying** the sales of *similar* items in the *Statistical Abstract* when data on the exact product is not available.
3. **Asking** friends and associates if they would buy a given item and what price they'd be willing to pay for it.

For lower-priced mass-distribution items such as portable personal CD and tape players, in-line skates, children's and adults' backpacks, and the like, you may not find as much statistical data available to you. Instead, you'll have to "feel out" the market based on:

1. **Observing** what's popular and selling today.
2. **Trying** to predict what will be popular tomorrow.
3. **Watching** to see if your predictions come true.

Recognize right here and now:

The low-priced, mass-circulation, fad-type item is more subject to public whim than the higher-priced, more useful item. So you'll usually have more trouble making market estimates for fad-type items.

Pick the "Ideal" Import

The "ideal" import for you will usually be:

- **Strong**—not fragile
- **Light**—not heavy
- **Safe**—not dangerous
- **Cheap**—not costly
- **Shippable** by air freight
- **Quickly** available
- **Unique**—not easily duplicated
- **Solely** available to you
- **Smaller** than competing items
- **Simpler** to use than other products

Now *no* import you will find will ever possess *all* these desirable features. But you must be able to compare prospective imports, one with the other, to see which is the most desirable. Also, you must be able to judge the probable troubles any import might give you.

To compare prospective imports, list their pros and cons. Then assign a number between 1 and 10 for each pro and con. Do this by assigning 10 to the strongest pro. The strongest con would get a negative 10.

Add up the numbers for each import. See which one has the highest score. This will usually be your best import. Give this import the most serious consideration for importing to, and selling in, your country.

For example, let's say import "A" has a pro score of 160 and a con score of -55. Its overall score equals 160 - 55 = 105. If import "B" had a score of 60—found the same way—then import "A" would probably be the more desirable one for your home-based business. You would—of course—also apply the other tests we discuss elsewhere in this chapter.

Where to Find Profitable Imports

To make your home-based importing as profitable as possible for the time you put in, you:

- **Should** pick products carefully
- **Make** fast, effective market surveys
- **Develop** import evaluations rapidly
- **Test** the market speedily
- **Move** into full-scale sales fast

You can find profitable imports faster if you know something about the publications and Internet addresses that can help you. To find suitable imports quickly, I suggest you subscribe to my monthly newsletter, *International Wealth Success*; details are listed at the back of this book. Send $24 for a one-year subscription—you'll be glad you did.

Other useful sources of information about available imports include:

- *Journal of Commerce*
- *Wall Street Journal*
- *Worldwide Riches Opportunities*, Volumes 1 and 2, available for $25 each from IWS.
- The Internet at *http://www.unzexport.com*

Decide How to Sell Your Imports

There are a number of ways you can sell an import in your home-based business. They include:

- Mail order and direct mail
- Sales to retailers
- Catalog house sales
- Wholesale to distributors

Let's take a quick look at each to see how you might use it in your home-based import business.

MAIL-ORDER SALES

Probably the most profitable way to sell your imports is by mail order. Why? Because you can get higher prices for specialty items offered direct to your customers through the mail.

But to sell any item by mail order you must know what you're doing. Other chapters in this book give you many hints on mail-order sales. But if you're new to mail order and direct mail, I suggest you get some training in these two great fields. You'll find the *Mail-Order Riches Kit* (K-4) at the back of this book an excellent self-study course for this field. It will give you the key data you need to start making money selling your imports from your home.

RETAIL SALES

You can sell imports to *retailers*—that is, large and small stores of all kinds—from your home-based business. You can make sales by mail, fax, or phone.

If you dislike selling on the phone, then you may find that you're not at a disadvantage. Why? Because you may be able to sell more of your imports from home by mail order and direct mail than by phone. So with a big payday in view every day, you can get into the mail and into ad pages to sell hard—without ever seeing a customer face-to-face!

So I recommend that you use direct mail/mail order, fax, or phone for selling to retailers as a way of making your fortune from home selling imports to firms that seek them. Many fortunes have been made selling imports of all kinds to retailers.

CATALOG HOUSE SALES

Catalog houses are familiar to most of us. The catalog house prepares a neatly printed annual or holiday catalog—or both—for distribution to prospective direct-mail buyers. Today, most such catalogs are printed in color and are handsomely illustrated. Many of these catalogs are also advertised, or carried on, the Internet, where they are easily accessed.

To make a hit with catalog houses, do what I do in my home-based import business. That is, build your fortune quickly by being sure to:

> Offer catalog houses as large a discount as you can, and larger than other suppliers offer the house.

This means you'll probably have to start offering a catalog house a discount of at least 45 percent—$4.50 off on an item having a $10 list or selling price. Then, this means that catalog houses will pay you $10 - $4.50 = $5.50 for the item. From this $5.50 you pay:

- Cost of the item
- Freight in cost
- Advertising cost
- Packaging cost
- Other costs

To be able to offer the biggest discount to catalog houses:

- **Buy** the item as cheaply as possible.
- **Price** items as high as possible, consistent with the market and the competition's prices.
- **Seek** large orders from every catalog house.
- **Limit** the number of free samples you give away.
- **Keep** all your operating costs as low as possible.

You can make millions in your home-based import business selling to catalog houses. But you have to be in complete control of your business.

If you'd like to deal with about 10,000 businesses selling products or services through mail order catalogs, send $75 to IWS, Inc., P.O. Box 186, Merrick, NY 11566-0186. Ask for our *Mail-Order Business Directory*, which lists about 10,000 catalog houses, including business-to-business and consumer catalogs. Each listing gives the company's name, address, telephone and fax numbers, contact name, sales range, price of catalog (most are free), and product lines handled. The directory is arranged in thirty-four product categories, with alphabetical index. Also included are some 500 foreign mail-order catalog companies. You can call (516) 766-5850 to order by credit card. Air mail delivery is an additional $10 in the United States, $20 overseas.

SALES TO WHOLESALERS

Wholesale sales of imports can relieve you of many head-aches in your home-based business—if you can find a few big-volume wholesalers. And what's a big-volume whole-saler? It's an all-out, gung-ho sales firm that really moves imports from your hands into the buyer's hands. It sells your imports to stores, catalog houses, mail-order firms, and others seeking imports in larger quantities.

Typical wholesalers I know operate from cheap office or industrial buildings. Their "furniture" is made of cast-off cardboard packing boxes, wooden fruit and vegetable crates, etc. Yet they make huge profits on imports because their:

- **Expenses** are low.
- **Turnover** of products is large.
- **Imported** items move in and out fast.

For example, one import wholesaler I know on the West Coast pays only $380 a month rent for a second-floor com-bined loft space and home near the waterfront. But, during the year of the writing of this book, he sold some $1.7 mil-lion in imports to retailers (stores, mail-order houses, and others). His profit on these sales was more than 12 percent—meaning he earned some $204,000 in his home business during the year. This BWB told me, "Success is earning more than your wife can spend!"

Retailers like him are constantly looking for new imports. Why? Because stores want new products. Such products are exciting and bring in lots of new customers and sales. This is what every wholesaler wants!

The Best Way to Sell Your Imports

The best way to sell your imports will vary with what you're importing. To find the best way:

Try each major sales method listed above—mail order/direct mail, retailers, catalog houses, and wholesalers—for your import(s).

Work with each method that produces enough sales; meanwhile, sell to every other market you can find for your imports.

You can make a big fortune from home-based imports. Just be certain—at all times—to:

- **Try to** improve the way you run your business.
- **Keep** searching for ways to make larger sales.
- **Think** success at all times.

Improve Your Methods

The only constant in life is change. Recognize this fact and resolve that the changes in your home-based business life will be for the better. Thus, every change you make will be

- An improvement of your business.
- Positive—not negative.
- Helpful to people, and yourself.

To improve your methods, get—and read—everything you can on the importing business. Go to the Department of Commerce Web site on the Internet and read the latest information about importing. Use the IWS *Export–Import Riches Kit* (K-17) at the back of this book to improve your know-how.

Two challenges you will meet in importing are: (1) when to order your imports; (2) what to do during costly transport strikes. Let's look at each.

Know When to Order Your Imports

If you're importing holiday decorations, you don't place your order in November for this year's holiday! "That's obvious," you say. Perhaps it is to you. But too many novice home-based importers do just that and are stuck with unsalable items for a year or more. The time to order holiday items is in the *previous* May.

As a general guide, consider using the Hicks Rule for Imports (HRI):

Order seven months in advance for repetitive holidays, five months in advance for repetitive seasons.

You may, as you advance your own home-based business, want to change these rules. Fine! I never wrote a "golden rule" yet. But these guidelines will serve as a starting point in developing your import planning. And when doing your import planning, just remember the other Hicks rule:

In business it always takes you longer and costs you more than you figure it will!

With that time-cost rule in mind, let's take a look at a major source of import delays—strikes of various kinds.

Be Ready for Costly Strikes

If we were to meet in person to discuss your home-based business's financial future, you'd probably hear me remark, within the first hour, "You have to 'beat the system'—but *you must use honest methods at all times.*"

Now such a remark doesn't mean I'm against "the system." Instead, it means I'm a person who wants to live within the system but at the same time accomplish much more than the average person does. You, I believe, must do the same— if you want to accumulate a large sum of money quickly and honestly in your home-based business.

To "beat the system" I mean that you:

• **Work** while others doze (such as on trains, planes, buses, etc.).
• **Act** while others delay to "think it over."
• **Overcome** while others succumb.

It's in the area of strikes that I suggest you spend a lot of time learning how to overcome while others succumb.

Here are a few helpful hints I've used profitably in my home-based business.

Don't Let Strikes Ruin You

I'm not against labor unions. As a seagoing deep-water Merchant Marine engineer I was a member of several unions. But in the import business there are so many strikes that can slow your business that you must be ready to overcome them. The possible strikes I'm talking about include:

- Trucker's strikes
- Seamen's strikes
- Longshoremen's strikes
- Tugboat strikes
- Harbor pilot strikes
- Shipyard strikes
- Airline pilot strikes
- Air traffic controller strikes
- Cabin attendant strikes
- Airport ground personnel strikes

Now keep in mind that such strikes can occur on both sides of the water. So strikes can really hurt you in your wallet. And—if you're like me—that's a very sensitive spot!

To prevent strikes from cutting into your import profits, take these steps:

1. **Use** the list of strikes above as a guide and prepare your own list of strikes that might hurt you in your home-based importing.
2. **Figure out** alternative shippers you could use, and ways of getting your import into the country—which is the usual problem in a strike.
3. **List** the alternate shippers you found in step 2.
4. **Contact** your alternate shippers—such as small trucking firms, airlines, shipping lines, etc. Find out what their fees are, their schedules, and other details.

5. **Try to arrange,** with each shipper, a strike plan—which is the service they would give you if a strike occurred.
6. **Make** complete notes, for each shipper, of the names, titles, phone and fax numbers, work schedules, and other relevant data, of important people at the alternate shippers, as you talk. Then you'll be ready to take action, if and when a strike occurs.
7. **Keep** alert to labor news in those industries that affect—or might affect—your business. Then you'll be ready for a strike before it occurs.
8. **Take** strong pre-strike action if nondelivery of your import items means a loss of steady customers. Do the same if you're in a seasonal business and a strike means the loss of your products for the entire season.

You can beat strikes in your home-based import business. But you must be prepared. Take the steps listed here and there will be few strikes that will beat you.

Keep Alert to Popular Fads

You can make a quick bundle of money in your home-based importing business from a popular fad such as in-line skates, personal CD players, American flag decals for windows, etc. But you must be alert so you can "tune in" on the fad while

- It is still new, and developing.
- You have time to design your product.
- You contact your overseas suppliers.
- The products are shipped to you.
- You begin your sales campaign.
- You get rich from the deal.

By keeping alert to new trends you will be able to move with speed, when you have to. And in today's fast-moving world, speed often means the difference between high profits and no profits!

Look Ahead to Your Import Wealth

You can get rich in home-based importing—if you really try. I'm just a skinny little guy—5-feet-10, 142 pounds. Yet with little more than one finger and a few minutes a week, I've supervised the selection and sale of imports generating more than $250,000 per year in sales.

Meanwhile, I'm a busy member of the Board of Directors of a multimillion-dollar capital lending and personal finance organization "crying" to make loans to people who need money. At the same time I'm president of a highly successful mail-order/direct-mail firm with import–export customers all over the world. And I conduct lectures and seminars worldwide. Meanwhile, my 106th book was just published. Now I'm not telling you this to please my ego. Instead, I'm saying:

> If one slender person can do all this, just imagine how successful you can be if you concentrate just on the importing business!

So you see, you can be a big success in your home-based importing business. Just recognize that you'll be most successful if you keep the following in mind:

- **Be aware** of possible import traps.
- **Recognize** the profitability of importing.
- **Have** a market before you import any product.
- **Make** sensible market surveys.
- **Pick** the "ideal" product for your business.
- **Develop** your import product from your ideas.
- **Decide** how to sell your import—use multiple outlets.
- **Improve** your methods as you gain experience.
- **Keep alert** to popular fads and the opportunities they offer.
- **Look ahead** to your import wealth.

This chapter shows you exactly how to take each of these steps in your home-based import business. Now all you need to do is *take the first step* toward your home-based import wealth. If you need help, call me—I'm at your service!

To get you started faster in your home-based importing, here are a number of hot imports. You can a start a business with each type of import. Concentrate on one type before you expand your business.

Hot Imports Worth Considering

Auto parts—for engines, brakes, fuel systems, electrical systems, tires, windshield wipers, etc.

Model airplanes, ships, military equipment—either finished production-line models of famous craft and vehicles, or custom-built special-order items.

Tools, hand and power—for home hobbyists and professionals, including hammers, saws, pliers, wrenches, power drills, power saw tables, chain saws, and self-powered outdoor tools.

Hair bows, bands, clips—for children and adults of all ages in varying colors, styles, and materials.

Office furniture—especially new designs reflecting the modern and different approaches to office working conditions.

Cotton socks, shirts, trousers, and other garments—for children and adults in new, and unusual, designs.

Cameras and video equipment for amateurs and professionals—specialty items for these markets are popular.

Peppers and spices for unique tastes are popular all over the world and are excellent import products.

Yarns and threads for the home and professional markets are always popular and sell well everywhere.

There you have nine hot import items. If any appeal to you, get started as soon as you can. And if you have any questions, please call me!

CHAPTER 5

Make Big Money in High-Discount and Liquidation Sales

You live in an age of discounting—everyone wants a bargain. We're all looking for a reduced price on whatever we buy—a car, furniture, food, vacations, and more. No one today wants to pay list price—we all want to boast about the shrewd deal we worked to get an excellent product or service.

You can earn money at home offering big discounts or liquidations on needed items. And you can often do this without ever seeing, touching, or handling the item or service. How? Here are two foxy-smart ways for you to cash in on this universal desire for a bargain and build a big home-based income.

1. Find items you can buy at a high discount.
2. Find buyers for these items and complete the transaction.

Both these steps are usually done by mail, phone, or fax, depending on your preference. Thus, you can "do the deal" all by mail, all by phone, or all by fax. Or you can use a combination of these methods—if you choose. Let's look at these two steps to see how easy they are for you.

Why Is the Surplus-Item or Liquidation Business Good for You?

There are a number of excellent reasons why this business is good for you. These reasons are:

- **You can start, and run, your business from home.** No office of any kind is needed—just a telephone and mailbox so you can receive letters.
- **You don't have to put up any money** of your own to start this business. Why? Because you can arrange a bank-to-bank transfer of funds from buyer to seller through your bank, with your profit staying in your account.
- **If you like to use the telephone,** you can get the toll-free 800 or 888 number of your supplier (the seller) and make your phone calls toll-free!
- **If you prefer to use the mail**, you can contact your seller and buyer for just the price of one First Class stamp for each.
- **You can combine mail and phone** by faxing your seller and buyer using their toll-free fax numbers.

Beyond all these reasons is one other. It's a five-letter word spelled M-O-N-E-Y! How much might you earn in this business? One expert says that people working full time at the distressed merchandise business can earn $250,000 a year. And this same expert says that part-timers working out of the comfort of their own home can average $40,000 a year! Just think what a difference in your lifestyle an extra $40,000 a year would make. Once you do I'm sure you'll give this business a close look!

How Do You Start in This Business?

That's easy. You just take a few simple steps.

1. **Decide what surplus items you want to locate** and place with a firm seeking them. The best surplus items to handle

are toys, tools, women's clothing, dungarees (Levi's 501's, etc.), videos, CDs, music tapes, children's cribs, sporting goods, sneakers, caps, sweaters, blankets, etc.

2. **Decide who might need your overrun items.** Typical buyers will include discount department stores, buyers' clubs, drugstores, military PXs, bargain basements, book clubs (for books), supermarket chains, mall wagon groups, etc.

3. **Contact your potential customer** by mail, phone, or fax. Say—for example—"WE CAN SUPPLY 1,000 matching necklace/earring sets at a very high discount. Call 123-4567, or write 210 Main St., Anytown 12345."

4. **Quote your price** when you get a call or letter from a prospective customer. When quoting your price—which includes your profit—tell the buyer it will be a bank-to-bank transaction because it speeds the sale.

5. **Talk to someone at your commercial bank** (it will usually have the initials N. A. after its name) about doing a bank-to-bank transaction for purchase and sale. Most banks will be glad to handle this for you for a small fee, which will be deducted from your profit. You can have a freight forwarder recommended by the bank handle the shipping.

Once you've decided this business is for you, you'll take a few simple steps. Here they are.

Decide Where You'll Find High-Discount Items

You must have a source of high-discount items to make money in this business. Your source can be near you—or distant from you. It makes no difference. You just have to be able to get products or services at a price that's way below what others have to pay. Typical sources of high-discount items include:

1. **Closeout specialists** who handle various products—such as children's clothing, videos, tools, auto parts, games, sporting goods, etc.

2. **Manufacturers** who have excess inventory, which they want to unload as quickly as possible to clear the way for new production.
3. **Overseas exporters** who have low-cost products that offer real value because their production cost is so much lower than if they were made in your country by people who are paid much higher wages.
4. **Special sales** of store closeouts, estate auctions, bankruptcy proceedings, businesses moving to a new location, department store returns, etc.

When you use any one of these sources for high-discount items, you deal by mail, fax, or phone. You don't have to travel to see what you're buying because most of the items are small and easily transported. Your biggest challenge is getting the lowest price possible for what you're buying.

In dealing with high-discount items you'll try to have as many sources as possible. Why? For a few important reasons, namely:

1. **The more sources you have**, the greater your chances of getting what you need at a price that beats your competition and allows you to make a sale at the highest profit possible to you.
2. **The more sources you have**, the greater the number of items you can offer to your buyers. With a larger number of offerings, your chances of making a sale are greater than with a smaller number.
3. **The more sources you have**, the easier it is to "play off" one supplier against another so you get a better price for what you buy. And the lower your price, the higher your profit on each sale.

To organize your sources, start a simple file folder marked *Merchandise Sources*. Using a single sheet of paper for each supplier, set up your source list this way:

MERCHANDISE SOURCES

Supplier Name: _____

Supplier Address: _____

_____

_____

Phone/ fax number(s): _____

_____

_____

Products/Services Offered: _____

_____

_____

Prices Charged: _____

_____

_____

Notes about this supplier: _____

_____

_____

_____

_____

Special shipping requirements of this item or service: _____

_____

_____

_____

_____

Other special considerations: _____

_____

_____

_____

_____

Will this supplier inventory my purchases until ready for shipment
to my customers? _____

The Fastest Way to Find High-Discount Sources

You can spend months looking for sources of high-discount merchandise. But with just one tip from a source book you can reduce that time to minutes. How? Use our *Directory of High-Discount Merchandise Sources* listed at the back of this book—and which you'll find at any large public library.

Or—if you'd prefer—use the list of trade associations and business groups that I give you below. To make use of their free help, take these easy steps:

1. **Decide** what types of surplus merchandise you'd like to handle and earn money from.
2. **Look up** the trade association listed below for that type of product.
3. **Call, write, or fax** the association, asking for the names of their members who might be offering high discounts on their products.
4. **Contact selected members** and ask for price quotations on their surplus items that they want to sell.
5. **Make an offer** to buy selected items based on your ability to find a buyer with a bank-to-bank transaction for the merchandise.
6. **Find your buyer** and collect your profit with just a few pieces of paper for the transaction. You never have to see, touch, or inventory the high-discount items or services you sell!

Trade Associations to Contact

PRODUCTS OF ALL TYPES

Adhesive & Sealant Council
1627 K St. NW, Suite 1000, Washington, DC 20006;
phone: (202) 452-1500; fax: (202) 452-1501;
Web: *http://www.ascouncil.org*

Aerospace Industries Association of America
1250 Eye St. NW, Suite 1200, Washington, DC 20005;
phone: (202) 371-8400; fax: (202) 371-8470;
Web: *http://www.access.digex.net/~aia*

Agricultural Retailers Association
11701 Borman Dr., Suite 110, St. Louis, MO 63146;
phone: (314) 567-6655; fax: (314) 567-6808

Air Conditioning & Refrigeration Institute
4301 N. Fairfax Dr., Suite 425, Arlington, VA 22203;
phone: (703) 524-8800; fax: (703) 538-3816;
Web: *http://www.ari.org*

Aluminum Association
900 19th St. NW, Suite 300, Washington, DC 20006;
phone: (202) 293-8500; fax: (202) 331-1362;
Web: *http://www.aluminum.org*

American Booksellers Association
828 S. Broadway, Tarrytown, NY 10591;
phone: (914) 591-2665; fax: (914) 591-2720;
Web: *http://www.ambook.org*

American Ceramic Society
735 Ceramic Place, Westerville, OH 43081;
phone: (616) 890-4700; fax: (614) 899-6109;
Web: *http://www.acers.org*

American Cloak & Suit Manufacturers Association, Inc.
450 7th Ave., New York, NY 10123; phone: (212) 244-7300

American Electronics Association
5201 Great American Pkwy, Suite 520, Santa Clara,
CA 95054; phone: (408) 987-4200; fax: (408) 970-8565;
Web: *http://www.aeanet.org*

American Floral Marketing Counsel
1601 Duke St., Alexandria, VA 22314;
phone: (703) 836-8700; fax: (703) 836-8705

American Hardware Manufacturers Association
801 N. Plaza Dr., Schaumburg, IL 60173;
phone: (847) 605-1025; fax: (847) 605-1093

American Home Sewing & Craft Association
1375 Broadway, Fourth Floor, New York, NY 10018;
phone: (212) 302-2150; fax: (212) 391-8009

American Luggage Dealers Association
610 Anacapa St., Suite G, Santa Barbara, CA 93101;
phone: (805) 966-6909; fax: (805) 966-5710

American Spice Trade Association
P.O. Box 1267, Englewood Cliffs, NJ 07632;
phone: (201) 568-2163; fax: (201) 568-7318

American Sportfishing Association
1033 N. Fairfax St., Suite 200, Alexandria, VA 22314;
phone: (703) 519-9691; fax: (703) 519-1872

American Surplus Dealers
2525 Ocean Park Blvd., Santa Monica, CA 90405;
phone: (310) 396-6006; fax: (310) 399-2662

Association of Home Appliance Manufacturers
20 N. Wacker Dr., Suite 1500, Chicago, IL 60606;
phone: (312) 984-5800; fax: (312) 984-5823

Beauty & Barber Supply Institute
11811 N. Tatum Blvd., Suite 1085, Phoenix, AZ 85028;
phone: (602) 404-1800; fax: (602) 404-8900

Business Products Industry Association
301 N. Fairfax St., Alexandria, VA 22314;
phone: (703) 549-9040; fax: (703) 683-7552

Carpet & Rug Institute
310 S. Holiday Ave., Dalton, GA 30720;
phone: (706) 278-3176; fax: (706) 278-8835

Diving Equipment Manufacturers Association
2050 Santa Cruz St., Suite 1000, Anaheim, CA 92805;
phone: (714) 939-6399; fax: (714) 939-6398

Door & Hardware Institute
14170 Newbrook Dr., Chantilly, VA 20151;
phone: (703) 222-2010; fax: (703) 222-2410

Electronic Industries Association
2500 Wilson Blvd., Arlington, VA 22201;
phone: (703) 907-7500; fax: (703) 907-7501;
Web: *http://www.eia.org*

Fluid Power Distributors Association
201 Barclay Pavilion West, Cherry Hill, NJ 08034;
phone: (609) 795-6113; fax: (609) 795-6362;
Web: *http://www.aid.net/fpda*

General Merchandise Distributors Council
1275 Lake Plaza Dr., Colorado Springs, CO 80906;
phone: (719) 576-4260; fax: (719) 576-2661

Home Furnishings International Association
P.O. Box 420807, Dallas, TX 75342;
phone: (972) 741-7632; fax: (972) 742-9103

International Institute of Synthetic Rubber Producers Inc.
2077 S. Gessner Rd., Suite 133, Houston, TX 77063;
phone: (713) 783-7511; fax: (713) 783-7253

International Sleep Products Association
333 Commerce St., Alexandria, VA 22314;
phone: (703) 683-8371; fax: (703) 683-4503

Jewelers of America
1185 Avenue of the Americas, 30th Floor, New York, NY
10036; phone: (212) 768-8777; fax: (212) 768-8087;
Web: *http://www.jewelers.org*

Motorcycle Industry Council
2 Jenner St., Suite 150, Irvine, CA 92618;
phone: (714) 727-4211; fax: (714) 727-4217

National Art Materials Trade Association
178 Lakeview Ave., Clifton, NJ 07011;
phone: (973) 546-6400; fax: (973) 546-0393

National Association of Music Merchants
5790 Armada Dr., Carlsbad, CA 92008;
phone: (760) 438-8001; fax: (760) 438-7327;
Web: *http://www.namm.com*

National Auctioneers Association
8880 Ballentine St., Overland Park, KS 66214;
phone: (913) 541-8084; fax: (913) 894-5281;
Web: *http://www.auctionweb.com/naa*

National Fluid Power Association
3333 N. Mayfair Rd., Suite 311, Milwaukee, WI 53222;
phone: (414) 776-3344; fax: (414) 778-3361;
Web: *http://www.nfpa.org*

National Grocers Association
1825 Samuel Morse Dr., Reston, VA 20190;
phone: (703) 437-5300; fax: (703) 437-7768

National Home Furnishings Association
P.O. Box 2396, High Point, NC 27261;
phone: (910) 883-1650; fax: (910) 883-1195

National Luggage Dealers Association
3338 W. Lake Ave., Glen View, IL 60025;
phone: (847) 998-6869; fax: (847) 998-6864

National Paint & Coatings Association
1500 Rhode Island Ave. NW, Washington, DC 20005;
phone: (202) 462-6272; fax: (202) 462-8549;
Web: *http://www.paint.org*

National Pasta Association
2101 Wilson Blvd., Suite 920, Arlington, VA 22201;
phone: (703) 841-0818; fax: (703) 528-6507;
Web: *http://www.ilovepasta.org*

National Sporting Goods Association
1699 Wall St., Suite 700, Mount Prospect, IL 60056;
phone: (847) 439-4000; fax: (847) 439-0111

Pet Industry Distributors Association
5024-R Campbell Blvd., Baltimore, MD 21236;
phone: (410) 931-8100; fax: (410) 931-8111

Specialty Tool & Fasteners Distributors Association
P.O. Box 44, Elm Grove, WI 53122; phone: (414) 784-4774;
fax: (414) 784-5059

Sporting Goods Manufacturers Association
200 Castlewood Dr., North Palm Beach, FL 33408;
phone: (561) 842-4100; fax: (561) 863-8984;
Web: *http://www.sportlink.com*

Toy Manufacturers of America, Inc.
200 5th Ave., Suite 740, New York, NY 10010;
phone: (212) 675-1141; fax: (212) 633-1429;
Web: *http://www.toy-tma.com*

Wallcoverings Association
401 N. Michigan Ave., Chicago, IL 60611;
phone: (312) 644-6618; fax: (312) 527-6774

Wood Products Manufacturers Association
175 State Road East, Westminster, MA 01473;
phone: (978) 874-5445; fax: (978) 874-9946

COMPUTERS AND DATA PROCESSING

Computers & Communications Industry Association
666 11th St. NW, Suite 600, Washington, DC 20001;
phone: (202) 783-0070; fax: (202) 783-0534;
Web: *http://www.ccianet.org*

Computing Technology Industry Association
450 E. 22nd St., Suite 230, Lombard, IL 60148;
phone: (630) 268-1818; fax: (630) 268-1384;
Web: *http://www.comptia.org*

National Association of Desktop Publishers
462 Boston St., Topsfield, MA 01983;
phone: (978) 887-7900; fax: (978) 887-6117

National PC Users Group
P.O. Box 1076, Lemont, PA 16851; phone: (814) 237-5511;
e-mail: *npcug@aol.com*

Recreational Software Advisory Council
1050 Waltham St., Suite 420, Lexington, MA 02173;
phone: (781) 860-9888; fax: (781) 860-9604;
Web: *http://www.rsac.org*

Software Publishers Association
1730 M St. NW, Suite 700, Washington, DC 20036;
phone: (202) 452-1600; fax: (202) 223-8756;
Web: *http://www.spa.org*

HOBBIES AND CRAFTS

Academy of Model Aeronautics
5151 E. Memorial Dr., Muncie, IN 47302;
phone: (765) 287-1256; fax: (765) 741-0057

American Horticultural Society
7931 E. Boulevard Dr., Alexandria, VA 22308;
phone: (703) 768-5700; fax: (703) 768-8700;
Web: *http://www.emall.com/ahs*

American Numismatic Association
818 N. Cascade Ave., Colorado Springs, CO 80903;
phone: (719) 632-2646; fax: (719) 634-4085;
Web: *http://www.money.org*

American Philatelic Society
P.O. Box 8000, State College, PA 16803;
phone: (814) 237-3803; fax: (814) 237-6128;
Web: *http://www.west.net*

American Rose Society
8877 Jefferson Paige Rd., Shreveport, LA 71119;
phone: (318) 938-5402; fax: (318) 938-5405;
Web: *http://www.ars.org*

Handweavers Guild of America
3727 Duluth Hwy., Suite 201, Duluth, GA 30136;
phone: (770) 495-7702; fax: (770) 495-7703

Hobby Industry Association of America
319 E. 54th St., Elmwood Park, NJ 07407;
phone: (201) 794-1133; fax: (201) 797-0657;
Web: *http://www.hobby.org/hia*

National Craft Association
1945 E. Ridge Rd., Suite 5178, Rochester, NY 14622; phone:
(716) 266-5472; fax: (716) 544-4699;
Web: *http://www.craftassoc.com*

SPORTS AND OUTDOOR ACTIVITIES

American Bicycle Association
P.O. Box 718, Chandler, AZ 85244; phone: (602) 961-1903;
fax: (602) 961-1842

American Bowling Congress
5301 S. 76th St., Greendale, WI 53129;
phone: (414) 421-6400; fax: (414) 421-3014

American Motorcyclist Association
33 Collegeview Rd., Westerville, OH 43081;
phone: (614) 891-2425; fax: (614) 891-5012

American Water Ski Association
799 Overlook Dr. SE, Winter Haven, FL 33884;
phone: (941) 324-4341; fax: (941) 325-8259;
Web: *http://waterski.net/ski/awsa/awsamenu.html*

Billiard Congress of America
910 23rd Ave., Coralville, IA 52241; phone: (319) 351-2112;
fax: (319) 351-7767; Web: *http://www.bca-pool.com*

National Archery Association
1 Olympic Plaza, Colorado Springs, CO 80909;
phone: (719) 578-4576; fax: (719) 632-4733;
Web: *http://www.usarchery.org*

Make the Sale and Build Your Fortune

Now that you've found your product or service, you're ready to make the sale from your home-based business to build your future fortune. To make the sale, take these easy, quick steps:

1. **Decide** where to advertise the products or services you have available for future customers.
2. **Pick** the publications, the Internet, or mailing list you might use to promote the low-cost products or services that you have available.
3. **Run** a short classified ad in your selected publications to test your market. Your ad might say—for toys you sell:

   TOYS AVAILABLE at high discount; all age groups.
   Call 123-4567 for full details and prices.

4. **Arrange** for the sale by phone, mail, or fax. Have the payment sent to your bank, as discussed earlier.
5. **Ship** the items to your customer. Go on to the next sale of products or services.
6. **Continue** selling until you reach the level of financial success you seek in your home-based high-discount business.

And remember: If you ever have any questions, call me—Ty Hicks, your author—and I'll be happy to try to answer them—at no charge of any kind—if you're a subscriber to one of my newsletters.

CHAPTER 6

FIND HIDDEN SUCCESS IN "PAPER" AND OTHER REAL ESTATE

REAL ESTATE IS a great home business. Some of my real estate BWBs are so close to their business that they live on the property that gives them their income! Could you ask for any closer ties? (These BWBs live in one of the apartments of their multi-family income buildings.)

Choose How You Want to Prosper in Real Estate

You can earn money in home-based real estate in two general ways.

1. **Invest small sums in "paper" real estate**—that is, *options* that allow you to control large pieces of real estate for a tiny amount of money. Your income comes from the difference between the cost of the property and the selling price you can get for it.
2. **Buy, and own, income property** of a type you feel comfortable with—such as residential (apartment houses), commercial (stores), industrial (factories), etc. Your income is derived from the rents you are paid, after you deduct the operating expenses.

Let's take a look at each type of real estate and see how you can earn money from it. And—if you'd like—you can run both types of businesses from your home and earn an excellent income.

How Options Can Help You Build Your Fortune

An option is a written agreement you have with the seller of a property to buy it at a stated price within a named time period—which could be thirty, sixty, or ninety days or more. If you do not buy the property within the option period (i.e., thirty, sixty, ninety days) you lose your option amount. But this amount is so small compared to the value of the property you control, and the profit you might make on its sale, that people shrug it off. For example:

> You find a multi-family building priced at $200,000. An option to buy it costs $100 with a sixty-day time period. You believe you can resell this property for $250,000 in less than sixty days. With a bit of advertising and a few phone calls you are able to sell the apartment house for $248,000. So your profit after expenses (including your option cost of $100) and closing costs of $11,000 is $248,000 - $11,000 - $200,100 = $36,900. Thus, for an investment of $100, you earned a profit of $36,900. And even if your option cost you $1,000 (which it probably would not), you'd still have a nice profit for a few days' work. Further, if you were unable to sell the property in sixty days, you would lose only $100 in the first instance, or $1,000 in the second instance.

All of your dealings with an option can be done from home—except for visiting the property you want to buy. Never take an option on real estate without seeing it with your own eyes! You might—if you wish—have a trusted partner or relative check a property for you. But—if you can—you're much better off checking it out yourself.

Some options can cost as little as $1. Such options are on property that is not in great demand. So while your option costs you little, the chance of selling the real estate will be smaller (usually) than for properties whose option costs more. (We've even heard of options that cost nothing—just your signature on a piece of paper—but the real estate sold fairly fast. See real-life examples later in this chapter.)

To help you understand options better, you should read the typical real estate option shown in Figure 6-1. This option is an example of one that might be used for your deals. Do *not*—however—use this option without the guidance of a competent real estate attorney, who will prepare your option for you.

What will be your game plan for making money from home in real estate options? Here's your ten-step game plan:

1. **Decide what type of property** you want to work with—that is, option and then resell either the property or the option itself.
2. **Look for such properties** in your area by regularly scanning the ads in your Sunday newspapers, and in any other local real estate publications you can find.
3. **Contact sellers** of suitable properties by phone, mail, or fax when you find one advertised. It is best to deal directly with a seller, instead of going through a real estate broker who might not approve of your offering an option on a property.
4. **Get full data on the property** from the seller. This will be supplied free of charge to you and will include the asking price, amount of down payment, income, expenses, real estate taxes, utility costs (water, sewer, etc.), and other important financial data on the property.
5. **Explore the sales possibilities** of the property. Is such property in strong demand in your area? Can you raise the asking price to a level where you can make a profit on this property? A real estate broker can help you answer these questions. (Note: A real estate broker may discourage your buying a property with an option, but the same broker will be happy to work with you on the sale of an optioned property. Why? Because he or she earns a commission on the sale!)
6. **Offer the seller an option to buy** the property if the numbers (your cost, potential selling price, and demand) appear to be satisfactory.
7. **Try to pay the least amount** for the option and get the longest time—more than thirty days and at least ninety days, if possible—for the option.
8. **Put the property on the market quickly**—the same day you and the seller sign the option. Use every means you

OPTION TO PURCHASE REAL ESTATE

___[Date]___

I hereby offer to buy the real estate located at ___[Address]___ and described in the attached copies of deed and title, within the next ___[Number]___ days, ending on ___[Date]___. In the event I do not purchase the above-described real estate within the next ___[Number]___ days, this purchase option will expire and any and all rights I have in this Purchase Option will become null and void, and the earnest money of ___[$ Amount]___ will be kept by the seller with no possible recourse by myself.

_____   _____
Signed—Optionee (You)   Signed—Optionor (Seller)

_____   _____
Date   Date

Figure 6-1. Example of an option to purchase real estate written by home-based wealth builder. Final option MUST be written by a qualified real estate attorney. Do NOT use this example for any actual real estate transaction.

can to get the property in front of its potential market. You want to sell as quickly as possible, even though a quick sale may produce a slightly lower price for the property.

9. **Get competent legal advice** every step of the way. Why? Because real estate today has many potential problem areas. Only with an experienced real estate attorney at your side can you avoid the traps that might exist.

10. **Go on to your next option deal.** Only by moving ahead can you build a big income from your home in the options field. You can—if you wish—pause and enjoy your profit from your first deal. But the best way to earn a large income in this field is to continue deal after deal!

You *can* earn big money in "paper" real estate from home. Just follow the ten steps outlined above to see what you can achieve without having an office, a large payroll, expensive machines, or any other problem-makers!

A Real-Life Option Success from Home

To show you how you might make big money in options, here's a real-life story from one of our IWS newsletter readers, who told me:

"I took an option on thirty-three single-family homes for 120 days for zero dollars—no money changed hands. The option cost of these homes at the end of the 120 days would be $796,000. If I could not come up with this much I would lose the houses. But by using creative advertising and sales methods I was able to sell fifteen of the houses for $748,000; my cost for these 15 houses was $392,000. So my profit, before ad expenses, was $748,000 - $392,000 = $356,000. I had the buyer pay the closing costs. The other eighteen houses sold for $565,000. My cost for these was $404,000; my profit before expenses was $161,000. So my total profit before minor expenses was $517,000. That's not bad for just about four months' work! Even if my expenses ran several thousand dollars (which they didn't), I'd still have a nice year's income."

The way this BWB accomplished this real-life deal working from his own home (he showed me all the paperwork) was by:

- **Knowing the area** these homes are located in. He carefully studied values and sales in this location for a long time.
- **Offering his buyers good value** for the price they paid, making it a win-win sale for the buyers and the seller—plus the issuer of the option.
- **Arranging the financing** so the buyers could get mortgages that were affordable and allowed them to earn money from the homes they bought.
- **Holding to his asking price** even though the buyers tried to "knock him down" in price to get a better deal.

Use a Land Contract for Other "Paper" Deals

When a seller is unwilling to accept an option on a property you want to control until you sell it, consider a *land contract*— also called a *contract for deed* or *installment land contract*. A land contract gives you control of a property, but it may cost you more than an option. Here's how a land contract works:

> Say you want to take over two buildings and the land they are on because you believe you can resell them at a profit. Or you might wish to hold these two buildings as sources of income after you refinance them to reduce the monthly mortgage payments. You work out a land contract with the seller that says that you will pay $400 down and $800 per month for five years, after which you will receive the deed to the property. When you receive the deed you will also have additional payments to make before you fully own the property. At any time during these sixty months, or thereafter, you can: (1) sell the property, or parts of it; (2) refinance the property; (3) take out an equity loan to get cash out of the property. You're in the driver's seat again because you can control the property and do what you wish with it.

"So what's the difference between a land contract and an option?" you ask. There are several differences:

1. **With an option**, you make only a one-time payment for the right to control the property.
2. **With an option**, you do not have to make any monthly payments to retain control.
3. **With a land contract**, you make a down payment of some amount to begin the deal.
4. **With a land contract**, you make monthly payments for a stated period of time, after which you are awarded the deed (ownership) of the property.

So how can a land contract work for you when you operate out of your home? Here's a real-life example from one of our readers:

> He bought twelve properties in the two- to four-family range in four months using a land contract on each. Working with a local lender he refinanced these properties and "mortgaged out" (that is, came away from the closings with cash in his hand) for a total of $40,000. He is holding these properties for the monthly cash flow he gets from them. As an aside, this BWB was able to buy these properties for 80 percent of their market value on the land contract and then refinance them at 85 percent of their appraised value.

You can do much the same in your own home business. All you need do is decide which type of paper you want to work with—an option or a land contract. Also, you will be prepared to work with either type, giving you greater flexibility in your dealings with sellers. Again—you *must* have the advice of a competent real estate attorney in all of these deals. Don't even think of trying to do one of these deals on your own!

For a comprehensive discussion of options, see the *Options Report* listed at the end of this book. It gives you a complete view of options and how you can use them. You'll find this big report both interesting and useful.

Figure 6-2 shows a typical land contract. This is presented only for informational purposes. For a land contract for a specific property, see your attorney!

LAND CONTRACT

_____[Date]_____

I hereby agree to buy the land and all improvements on it at

_____[Address]_____ , described in the copies of the deed and title

attached, for _____[$ Amount]_____ paid in _____[Number]_____

installments of _____[$ Amount]_____ monthly for the next

_____[Number]_____ months during which time I may use, occupy,

and collect income from said property. Within 30 days after

completion of the stated number of payments I will receive the

deed to and title for the above-named property. In the event I fail

to make full payment as described above, the property will revert

to the seller and I will not have any further right to use or occupy

this named property.

_____   _____
Signed—Buyer   Signed—Seller

*Figure 6-2. Example of a land contract written by home-based
wealth builder. Final land contract MUST be written by a
qualified real estate attorney. Do NOT use this example for
any actual real estate transaction.*

Build Your Home Fortune with Real Estate You Own

When you work with options, you almost never own the real estate. And you don't buy the real estate for monthly income. Instead, you're in the "flipping" business—that is, you take control of real estate to flip—sell—it for a profit.

With a land contract, you approach real estate ownership. But you need not own the real estate to profit from it. You can sell the real estate—that is, flip it—if you want to.

When you own real estate, you seek a monthly income from it in the form of rent payments from your tenants that exceed all your expenses for the property, including your mortgage payments. Your monthly profit can easily exceed $5,000 in larger properties. Meanwhile, the depreciation deductions that you are legally entitled to take can reduce your tax on this income to zero. Could you ask for a better deal?

But real estate ownership does require certain tasks from you, or from one of your helpers. You will need to:

1. **Find a suitable property** that appears to have sufficient cash flow to meet all its costs, plus paying for the mortgage.
2. **Work out a deal** so you can buy the property with a suitable down payment (that is, one you have, or can borrow).
3. **Buy the property** at a price that allows you to "make a buck" after you do any needed work on it and get it in suitable shape.
4. **"Shape up" the property** so its condition meets your approval and it delivers the cash flow you seek for it. This will typically take you six months after you take title to the property. As you gain more experience, you can cut this time to three months, or less.
5. **Continue to expand** your real estate holdings until you achieve the home-based income you seek. This may take anywhere from three to five years, depending on your income goals.

Let's see how you can build your home-based fortune in real estate you own, starting with little—or no—cash. You'll find it's lots of fun—and can be highly profitable for you!

Use the Zero-Cash Way to Real Estate Wealth

Almost every BWB I meet who likes real estate as a way of building home-based wealth has these two characteristics:

1. The BWB can easily—and quickly—find good income properties in his or her area.
2. The BWB does not have the cash down payment needed to take over the property he or she wants.

What can these BWBs do to get the properties they want? My answer is—and has been for many years—*borrow the down payment money you need!*

Why do I recommend that these BWBs borrow the down payment money for the income real estate they want to own? For these four important reasons:

1. **Borrowing the down payment money** is usually the only way these BWBs have to get into profitable income real estate they can run from home.
2. **Borrowing the down payment money** gives these BWBs greater incentive to work for their success. This means they have a much greater chance of hitting it big in this business—which is almost foolproof. Few people fail in income real estate ownership anywhere in the world.
3. **Borrowing the down payment money**, and repaying the loan, gives a big boost to the BWB's credit rating, allowing him or her to borrow more in the future. This means the BWB can expand small real estate holdings to large ones, increasing his or her monthly positive cash flow (PCF). You will never go wrong with a rising cash flow!
4. **Borrowing the down payment money** can be your key to wealth success today because PCF properties are easy to find when you have the down payment money!

Now you need not believe what I say. I respect you for that, good friend of mine. But you might like to glance over a few recent comments from my readers who tell me about their business success in letters, phone calls, and faxes. Here are a few, which you'll find interesting. The first success story, from Colorado, was a no-money-down deal:

> "I own a fourplex and one threeplex that I bought with no money down. These two bring me a cash flow of about $1,000 a month combined. This is great! I'm also starting a mortgage brokerage firm."

Another reader, writing from the Philippines, used no money down in an overseas real estate transaction:

> "Two weeks after reading your real estate book, I acquired my first property with our community mortgage fund for $385,000 Philippine. Using three loans, I got $1,960 P cash without putting any money down, so I mortgaged out. I got another property for $300,000 P. I will get a second mortgage on it and use the money for expansion and business." So you see, the borrowed down payment works worldwide!

This reader, who called from North Carolina, used a credit-card line of credit to finance an income real estate deal:

> "I have $1,000 per month positive cash flow from six apartment units and five houses I took over using my credit cards and a loan from a small bank. Getting these units really gave me much greater confidence."

A reader from Georgia owns multiple rental properties in different states:

> "Currently we have three single-family rental homes, two in Colorado and one in Georgia. We are always looking for more and have no problem finding positive cash flow properties. Lenders will easily give 75 to 90 percent mortgages."

I have thousands of similar letters from all over the world. Each was voluntarily written to me to tell me of the success each person achieved. You are welcome to inspect any—and all—of these letters at your leisure. All I ask is that you give me a few days' notice so I can get the letters out of the safe-deposit box where we keep them.

Consider Six More At-Home Real Estate Businesses

There are a number of other "paper" real estate businesses you can run from home. Full data on your earnings opportunities with each of these businesses is given in the listing at the end of this chapter. Here are six other "paper" real estate businesses you can run from home:

1. **Locate foreclosure properties** for others—and even yourself. When you locate foreclosures for others, you charge them a fee for each property you find. This fee can vary from as little as $10 to as much as $1,000, depending on the amount of work you do and the need for the property. You get your information from banks, sheriff's offices, the Internal Revenue Service, HUD (Department of Housing and Urban Development), city tax collection offices, etc. You can mail or fax to your clients the data you produce on foreclosures. And you can collect this data the same way—by mail or fax. All of this you can do from the comfort of your own home—be it an apartment, a trailer, a boat, or a rented room in a hotel. The person seeking foreclosure information doesn't care where it comes from as long as it is accurate and can help him or her earn money!

2. **Find cash for people who want to cash out of a mortgage** they're holding. People who sell real estate to others—homes, commercial buildings, factories, etc.—often accept part of the down payment in the form of a promissory note. This note, when backed by real estate, is called a *second mortgage* or *purchase-money mortgage* (PM). Such mortgages typically run 60 to 180 months, with a monthly payment of principal and interest (P&I). Many holders of such mortgages get weary of the monthly payments, which they must record, deposit, and keep track of twelve times a year. Other holders have a financial emergency requiring quick cash. Or a child may reach college age and the mortgage-holder is faced with a big tuition bill. What can be done? The mortgage holder can cash out— that is, sell—the mortgage for quick cash, which will solve his or her emergency or other difficulty. You bring the

seller and buyer of the mortgage together and earn a fee for doing so. It's a win-win situation: The seller gets cash; the buyer gets a steady stream of payments at a known interest rate, all secured by a piece of real estate that—in general—rises in value as time passes; and you get a fee working from home using the mail, fax, and phone. You're a mortgage cash-out broker! You can earn a significant income in this business with nationwide clients.

3. **Make real estate surveys for clients** who are thinking of buying, or selling, a property. You must study to qualify as a surveyor. Some states have colleges and other schools that offer courses in real estate surveying. A license may be required in your state. Check with your state's real estate department, which you'll find listed in your large-city phone book. Real estate surveys can be a great business because they help you learn all about values, problems, and opportunities in your area. You may even decide to use some of this data for your own business purposes. It is legal to do so!

4. **Appraise real estate for a fee in your area.** This is another "paper" real estate business that requires training—and possibly—a license. But your rewards—working from home—can be significant. You do need appraisal experience before you can start earning money as an appraiser. The best way to qualify is to take a course at a local college or technical institute and then work in the field as a trainee with an experienced appraiser to gain the needed know-how. Once you know enough—and have passed any state requirements—you can go out on your own. Besides earning a nice income as an appraiser you can also get a good handle on the properties in your area and their true value, should you ever decide to become an owner of income real estate.

5. **Become a mortgage payoff advisor.** Many people, when first buying a home or an income property, do not take time to figure the total cost of a thirty- or forty-year mortgage. For example, if you pay $1,000 a month on a thirty-year mortgage your total cost will be 30 years × 12 months/year × $1,000 per month = $360,000. If a person makes just one extra payment a year, he or she can reduce the total cost to about $320,000, saving $40,000. You

can earn money at home showing people how to reduce the total cost of their mortgage. Using readily available computer programs, you can show clients the effects of making an extra one, two, three, or more payments per year on their mortgage. For this guidance, you are paid a generous fee—working out of your own home. While a computer can make advising your clients easier and faster, you can get along without one by using manual savings tables. The calculations are easy and you can do them in just a few minutes. Your earnings at home can improve your lifestyle enormously!

6. **Run an apartment rental agency.** In most large cities there is a constant influx of young people seeking jobs and careers. Since almost none have relatives in "the big city," they seek apartments, rooms, sharing, or other arrangements until their salaries become large enough for them to buy places of their own. You can earn a nice income serving the needs of these people—again in a "paper" real estate business. As research into the income potential for you in this business, you can contact some local apartment rental agencies (see your yellow pages under "Apartment Referral Service" or "Apartment Sharing Service"). Call and get full details on charges and other costs. Ask for info on what areas are popular, how many apartments or rooms are available, etc. With this info in hand you should be able to decide if you could earn a suitable income in this "paper" real estate business in your area. The table at the end of this chapter gives you the typical income you might earn in this excellent business.

Money Brokering: Another "Paper" Real Estate Business

There's an ancient quotation that says, "Water is the universal solvent." I disagree with this. The real truth is that "Money is the universal solvent!" To verify this, listen to conversations in restaurants, at meetings, during parties, etc. You'll often hear the remark "It always comes down to money!"

What does this mean? It means that in business, money is almost always the deciding factor in a transaction. So, too, in real estate—it always comes down to the money! You can earn money catering to this situation. How?

By acting as a source of funding for real estate deals. You become a *money broker, financial broker,* or *financial consultant,* depending on which title you prefer. You're a middle person between the borrower and the lender. You're paid a fee—usually by the borrower—for finding a needed loan. And if you deal with lenders who say "Brokers Welcome," "Brokers Protected," etc., the lender will cut your check from the loan proceeds. Many money brokers prefer this arrangement. But I can tell you this:

> In more than thirty years of dealing with brokers raising money for real estate and business activities, I've never seen—or heard of—one broker who hasn't received the fee he or she deserved after the successful completion of a deal!

So you can stop worrying about not getting paid. As long as you have a signed written agreement with your client, you *will* be paid! So quit your worrying and get to work!

Many of my readers have done well raising money for others (and themselves) as money brokers. In the real estate field they use our *Low-Cost Real Estate Loan Getters Kit* (see Figure 6-3) to get thousands of sources, and proven procedures for raising money for a variety of property types and situations. You—too—can probably do the same.

This big kit also gives you legal, legitimate, and approved ways to operate your business without a special real estate license. You will—however—need a simple no-examination business registration license, which costs a few dollars, if you operate your business under an assumed name.

Good Reasons for Being a Home-Based Money Broker

There are several attractive aspects to being a home-based real estate money broker. These are:

1. **You do not have to beg people** for business; they beg you to handle their deals!

There's a better way to **MORE**

LOW-COST
REAL ESTATE
FINANCING

100%
FINANCING
NO DOWN PAYMENT
NO CLOSING COSTS
NO POINTS
NO MAINTENANCE WORRIES
NO NEGATIVE CASH FLOW

100% Financing!
110% Financing!
120% Financing!

__GET ALL KINDS OF REAL-ESTATE LOANS FASTER!__
Take the hassle and delay out of getting a
real-estate loan! How? By using the IWS
__REAL-ESTATE LOAN GETTERS SERVICE!__ This __NEW__
service from Ty Hicks gives you:
**Proven ways to get loans
**Forms for fast loan approval
**Names & addresses of lenders
**Step-by-step tips for borrowers
**Keys to getting __ANY__ type of
real-estate loan today
**A turn-key business for you in any
state, city, or county
**Ways to earn __BIG__ commissions
from the easiest loan ever
**Speedy decisions--sometimes in
just an hour
**Built-in collateral--no credit
check hassles
**Sources of the unusual and hard-
to-get real estate loan

__YOU CAN USE THIS SERVICE__ to get loans for

100% Financing!
110% Financing!
120% Financing!

your own real-estate deals, or for deals
that other people have! Ty Hicks gives __YOU__
complete support in this service--giving
you the forms you need, the lenders you can
work with, and advice over his hotline!

__GET REAL-ESTATE LOANS__ for any type of deal,
from single-family homes to office-complex
developments, etc. If it's real estate, this
service can help __YOU__--with 1st, 2nd, 3rd--
even 8th mortgages! Get money for raw land,
air rights, shopping centers, garden/senior
citizen apartments, marinas!

__MEGA-MORTGAGES INTO THE MULTI-MILLIONS__ are
there--just for the asking! Don't let them
go to waste! Get in on the real estate boom.
Be part of the lending spree that's putting
billions into new and used real estate every
year! Know who's lending for what use!

__TO START USING THIS SERVICE__ send $100 __TODAY__
to IWS, or call in your credit card order!

SUCCESS STARTS
HERE!

Send your check or money order for $100 to
IWS, Inc. at the address at the right. Or
call Ty Hicks at 516-766-5850 from 9am to
4pm New York time or from 8pm to 10pm at
516-766-5850 with your VISA or MASTERCARD
order. If ordering by mail, give card no.,
expiration date/signature, and phone number.

MAIL THIS COUPON NOW OR CALL IN YOUR
CREDIT CARD ORDER! DON'T WASTE TIME!

Send me the REAL-ESTATE LOAN GETTERS SERVICE.
Here's $100. Or charge my credit card at left.

NAME_____ PHONE NO._____

ADDRESS_____ Apt/Suite #____

CITY_____ STATE___ ZIP_____

Send to: IWS, Inc. 24 Canterbury Rd
Rockville Centre NY 11570

To order by Credit Card, call Ty Hicks at
516-766-5850, day or night. Have card ready!　C-6

Boxed items are statements some lenders
make about their loans.

Figure 6-3. Details about the Low-Cost
Real Estate Loan Getters Kit from IWS, Inc.

2. **Lenders welcome you** when you bring them solid deals from which they can earn interest and fees. You do not have to beg for money!
3. **Borrowers recommend you** to their business associates and friends, helping your business grow, free of advertising costs. As is often said, "The best kind of advertising is word-of-mouth—which also happens to be free!"

While you can get started as a real estate money broker on your own, by studying information in a public library, you can save lots of time and begin earning money sooner by using a planned study program such as that shown in Figure 6-3. You can earn its cost ten times over—or more— on your first deal!

Make Cold Cash Working with "Hard Money"

Another "paper" real estate business is "hard money." "What's *hard money?*" you ask. It's *high-interest money*—that is, money borrowed at a higher rate of interest than conventional going rates. Thus, when normal rates are 7.25 percent for a long-term first mortgage (fifteen to thirty years), hard money rates might be 16 percent, or higher, for the same mortgage.

The best investments for hard money are usually in commercial real estate. Why? Because this type of real estate is easier to appraise, is often newer, and may have fewer tenant problems than other types of real estate. For a comprehensive approach to this type of "paper" real estate business, use the *Hard Money Real Estate Kit*, listed at the end of this book. Again, you can also study this field on your own to get started in this great business.

Get in on One of the Newest "Paper" Real Estate Businesses

One of the newest "paper" real estate businesses being run today is the Real Estate Investment Trust, shortened to REIT, and pronounced to rhyme with *feet*. A REIT is defined in a businessperson's terms as: *a corporation, trust, or association in which at least 75 percent of its gross income comes from rents on real estate, mortgage interest, sale of real estate, or dividends from real estate. In any given year, a REIT that pays out 95 percent of its income to its shareholders pays no income tax. Shareholders, however, must report and pay income taxes on any dividends they receive from the REIT.*

Today REITs are a popular form of real estate ownership. They are sometimes called "mutual funds" of real estate. You can form your own REIT to invest in any type of property, such as:

- **Residential real estate**—apartment houses, townhouses, senior-citizen residences, etc.
- **Commercial buildings**—offices, stores, shopping malls, plazas, etc.
- **Medical facilities**—hospitals, nursing homes, professional suites, hospices, etc.
- **Industrial and warehouse structures**—factories, mini-storage buildings, assembly plants, etc.
- **Recreational facilities of all types**—golf courses, tennis courts and buildings, marinas, private airports, swimming pools, etc.

Thus, you can say that if land and a structure of some type are involved, a REIT can be used to finance it. Most REITs raise money in multimillion-dollar amounts from the public. But there are privately financed REITs also. Much depends on the amount of money needed and the purposes for which it is to be used.

You can form your own REIT by taking some simple steps. Once you take these steps you will need an attorney to read and approve of your plan. Here are the six easy steps to form a REIT:

1. **Prepare a business plan** telling what types of properties your REIT will invest in, and the general location of your properties (East, West, nationwide, etc.).

2. **Estimate how much money you'll need** to get from the public or private investors to buy the number of properties you seek, or finance the number of mortgages you plan to fund, etc.

3. **Tell your investors what types of returns** you'll aim for when you put their money to work in the REIT. You are not allowed to guarantee a specific return. However, you can tell investors what level of return—6 percent, 8 percent, etc.—you'll aim for when you purchase properties, lend money, or engage in other real estate activities.

4. **Use drawings or photos of the types of properties** you plan to invest in. These illustrations will interest your investors and make them more likely to put money into your REIT.

5. **Select a descriptive name for your REIT.** For example, if you use *Greenlawn Shopping Malls,* your investor knows from the start what types of properties you'll invest in. The same is true of *Riverfront Office Towers* or *Parkside Garden Apartments.* Each such name conveys a favorable image for your potential investors. The hope is that the name will help encourage them to put money into your REIT— which is what you want.

6. **Be sure to give an exact amount** that you want to raise for your REIT. The smallest you should look for is $500,000; for large REITs, you can seek $50 million, or more. And the larger amounts are sometimes easier to get because investors feel safer when there are big sums in the business. Aim high—it could be your biggest chance to make it in your own home-based business!

Six High-Earnings-Potential "Paper" Real Estate Business for You

Here are six "paper" real estate businesses you can run from home. We discussed them earlier in this chapter in detail. Table 6-1 gives you details on your potential earnings, money required to start, time to your first earnings, and the equipment you can use. Note that you can start with rented equipment. You don't have to own a business machine to use it!

Good luck in your real estate ventures from home. Remember—at all times—you have a good friend in your author, Ty Hicks. Call me—I'll answer on the first ring!

Table 6-1. Six "Paper" Real Estate Businesses That Can Make You Rich

Name of Business	What You Do	How to Find Clients	Money Required to Start	Annual Earnings Potential	Time to First Income	Equipment Needed
Foreclosure Locator and Advisor	Find foreclosure real estate for people.	Ads in papers, magazines.	$200 to $600	$6,000 to $20,000	4 to 6 weeks	Desk, phone, PC, fax, typewriter.
Mortgage Cash-out Broker	Get cash for people holding a mortgage.	Ads in papers, magazines.	$300 to $800	$12,000 to $100,000+	4 to 6 weeks	Desk, phone, PC, fax, typewriter.
Real Estate Surveyor	Survey properties.	Ads in papers, yellow pages; contact real estate brokers.	$200 to $700	$8,000 to $36,000	12 to 14 weeks	Desk, phone, PC, fax, typewriter.
Real Estate Appraiser	Appraise local real estate for buyers and sellers.	Ads in local papers, magazines.	$400 to $900	$12,000 to $60,000	8 to 15 weeks	Desk, phone, PC, fax, typewriter.
Arrange Faster Payoff of Home Mortgages	Put homeowners in touch with mortgage firms.	Ads in local papers, magazines.	$200 to $800	$20,000 to $100,000	3 to 6 weeks	Desk, phone, PC, fax typewriter.
Apartment Rental Agency	Find tenants for local apartments.	Classified ads in local papers.	$500 to $600	$5,000 to $75,000	4 to 6 weeks	Desk, phone, PC, fax, typewriter.

CHAPTER 7

STAKE YOUR CLAIM IN THE MULTI-BILLION-DOLLAR INTERNET MARKET

WHEN YOU HEAR the words *Internet, Information Superhighway,* or *World Wide Web,* do you think of your future home-based fortune? Or do you feel out of touch with what the person is saying? Either way, this chapter shows you how you can turn the Internet into *your* road to riches—even if you don't own or use a computer! You'll soon see why you—as the owner of a home-based business—have every reason to start and grow your fortune in the exciting world of the Internet.

You can't ignore the Internet. Like it or not, the Internet is here and it's *not* going to go away. Here are a few reasons why you should think of putting your business on the Internet—Net for short:

- **The Net is an enormous TV-like channel** you view on a personal computer (PC) screen. Its "programs" cover nearly every aspect of human life and business. Experts predict that—eventually—the Net will cover every aspect of life.
- **The Net is the world's largest advertising network** and reaches people everywhere who have computers.
- **The Net allows people to order products or services** from you—from anywhere in the world.
- **The Net allows people anywhere to send you payments** for your products or services—quickly, easily, and at low cost.
- **The Net allows you to promote your products** and services to people everywhere in the world who might be interested in buying them from you.

- **The Net allows you to make announcements** of interest to people thinking of buying your offerings.
- **The Net allows you to exchange** interesting and useful information with people anywhere.

You might say: "But haven't people done these things for years without help from computers? What should the Net matter to me?" The answer is that—in general—on the Net each of these tasks can be done faster, cheaper, and more efficiently by more people than ever before. And each of these tasks—getting orders, promoting your business, sharing information, etc.—are keys to your home-based business success! The Internet can help you make more money—faster!

Unlimited Opportunities on the Net

At this writing, some 60 million Americans are shopping on the Net. And do they shop! For the most recent twelve months, sales on the Net reached $3 billion. Worldwide sales on the Net will reach $1.5 trillion in just a few years, researchers say. (That's a big "T" in that number).

Not bad for a business many people are still learning about. And those 60 million Americans we mentioned are just a part of the wonderful world of potential customers that you—as a home-based BWB "shopkeeper"—can reach online (on the Net). Add to this *business-to-business* (B-to-B for short), where you're selling to another business instead of a consumer. Then add sales to customers from other countries. The opportunities for your home-based business become virtually unlimited!

Another great benefit of having your home-based business on the Net is that you can sell to customers around the world—just as easily and as quickly as you'd sell to someone across the street. What's more, on the Net people see your business as just as "big" and just as important as the next person's. Thus, the owner of a small startup home-based business may pull profits from across the world just as easily as the biggest firms.

Make Money on the Net—With or Without a Computer!

The future is bright for home-based business on the Net. Why? Experts say the number of people shopping on the Net will double each year. Sales will rocket through the roof! Some of these sales should be yours.

You can *claim your share* of this exploding market, promoting your home-based business and getting checks or credit-card payments from around the world. Best of all, you don't even need to own—or use—a computer to get started.

In this chapter you'll learn the simple steps you can take to start in the wonderful world of the Net without even owning, renting, or using a computer.

Your Way to Internet Success Today

Getting to know, and understand, the Net takes some work. Why? Because it is different from typical media—magazines, newspapers, TV, radio, etc. The words used to talk about the Net are different from the other media. So, too, are the publications and people who serve the Net. But it's easy—and fun—to explore the Net to learn more about it and how you can make money from it in your home-based business. And—best of all—you do not need a computer, or computer know-how, to benefit—moneywise—from the Net!

A few years ago I, too, knew little of the Net, and what it offered. Yet I sensed that it held much promise for home-business people like myself. So I:

1. **Had my newsletter,** *International Wealth Success,* put online (that is, on the Internet) for anyone who wanted information about the newsletter to see it.
2. **Included with the newsletter** sixteen pages from our catalog describing our many products.
3. **Used the World Wide Web** (Web for short) to carry this information to potential viewers on the Net.
4. **Opened my home-based business** to a whole new group of customers around the world.

5. **Caused sales to rise significantly,** bringing in people from all over the world—sooner and at lower cost than using the regular mail system, as we had for years.

If I had shied away from the Net—as many BWBs do—these new customers would never have seen our home-based offerings. So don't say: "I'm not into computers. I don't see what the Internet has to do with my home business!"

"It has *plenty* to do with you," I reply. "Just look at what it has done for my home-based business. It could do more for yours!"

Today there are thousands of successful home-based businesses getting a good portion of their income off the Net. I know many of these BWBs. And I want *you* to be one of the next to tell me, "The Internet has my business booming! Thanks for pushing me into it."

The World Wide Web—Where the "Right" Business Makes Millions

The World Wide Web contains *home pages* for advertisers, allowing people to "access" them—that is, look at the pages on the screen of their PC using a *Web browser.* A home page is a unique location for your business that has its own address—just like you have an address for your home—be it an apartment, a house, a trailer, etc. For example, the IWS Internet address is *http://www.clickserver.com/iws.* This tells you that we're on the Web, a mall (which is a collection of advertisers in one area—just like a shopping mall), and that this is a commercial (moneymaking) activity (*.com*).

The World Wide Web makes many BWBs' dreams—large and small—come true. Here's a true-life, dream-come-true, home-based business adventure of two BWB brothers on the World Wide Web:

THEIR HOBBY

The two brothers are music buffs and are avid collectors of compact discs (CDs) and records. As a hobby, they bought, traded, and sold hard-to-find used and new recordings with friends. They know the best places to get recordings at bargain prices. But their hobby was just that. Sometimes it earned a few dollars for them; sometimes it lost them a few dollars. Both in their twenties, the two men scraped by on low incomes from ho-hum jobs.

THEIR BUSINESS STARTUP

One day one of the brothers suggested that they take a shot at turning their hobby into a home-based record- and CD-selling mail-order business they would later try on the World Wide Web. Mail order—they agreed—was the first step for them. The Web could come later.

It took several months to get a Web site (an Internet "storefront" with its own address at which customers can find you). At this site people can place orders for CDs or records, inquire about music that interests them, or just make comments about music, musicians, or recordings.

To access the brothers' Web site, anyone with a PC and access to the Internet types the Web site address into their Web browser to get to the home page—which is like the cover page of a catalog. Customers can then select the names and titles of music they would like to see. A list of CD titles appears on the customers' PC screen, complete with prices and an order form. Small photos of the CD cover art can also be viewed on the screen.

PLACING ORDERS

Customers place orders from their computer by typing their name, address, telephone, and credit card number into an onscreen form. Or they can telephone this information in to the brothers' firm. (This is just one way the Net can be used to order—there are many others.)

HOME-BASED BUSINESS SUCCESS

In each of the two years the brothers have sold CDs and records on their Web site they have had nearly $10 million in sales! And they have nearly 200,000 customers, and millions of visitors (a person who visits the Web site and looks at it, but does not buy anything). Their business is one of the top three CD sellers on the Net. They hold nearly half the market. After this success, the two brothers decided to take their company public—that is, sell stock in their firm. Doing so they raised $60 million! Not bad for a home-based business that started as a hobby.

Features of a Successful Online Home-Based Business

What does this real-life business experience tell you about home-based Net businesses? It shows several important points that are valuable to every home-based BWB. These points can be the key to your future success, namely:

1. **It *is possible* to get rich in a home-based business on the Internet.** These two BWBs would have had much more difficulty achieving the same success *offline* (that is, in a store or other non-Internet facility). Their Web site gives customers lightning-fast ways to buy CDs and records. No need to hop in a car, battle traffic on the way to the shopping mall, find a parking space, and then learn that the CD you want isn't in stock! Customers on the Net greeted the brothers' business with open arms and full wallets. Word about the business spread fast, causing music lovers from all over the world to access the site and spend their money at the brothers' online store.

2. **Be among the first to sell your product or service** online and you'll have an opportunity to succeed in your home-based business way beyond your wildest dreams. The brothers were among the first to open a CD store on the Net. Today they have nearly half the $20 million CD market on the Internet. Still, there's enough demand for CDs to keep other large CD vendors and numerous small ones busy, successful, and profitable on the Net!

3. **Look for a good "fit" for your business on the Net.** For example, the brothers offer great convenience in buying a moderate-priced product. So, too, does IWS, with our newsletters, books, and kits. If your business requires face-to-face discussion with your customers—such as home repair—it may not be too good a fit for the Internet. Such businesses generally do better with traditional promotion methods—yellow pages ads, newspaper ads, etc.

4. ***Emphasize impulse sales* of your products or services.** The Net is a great place for impulse sales. Stores in shopping malls place products in racks near the checkout counters because customers like to grab a few items *on impulse* just before checking out. Impulse sales are a "bonus" feature for home-based businesses selling on the Net. Also, Net customers can buy from you any time of the day or night,

from anywhere in the world. And you don't have to be sitting at a telephone taking orders. All of this can be done for you at low cost. So you sell more sooner, especially if your products or services are low- or moderately priced. What more could a home-based BWB ask for?

5. **Don't build a big inventory at the start.** The two brothers couldn't afford a store full of CDs at the start. But their familiarity with suppliers allowed them to order (and deliver) quickly the needed products as soon as the orders came in. Today they can afford to maintain a large inventory. You will go through the same steps. But keep your inventory small at the start!

6. **Get your Web site free of charge at the start**, when money is usually limited for home-based BWBs. The brothers did this and it saved them lots of money. IWS did it this way, too. There are several Internet service providers who offer free Web sites—see the resources at the end of this chapter. Later, you can rent space on a Web server— essentially renting a Web site—that comes with lots of the "extras," if you wish. Such a site may offer credit-card processing, home-page design, plus other features, which will free you from these tasks.

7. **Promote heavily on the Internet**—your costs can be very low. Keep this fact in mind when considering taking your business on the Net. Promotion can bring sales at a much lower cost than advertising. Result? You earn more in your home-based business.

Is the Internet for You and Your Business?

Not every home business on the Net will become as big as the CD-selling brothers above. Nor will the Internet solve all your money concerns. But the brothers' story shows it is possible to make it big with a home-based business on the Net. Here are some more ideas you might want to think about when considering using the Internet in your home-based business:

1. **Do you want to receive orders more quickly** than through traditional methods—such as mail order, direct mail, or

telemarketing? Remember: Customers on the Net usually expect a faster turnaround from you. Some BWBs like a more leisurely approach to their business and dislike rush shipments.

2. **Do you seek low promotion costs?** If you do, then the Internet can be a big help to you. Why? Because your promotion costs for your home-based products can be nearly zero. Could you ask for a better deal?

3. **Do you want to send press releases or "freebies"** to keep your customers informed and win their loyalty? The Internet—through e-mail (electronic mail) and mailing lists—makes this cheap and easy to do. It's ideal for the home-based business startup BWB who usually has only a small amount of money at his or her disposal.

4. **Do you want to open your business** to a new group of customers, even if you're taking a small risk to do so? The Net will give you a whole new world of potential buyers who seek what you offer—either products or services. That's why we say: You cannot ignore the Internet in your home-based business!

The ability to buy and sell on the Net gives both you and your customers a new way to do business. Commercial online services such as America Online (AOL) and CompuServe offer many of the advantages the Internet provides, but usually at a slightly different cost. Web sales are the wave of today and the wave of the future. Thus, your Internet sales will add to your other sales through mail order, direct mail, telemarketing, TV infomercials, radio ads, word-of-mouth, and so on. While you may not use all these methods, the Internet will supplement whichever ones you do use. If these possibilities sound attractive to you for your home-based business, you should consider getting on the Net—*now!*

Take a Sensible Approach to the Internet

You can rake in big bucks on the Internet while you build your home-based fortune in traditional ways. The sensible approach to the Internet uses these ideas:

- **Treat the Internet as a way to** *increase* **existing sales** and expand your customer base worldwide.
- **You must first have a good business idea** to succeed on the Internet, along with a plan for your business.
- **Remember—the Internet is just like the "real" world.** Thus, it has its share of people who want to profit from the newcomer. Or they will try to sell you success as part of a "canned" marketing scheme.
- **Follow your dream of your own home-based business** rather than buying into someone else's prepackaged plan.

For those people who are willing to take this sensible approach, the basic question they should ask themselves is: "Can I afford to be on the Internet?" But the really important question is: "Can I afford *not* to be on the Internet?"

Ten Top Reasons for Putting Your Home Business on the Net

The future is so promising for your home-based business on the Internet that I want to give you the strongest motivation I can to get you on the Net as soon as possible. Here are ten powerful reasons why you and your business should be on the Net:

1. **The easiest and quickest way** to get information about your business out to the entire world is via the Net.
2. **Anyone can get on the Net**—there are no restrictions of any kind for businesses in legitimate activities.
3. **Faster sales and communications** offered to every business by the Net mean lower costs and higher profits—all of which show up in your business bank account.
4. **You'll have thousands of "channels" (places)** in which to promote your business on the Net. Later in this chapter, you'll find several free ways to get on the Net.
5. **You'll make big savings on supplies** (paper, envelopes, stamps, and so on) when you do business on the Net, compared to traditional forms of promotion and advertising. These expensive materials are not used on the Net.

6. **You can work up from "little guy or gal"** to "big guy or gal" status faster on the Net than on any other promotional medium.

7. **Potential competitors may be starting to do business** on the Net. Wouldn't you rather beat them to it so you sell more—sooner?

8. **You can get lots of free business information** on the Net. Much of it will be helpful in starting and expanding your home-based business. You'll find a number of sources of such information at the end of this chapter.

9. **You can do most of your advertising and promotion** on the Net yourself—thereby saving time and money that you'd have to spend with others to do the work to "make right" what they didn't get right the first time! You know—and understand—your home-based business better than anyone else!

10. **Being on the Net increases the credibility** of your business. You appear more business-minded and forward-looking to bankers and other lenders from which you might seek loans for your business. And your customers think more highly of you for the same reasons. So they buy more!

Rocketing Potential—60 Million Customers and Counting!

When you put your business on the Net, you get an Internet address for your home-based business. Then you can advertise on the Web, or put your catalog on the Net for people worldwide to see. In doing so you'll be joining some 80 percent of the Fortune 500 companies who are on the Net. And you can be certain those companies are on the Net because they believe it's good for their business. Just like it will be good—great—for your business!

Using the Net, your small home-based business can attract customers as easily, and as effectively, as larger, older firms. And for you the risk is low—especially if you start on the Net free of charge. You can take easy, no-risk steps to move into a strong sales position.

No firm—large or small—can ignore 60 million potential customers. That's why we urge you to get on the Net as soon as you can with your home-based business. If you're questioning what kinds of home-based businesses do well on the Net, here are a number of them.

Successful Home-Based Businesses on the Internet

The number of ways you can make money on the Net is limited only by your imagination. Home-based business owners are particularly lucky because the Net allows them to run almost any type of business from home. Here are typical categories of businesses that do well on the Net. Remember: You *never* see, talk to, or otherwise face a customer when you make a sale on the Net. It all takes place electronically, onscreen using words and pictures:

1. **Selling information products**—books, courses, kits, yellow pages, databases, business research tools.
2. **Selling subscriptions** to newsletters, magazines, journals, newspapers, trade publications, bulletins, etc.
3. **Selling commercial products** of all types—from asthma medicine to xylophones—to both individual consumers and companies worldwide. Millions of fortunes are being made this way on the Net today.
4. **Selling custom-made products to consumers and firms worldwide.** For example, you might sell handmade dolls, teddy bears, artwork, model ships, etc. There is an enormous market for such custom-made items all over the world. You can cash in on it—today!
5. **Selling advertising and ad products** such as the "banner" ads used on the Internet, plus the more traditional types of ads used in all kinds of media—magazines, newspapers, books, newsletters, etc.
6. **Selling promotional services other than advertising** such as that done by the owners of online malls and organizations, providing a central place on the Net where you can find a particular business or service. This type of business is best suited for experienced Internet businesspeople.

You can get into this business after you've learned the ins and outs of the Internet.

7. **Selling consulting services of all kinds** to people and businesses that need them. Typical topics you might help people with by consulting with them for a fee include being a financial broker to find loans, information about and guidance for getting grants, import–export, mail order, etc. Almost any topic for which people need advice and guidance can be a subject for your consulting skills. And—again—you never see your client! It's all done electronically, onscreen, with words typed by you and your client. One-finger typing is fully acceptable because your client doesn't see your hand when you're typing! (Your author is a one-fingered typist who has produced millions of words sold round the world in the 106 books he now has in print.)

8. **Selling other, miscellaneous products or services** you develop on your own, have someone else develop for you, or take on to sell from a developer. This is where your imagination can come in and develop, or help sell, an unusual item that you see is needed by certain groups or types of people. Many of the world's biggest sales breakthroughs have been made by home-based BWBs who see the need for miscellaneous products or services. They find what's needed and run with it—to the land of gold!

As you can see, some of these businesses fit into more than one category. So you can sell many of the items listed to both consumers and to businesses (B-to-B). For example, in my business we sell to individuals, businesses, libraries, colleges and universities, military personnel on ships and Army and Air Force bases, government agencies of many types, overseas consumers, plus dozens of other types of buyers at home and abroad. You—too—can do the same in your home-based business!

What Kinds of Products and Services Can You Sell Best on the Internet?

The kinds of products and services that sell best on the Internet are those that take advantage of the convenience of the Net. You saw this for the CD business earlier. Another such business is the world's largest florist. Using its Web page and a toll-free number you can have flowers delivered almost anywhere. At this writing, the company is earning some $10 million a year (about 10 percent of its annual revenue) from its Web site and other online services. Again—the answer is convenience, combined with superb service and outstanding reliability of delivery.

Products and service that sell well on the Net include:

- **Most products sold by catalog or mail order** will also sell well on the Net.
- **Custom-made products or services** that fill a specific need for people and companies.
- **Offbeat or unusual products or services** often attract online attention and sell strongly.

You would not—in general—try to sell items people can get at the corner store. Thus, few toothbrushes are sold on the Net. Likewise with daily food and beverage purchases. But special cheeses (offbeat or unusual), rare cigars, and long-aged wines can—and do—sell on the Net.

Where face-to-face selling is needed to close a deal, the Net doesn't help too much. The Net can give lots of preliminary information that's useful in setting the scene for the closing. But the actual closing takes place offline—i.e., not on the Internet.

Remember: You can use the Net to bring people into your home office to complete a deal. Then you have the face-to-face meeting needed to present, and sign, papers and other documents.

E-mail and Newsgroups: Low- and No-Cost Promotion Tools

The CD and newsletter home-based businesses mentioned earlier make actual sales on the Net. Now we'll look at a home-based business using the Net to reduce promotion costs by utilizing Internet newsgroups, mailing lists, and e-mail.

A reader of my newsletter has a home-based business selling health foods and vitamin supplements by catalog and mail order. She has been very happy with the business since she started it. But she often calls to complain about one costly problem:

- **The cost of mailing her catalog** through the Postal Service is too high, she says. Her catalog contains descriptions of the products, along with their prices, and an ordering sheet. She sends this catalog to a list of names she rents from a list broker.
- **Mailing 5,000 catalogs at about 50 cents each** costs $2,500 per mailing. So one day I asked her if there was any way she could use e-mail (mail sent electronically over the Internet or over a commercial network such as America Online) to lower her cost. Her eyes lit up as she told me she had recently learned from a friend that there are newsgroups and mailing lists on the Net that discuss health foods, vitamins, and related topics.
- **Newsgroups and mailing lists** allow anyone to send comments and questions on the group's topics and to read replies from other group members. For example, a health-food enthusiast in California might "subscribe" (usually free of charge) to a newsgroup for health-conscious people. Every time this person turns on her PC and connects to the Internet she gets the day's newsgroup discussion and the latest on health foods.
- **If you publish a catalog** for your home-based business, many of these newsgroups will be happy to put your catalog on the newsgroup's server (a computer), free of charge. People in the group can then read about your products from their own computer.

I encouraged this BWB selling health foods and vitamins to:

1. **Make a list** of Internet newsgroups and mailing lists dealing with her topic using the Internet yellow pages.
2. **Get the name** of the person (known as the administrator or moderator) in charge of each group.

3. **Ask the administrator** if he or she would place her catalog on the group computer and send an announcement to the group detailing this. Most administrators will be happy to do so.

"Great," said my BWB reader–friend. "I'll immediately do as you suggest. My friend said he'd help me and let me use his PC." Then the BWB asked me, "Since I'll be sending the newsgroup administrator my catalog, why not send ads or fliers directly to the group itself?"

At that point I decided I had to tell her about the "right" and "wrong" uses of e-mail. I didn't want her to make a silly mistake that could be bad for her business.

Use E-mail Effectively and Avoid Mistakes

The mistake I warned this highly competent BWB to avoid is a way of using e-mail that's called *spamming*. It means the sending of *unsolicited* e-mail (spam)—particularly to a group—on the Net. Newsgroups are formed to promote serious discussion—not as a medium for advertising. So the simple advice is:

Don't spam—ever!

My reader–friend thanked me and said she would never send unsolicited mail to newsgroups.

Here are important pointers about sending catalogs and other advertising to newsgroups:

• **It's all right to send catalogs and other ad material** to people who request it. For example, our BWB reader received some 1,000 names and e-mail addresses of people who wanted information on vitamins and health food. Sending e-mail to such people is *not* spamming. So I encouraged my BWB reader–friend to send her catalog to the e-mail list. I added, "Just be sure to use the list of people who requested the catalog or ads!"

- **You can save significant amounts of money** on mailings done via e-mail. This BWB will save $500 to $2,000 per year, depending on how many catalogs she mails each year. The Internet mailing doesn't cost her a penny and she reduced her post office mailing by 1,000 copies of her catalog. She now asks her new customers to supply their e-mail address with their order. This enables her to e-mail catalogs to them, saving her even more money. She has even received a number of orders for her catalog via the newsgroups. And whenever she updates her catalog she sends an updated e-mail copy with a short message about the update to the newsgroup administrator.

Basics of Dealing with Newsgroups and Mailing Lists

When selling a product or service on the Net, it's always a good idea to follow a few simple guidelines:

1. **Read some of the messages carried by a newsgroup** before you send a message of your own to the group. Many groups have a list of *Frequently Asked Questions (FAQ)* that can give you information on how the group works. If you don't have a computer, you can go to your local library or high school and ask to be allowed to download and print out a copy of the FAQ for the group.

2. **Do not send advertising to a group.** But you can send helpful messages and can include a brief "signature" at the end of your message. For instance, the BWB who sells vitamins and health foods eventually became a popular "voice" in one of the health-food groups, where she shares her knowledge with others about vitamin safety and uses. She never tries to push her products directly to the group in their discussions. But many people from the newsgroup buy her products because they feel she is helpful and trustworthy. She even wrote a FAQ on selecting the best vitamins for one's money.

3. **Get additional free promotion for your home-based business** using these simple methods:

- **Form your own Internet mailing list** or newsgroup.
- **Post press releases** about your product at relevant Web sites.
- **Submit your Internet address(es)** to the most popular *search engines*—see listing at the end of this chapter for businesses that will do this for you.
- **"Trade" ads** with other businesses on the Web to get free ads—see data at the end of this chapter.
- **Join** *Webrings*—groups of like-minded people and organizations that "link" together, so visitors to one site in the ring will move on to visit other sites in the same ring.

Let's Put Your Business on the Internet

Your future is bright in a home-based business partly promoted on the Net. You will also promote it by other means—such as direct mail, mail order, space ads, telemarketing, TV, etc.—if such methods are profitable. The number of people shopping on the Net will double each year, experts say—sending sales through the roof! So let's take the needed steps to put your home-based business on the Net.

To show you how to put your business on the Net, I'll use a business that is most familiar to me—my newsletter, *International Wealth Success*, which I put on an Internet mall two years ago. The steps you'll take to put your business on the Net will be the same as the ones you take here. Why do I use my own business to show you how to put *your* business on the Net? Because:

- **I founded**, and have run, this great newsletter for more than thirty years.
- **The IWS newsletter**—and the books, kits, and services we've added over time—have been selling successfully on the Net for two years.
- **This newsletter** was put on the Net without my using a computer! (Of course, I use a computer in our business, and for my writing, but not for putting my business on the Net.)

Here's how your home-based business can get on the Internet free of charge to you:

1. **You started your business and built it up** over the years by giving good, solid products and attentive service to your customers. This is what we do at the IWS newsletter. For the duration of this example, we're assuming you're the publisher of the IWS newsletter.

2. **During the years you've been publishing your newsletter**, you've added new books and kits in areas of small business where people need help—import–export, mail order, real estate, etc. You've also prepared, and published, a forty-eight-page catalog of your products, which people seem to like.

3. **You're approached by a Web site provider** who volunteers to put your catalog and newsletter on the Net free of charge. This Net provider wants no money up front. All he needs is a copy of your catalog, from which he'll set up some sixteen pages on an Internet mall, along with a number of other advertisers.

4. **Your mail-order and direct-mail businesses are booming** for your newsletter, books, and kits. But you don't want to be left out of this new media. So you agree to go on the mall on a nonexclusive basis—that is, you can set up your own Web page, or go with other providers, if you choose to do so. Your mall provider agrees to this, you give him a copy of your forty-eight-page catalog, and he gets his people to work on it. You want to keep yourself open to new opportunities, so you always have your eyes and ears open, watching and listening!

5. **You are offered a deal** in which your provider will receive a 25 percent commission on all sales from your Web catalog. The provider will process the credit-card charges and you will fill the orders as soon as you receive payment from the provider, plus data on what was ordered, and by whom.

6. **Your provider puts your catalog on the Net** and within days the orders come pouring in. Your business prospers and you're delighted to have another way, and medium, to promote your products.

To help you get your free Net listing, we'll give you a number of organizations that can get you started (see the list at the end of this chapter). No matter what home-based business you may have, you can follow the six general steps listed above. But let's take a closer look at the exact steps you can take to put your home-based business—which has a catalog of products—on the Net.

Basic Steps for Putting Your Catalog Online

Here are detailed steps you'll take—or someone will take for you free of charge—to get your home-based business catalog online:

1. **Find a sales method that's a good "match"** for your type of home-based business. Your sales method must work together with your home-based business. If it does not, your sales will probably be small. Sales methods worth considering include:

    • **Online catalogs** of all kinds that people (your prospective customers) can read onscreen and print out from their computers.
    • **Internet "malls,"** such as the one mentioned above, where a number of businesses form into groups, usually paying a "host" fee for their space in the mall—just like rent in a shopping mall. (Some malls even offer free space, as mentioned above.)
    • **A Web page or site** on the Web, which are individual "storefronts" (also called a *home page*) offered by a number of Web providers.
    • **One-shot ads** that are sometimes run free; or you can run ads continuously, paying for them or working out a deal for free ads.
    • **Announcements,** press releases, or ads you send out through Internet mail to lists, newsgroups, forums, e-zines, or individuals.

2. **Pick the sales method(s) you want to use on the Net.** As publisher of the IWS newsletter (returning to our earlier

example), you decide to use the online catalog method. Why? Because it makes a perfect fit between the Net and your home-based business. Since you already have a forty-eight-page printed catalog, most of the work is already done. And even after you put the catalog up on the Net you can still send out printed copies to people who don't, or don't want to, use a computer. So you're not restricting your sales in any way by going on the Net. Instead, you're expanding your sales opportunities! And your previous experience shows you that people buy and buy from printed descriptions of your products. Further, when you look around at Internet companies that put catalogs on the Net, you find several willing to put your catalog up free, or nearly free, of charge.

3. **Find a company, or person, that will "host" your catalog online.** A host is a company or person with a computer (a *server*) that allows you to put your catalog, samples of your newsletter, etc., on his or her computer so people can see your information online—that is, on the Internet. You can find host companies in the yellow pages under headings such as "Internet Services." Or you can do a search on any popular Internet search engine for words such as *Internet service provider, catalog host,* or *online catalog.*

4. **Choose the catalog host you wish to use.** Host firms may offer you several different arrangements for putting your catalog online. As publisher of the IWS newsletter, you're offered:

   • **Free catalog hosting** based on a sales commission. Your catalog is put on the Net free of charge. The host firm takes a 25 percent commission on each sale, as mentioned earlier.
   • **Per-inquiry arrangement** in which you pay the host 50 cents for each inquiry you're sent for your catalog. Again, your catalog is put on the Net free of any charge to you. This method helps you build your mailing list.
   • **Rental fees,** where you pay the host a monthly or annual rental fee for putting your catalog online. This type of deal is good for large, established catalogs that find the rental fee easy to pay.

5. **Start selling your products or services on the Net.** This is the easiest step of all. Just follow the host's directions for supplying your catalog data. Then watch the orders roll in. Look back at these steps and you'll see you've taken them all without your own computer! To see the results of your work, look them up on a friend's computer at *http://www.clickserver.com/iws.* I'm sure you'll like your work!

Getting by on the Net in a Home-Based Business Without a Computer

You *can* get started in your home-based business on the Internet without a computer, as we just saw. Here are additional steps to help you. But remember this: *You will eventually have to get a computer for your business. And the sooner you do, the better!* Here are the suggested steps:

1. **Use the telephone, fax, and postal mail** to promote your business on the Internet. Most forms of promotion (catalogs, fliers, press releases, etc.) can be sent by traditional means to the person requesting them on the Net.
2. **Request information** from Web sites, online malls, or newsgroups by telephone, fax, or postal mail. Listings of many popular sites can be found in Internet yellow pages in books in bookstores and libraries.
3. **Borrow a friend's computer** for a few hours a week and access the Web. Further, your friend may teach you a lot about the computer that will increase your home-based business income.
4. **Contact nearby public libraries**, colleges, universities, and schools to see if you can use their computers for free. Or take a low-cost computer course (sometimes just $15) and use the computer time for your home-based business.
5. **Look for coffeehouses and other establishments** offering free access (the cost of a cup of coffee) to their computers. You'll find lots of such computer coffeehouses in larger cities.
6. **Check your local copy shop.** It may offer computer access for a nominal fee.

Ideas for Good Home-Based Businesses on the Net

Now that you know how to get on the Net free of charge, here are some home-based businesses you might like to consider running on the Net. Or you may be able to expand your present business to include one, or more, of these.

PRODUCTS AND SERVICES FOR PERSONAL OR SPECIAL INTERESTS

Family tree research—there's an enormous interest in family roots. You can serve this interest with reliable data on the origin of various families.

Religious holiday supplies, gadgets, and devices for Christmas, Hanukkah, Kwanzaa, and others are popular year-round, all over the world—which can be reached by the Net.

Paper stationery of all kinds—especially customized letterheads, envelopes, business cards, and so on sell well on the Net. You should have a special skill for preparing such stationery, or you should have access to a printer that can handle this work.

Hobby products of all kinds—model ships, aircraft, helicopters, radio controls, and so on sell well on the Net. So if you have a special knowledge or skill in a hobby area, consider selling it on the Net.

Sports products of all types—especially for specialty sports such as white-water rafting, hiking, soccer, lacrosse, ice hockey, in-line skating, etc. Sports enthusiasts buy and buy—especially if you have what they need.

Auto, boat, and airplane products that appeal to owners of popular makes—such as Ford Explorer, Dodge Caravan, Mercedes S420, Ford Mustang, Chevy Blazer, Plymouth Voyager, BMW, Cadillac Catera, Lincoln, or Chrysler cars; Hatteras and Chris-Craft boats; and Piper Cub airplanes. Key rings, lapel pins, belt buckles, and so on are all popular with such owners and can sell well on the Net.

HOME AND LEISURE-TIME PRODUCTS

Gourmet cooking equipment is popular around the world. As families spend more time at home on weekends, the backyard cook has been spending more and more money on fancy devices to improve the output of his—or her—stove.

Specialty foods, cheeses, meats, candies, and other delicacies for regular and special holiday consumption continue to rack up huge sales on the Net. If you can supply these items, your future is bright.

Sportswear of all types—Northern, Western, Southern, etc.—is highly popular on the Net. It's "in" to wear sports clothing of many types—even if you're not into sports! You can make money from this craze, which never seems to end. Start now!

INFORMATION SERVICES OF MANY TYPES

Training programs by mail and e-mail are offered on the Web. You can teach either skills that you have, or skills that are in demand, using the part-time services of competent teachers who need extra income.

Matchmaking and dating services—both social and business are a rage today. What with unknown social backgrounds for potential marital partners, and varying business histories, matchmaking services are on a roll.

Travel services, including research into laws and customs in foreign countries, is highly popular—especially with the various terrorist acts that seem to occur continuously, worldwide. These services can be offered to individuals or companies, or both. Just be sure to know your laws and customs backwards and forwards!

Market research reports of special fields can sell at anywhere from $895 to $12,000 each, depending on the field and the depth of the coverage of the report. Such reports are sold to companies, not individuals. Yet if you sell ten reports at $5,000 each, you bring in $50,000; sell fifty and you gross $250,000. Not bad for less than a year's work!

Tapes of local and regional sporting events are popular with sports buffs. You have to arrange to either obtain such tapes, or have the events taped. Sports have replaced almost every other interest in the world today. So you CAN make big money making sporting events available on the Net.

Plus—of course—the many other Net businesses mentioned earlier in this chapter and elsewhere in this book. Look them over and decide if any are worth including in your home-based business. Who knows, you may join the home-based book publisher whose business is grossing $300 million a year! Just think what you could do with an income of that size. It *IS* possible—if you work at it!

Industry predictions at the time this book is being written are helpful to BWBs seeking a direction for their home-based business. The most popular Internet businesses, based on the dollar amount of projected sales, in descending order, are:

• Travel—airline, cruise ship, and other tickets
• Personal computers—hardware of all types
• Entertainment—CDs, tapes, etc.
• Books and music
• Gifts, flowers, and greetings
• Clothing and footwear of all types
• Food and beverages
• Toys and home supplies
• Jewelry
• Consumer electronics
• Sporting goods

There's your list. Take your pick! Your home-based business future fortune can be made on the Net. Start now. It's never too late to get rich!

Resources Available Free of Charge on the Internet

Here are a number of resources that are available free of charge at the time this book is being written. Since there are constant changes, we suggest you check each resource yourself. These sources can be accessed using a standard Internet connection and any of the sources of access to computers mentioned earlier in this chapter.

FREE GUIDES TO THE WEB

Snap Online! CD-ROM   *http://www.snap.com* or
and Web site   *http://www.cnet.com*

Hitchhiker's Guide   *ftp://nic.ddn.mil/rfc/rfc1118.txt*
to the Internet

INVENTORS' NEW PRODUCTS SITE

New Product Creation   *http://www.elect-spec.com/*
and Inventors' Site   *new-prod.htm*

INFORMATION ON INTERNET MARKETING

Web Marketing   *http://www.wilsonweb.com/webmarket*
Info Center

Internet Publicity   *http:/www.olymps.net/okeefe/pubnet*
Resources

Myths of Web Marketing   *http://www.jaderiver.com/glossary.htm*
and Marketing
Manager's Plain English
Internet Glossary

Internet Advertising   *http://www.admedia.org/internet/*
Resources Guide   *introduction.html*

Nuts and Bolts   *http://nans.com/MouseTracks/*
Marketing on the Net   *NutsandBolts.html*

GENERAL HELP FOR SMALL BUSINESSES

Edward Lowe Foundation   *http://www.lowe.org*

Home Business   *http://homebusinessmag.com/hmbg/*
Magazine   *index.html*

SmallBizNet   *http://www.lowe.org/smbixnet/sites/*
                              index.htm

Small Business   *http://www.sbaonline.sba.gov/starting*
Administration

Who's Marketing Online   *http://www.wmo.com*

Free Online Advertising Discussions

Net Advertising Discussion	*http://www.exposureuse.com/ i-advertising*

Free Web Site Listings

Exploit Submission Wizard	*http://www.submissions.com*
Link Master	*http://link master.com*
Submit It	*http://www.submit-it.com*

Free Banner Ads (which are placed on home pages)

Internet Link Exchange	*http://www.linkexchange.com*

Other Sites of Interest

Beatrice's Web Guide	*http://www.bguide.com*
Internet Fraud Watch	*http://www.fraud.org*
Internet Scambuster	*http://www.scambusters.org*
Women's Wire	*http://www.womenswire.com*
Directory of 2,500 Malls	*http://nsns.com/MouseTracks/ HallofMalls.html*
Links to More Than 200 Web Directories, Search Engines, and Link Services	*http://www.GoNetWide.com/ gopublic.html*
International Wealth Success Newsletter, Books, and Kits	*http://www.clickserver.com/iws*

CHAPTER 8

PROVIDE QUALITY
CHILD CARE AND PROSPER

WHAT IS THE working world's biggest problem today? And how can this biggest problem be solved? Can you earn money from home by solving this problem?

The working world's biggest problem today is not jobs, *not the minimum wage, not overtime, not salaries.* Instead, the working world's biggest problem is the safe, reliable care of working parents' children while the mother or father is at work. You can earn big money helping solve this problem. How?

1. **By finding suitable child-care** providers (basically baby-sitters);
2. **By being able to recommend suitable baby-sitters** that parents can trust;
3. **By recommending baby-sitters parents can employ at a reasonable wage** that will not eat up every penny the working parents earn from their jobs during their employment hours.

One Way to Get into a Booming Home Business

You can get into this booming field without ever having to look at a baby, feed a screaming infant, amuse a bored two-year old, or do any other similar child-care tasks. How can you get into this big-money field? You can:

1. **Open—in your home—a child-care referral service** in which you find qualified baby-sitters for working parents in your area for a fee.
2. **Screen applicants** who answer your short and low-cost classified ads for work at home.
3. **Gather data** on the applicants by mail, fax, and phone from previous employers who will help you free of charge.
4. **Build up a file of data** on each applicant; you can then furnish the data to the parents and earn a fee for your work.
5. **Act as a finder**—not an employment agency. You do not need a license of any kind to run this business, unless you use an assumed name. Then you will register your business name for a few dollars, without taking an examination of any kind. You just fill out a one-page form.
6. **Never meet an applicant face-to-face** unless you want to do so because you enjoy it.

"What work will I do?" you ask. You'll run a *child-care referral service.* That is, you'll do the following:

1. **Offer** to supply the names, addresses, and telephone numbers of qualified baby-sitters for a fee paid to you by the parent(s).
2. **Guarantee** that the baby-sitter will work a certain number of days or weeks, depending on the arrangement you make with the parent(s).
3. **Find** ongoing baby-sitting providers for your client as time passes and the children grow.

You can do all your work by mail, phone, and fax—never leaving your home except to go to the local mailbox to drop some letters into it. (Or you can have someone do this for you.)

In evaluating a potential baby-sitter's qualifications you are *not* acting as an employment agency. Hence, no license is required. And if you run your business under your own name, you need not even register the business in most localities. (Be sure to check with an attorney about the laws in your area.)

By running simple classified ads in your local daily or weekly newspaper under a suitable heading—such as *Baby-sitters Available* or *Child-Care Service*—you can start earning money in the first week you're in your own home business! Your ads might say:

Do you need a reliable baby-sitter? We can recommend one. Call 123-4567 for info.

Want to take a trip and leave the kids home? We can recommend a capable baby/child-sitter. Call 123-4567 for info.

Your job in your home-based business will be to recommend qualified baby-sitters for: working mothers or fathers; parents who want to travel or vacation without the kids; parents or guardians needing baby-sitting service for any other nonmedical reason. Note: You should supply baby-sitters *only* for healthy children. When a child has medical problems of any kind it is better to leave baby-sitter selection to agencies equipped to handle such referrals.

You can earn from $12,000 to $48,000 a year in this business when you run it from your own home. For higher earnings, you will probably need an office and two part-time helpers to handle the increased volume of work. When you run your business from your home, you'll need a desk, phone, typewriter, PC, and fax. For full details, see the book *How to Run a Profitable Child Care Referral Agency* by William Frederick, described at the back of this book.

Provide Baby-Sitting Info from Home and Earn Big

If you want to work at home only by mail, fax, or phone—or solely by just one of these communication methods—consider preparing a listing of companies in your area offering child-care services to their employees. For example, one national company offers employees:

- **Child care** for children six weeks to six years of age.
- **Flex-time** for working parents of these children.
- **Two years** of part-time work for new mothers.
- **6:30 A.M. to 7 P.M.** child care for these children.

- **Learning** environment for the children—ABCs and 123s for the kids.
- **Arts** and crafts.
- **Hot**, balanced meals.
- **Song** and dance activities.

Most working parents are so caught up in their sitter problems that they don't have the time or energy to research what local firms offer in the way of child care. You can easily do this research and sell the results in the form of a simple list for anywhere from $25 to $100 per copy. Parents will be glad to pay such prices if the information will help them solve the working world's biggest—and their specific—problem.

How can you help these parents while earning a nice income from home? Here's your answer:

1. **Go to your public library** and ask for a state business directory. They're available for almost every state, or for several states in one volume.
2. **Look for companies** in your city or town and in nearby ones where people might commute to jobs.
3. **List the companies** you find, along with their addresses and phone numbers.
4. **Write a letter**, such as that in Figure 8-1, to the Director of Human Resources. Ask for data on their child-care programs for employees.
5. **Assemble the data** you receive into a small typewritten list. You can use a layout similar to that in Figure 8-2. Or you can vary it, using something you think is better.
6. **If you have any questions**, call the Director of Human Resources and ask for clarification. Make note of the director's name, the date and time you spoke to him or her, what they told you, and so on. Keep this in the company's record—which I suggest you keep in an individual file folder. You'll always have this info to back up what you say in your list.
7. **Advertise your list** in local daily and weekly newspapers, in church and synagogue newsletters, in industrial and business magazines serving your area, and in any other publication read by parents—married or single. Use

___[Date]___
J. J. Doe, Director of Human Resources
ABC Corp.
123 Main St.
Anytown, XX 12345

Dear Mr./Ms. Doe:

I am compiling a listing of child-care services offered by companies in the
_____ geographic area. Since your company employs people in this
area, I'd like to have answers to the following questions:

  1. Does your firm offer child-care services for its employees?
  2. If you do, please describe these services below:

Services offered _____
Eligible employee _____
Hours that service is offered _____
Is flex-time offered? _____
Ages of children served _____
Features of the program: _____
_____
_____
Are meals offered? _____
Education offered? _____
Arts & crafts? _____
ABCs, 123s? _____
Other services offered _____
_____
_____
How long has this program been offered? _____
Remarks _____
_____
_____
Telephone number for employees to call _____
Contact name _____
Contact title _____

   Thank you for providing this information. We will send you a free copy of the
listing as soon as it is offered for sale. Having this information available on a wider
basis could attract better-qualified and more loyal employees to your company.
   A stamped, self-addressed envelope is enclosed to make your response easier
and faster.

Very truly yours,

___[Your Signature]___

Figure 8-1. Sample letter seeking data for child-care listing.

ABC CORPORATION

123 Main St.

Anytown, XX 12345

Phone: 123-4567

Fax: 123-6789

e-mail: abc@anytown.com

Child-care services offered: Receives children of employees from 6:30 A.M. on. Cares for them until 7 P.M., five days a week for non-shift workers. Offers shift workers the same hours on weekends. No services offered on official company holidays. Meals, learning activities, and on-duty nurse included. Weekly cost is $_____, deductible from the parents' salary, if desired. Number of spaces available for children: 36. Usual waiting time to enter child into program: 2 weeks.

For more information, contact: Ms. A. A. Doe, Director Human Resources, 123-4567; fax: 123-6789.

Figure 8-2. Typical entry for child-care listing.

short classified ads. Here's a typical one you might wish to consider:

Earn while your child gets top-notch care. Learn which local companies offer child-care services for their employees. Call 123-4567 for details and price of helpful local listing.

Now let's look at your income potential from such a list. If you price it at—let's say—$75 and sell 100 copies, you'll bring in 100 copies × $75 each = $7,500. Sell 500 copies and your income will be 500 × $75 = $37,500! Not bad when your list might run ten to thirty pages, 8½ × 11 inches, depending on the number of firms in your area. You can produce these in typed form and have them copied at a local print shop for just 5 cents a page. Your profit will be enormous.

What's more, you can expand your child-care list sales to every major city in your state—still working from home. All you need is that industrial/business directory in your local library, plus a few pieces of paper and some stamps!

REAL-LIFE LIST SALES

A friend of mine, Jeff, is handicapped and must work from home. He developed a child-care listing of local companies and sells it in his large city. He sells several thousand copies a year at $25 each. This price was selected because most of the workers in his city are blue-collar shift employees. A higher price might reduce sales. Jeff hasn't gone beyond his own city because he's happy with the $75,000-plus that he's earning every year from his own home. His listing is so valuable that companies are sending him data free of charge to be included in his next printing! Jeff would never leave his lucrative home business because it's too profitable—and he said goodbye to cranky bosses a long time ago!

Once your listing is established for sale, you can put it online. All you need do is get an Internet home page. Then you can advertise your directory, giving a few sample listings (see Figure 8-2) to entice parents to order it from you. With a credit card merchant account you can take orders online and ship the same day, or the next day. Your home-based business world is almost unlimited!

Other Profitable Home-Based Child-Care Businesses

Here are a number of other home-based child-care businesses you might wish to consider. While none of these may appeal to you, one or more might suggest a child-care business you'll like. I see part of my job as an author as the task of suggesting ideas to you that might suggest other—better—ideas from your mind! So let's see what good ideas you can come up with.

Summer Camp at Home for Kids

If you have lots of space at home—such as on a farm or ranch—you might wish to consider running a summer day camp for kids. At the start you can have the parents drop the kids off at your facility. As your business grows, you can hire a part-time bus driver to pick up the kids and return them late in the day. You will—of course—raise your price when you have this pickup and drop-off service. Activities you'll conduct for the kids include:

- **Games** that teach kids lasting values—such as friendship, respect for others, and gentle competition.
- **Hand skills**—woodcarving, sewing, painting, sculpture, weaving, etc.
- **Sports**—basketball, soccer, baseball, swimming, hiking, football, handball, etc.

For a ten-week summer season, figure an income of at least $1,000 per child—with $2,000 and $3,000 per child being possible in upscale areas. Your costs will be minimal because you'll be using land that would otherwise be vacant. Be sure to check local rules covering summer camps.

Baby-Sit at Home During the Day

If you like working with children, you should consider running a baby-sitting service in your home. Depending on the rules in your area, you might be able to care for six children without any special license requirements. Beyond this number, you may require a license. The rules vary from one locality to another. Typical rules require at least:

- **A sleeping area** for each child in which the lights and drapes can be lowered to simulate nighttime conditions.
- **A play area** where children can play with toys, dolls, stuffed animals, etc.
- **A dining or feeding** area in which the children will receive wholesome meals.

To be successful in this business you *must* like children! You really can't make big money unless you enjoy working with children. Your income can run from $100 per five-day week per child to as high as $300 per week per child, depending on the area and the type of clients you have. With six children you can earn from $30,000 a year for fifty weeks, to $90,000 a year. Not bad when you don't have any travel or dress-up clothing expenses. And you can pay your helpers near-minimum wage because they will come from the local area and will also have minimum expenses.

Run Tours for Children

You can help parents cope with child-care needs by running tours for children. Typical places you can tour include local museums, libraries, historic sites, city facilities—waterworks, power plant, bus maintenance garage, mayor's office, etc.—that have educational value for the children. Typical tours will be run once a week for four to six hours. Tours do not provide full-time care. But they can give parents a respite from the daily care of screaming youngsters who—after a while—can get on one's nerves, no matter how patient or understanding a parent may be! Just ask any struggling parent and they'll tell you how it is. Your tours can be conducted:

- **By bus**, which you hire for the day, week, or month, depending on how long you'll need the vehicle.
- **By boat** for water tours of harbors, bays, rivers, or nearby ocean waters for whale watching.
- **By auto**, when you have only three or four children to tour—just be sure your auto insurance is paid and covers your risks.

You price tours based on their duration and whether you provide pickup and drop-off service. Rates can range from a low of $10 per child per tour to as high as $150 per child per tour, depending on tour duration, food supplied, guides, pickup and drop-off, etc. Don't get into children's tours unless you: (a) like kids, (b) enjoy moving about and answering questions, and (c) like a home-based business in which you work out of your home!

Conduct Specialized Schools for Children

Lots of children today need specialized education. Such education can range from math tutoring to golf or tennis lessons, training in social manners (also called etiquette), and so on. You can run such specialized schools in your home for just one child, or for as many as six. Much depends on what you teach (or hire others to teach), and the demand for lessons.

Specialized schools can be run during normal class hours, or after hours in the afternoon or evening. Again, much depends on the educational needs of the children in your area. Probably the most common needs are for tutoring in various high school subjects—math, English, science, etc. So if you're proficient in one of these and you like to teach, you can start your own home business in just a few days.

In running a specialized school for children you help parents in several ways. You:

1. **Occupy the child's time** for a few hours, freeing the parent to do what he or she pleases.

2. **Relieve the parent(s) of the chore** of trying to teach the child what he or she needs to know to pass the subject, or gain proficiency in a skill.
3. **Give the parent(s) a good feeling** about meeting his or her responsibility for educating the child in a proper manner.
4. **Free the parent of the worry** over a child who may be getting failing grades in school while the rest of the kids in the neighborhood are winning prizes and scholarships for their marks.

You price specialized education depending on the course, its importance to the child and parent, and the number of hours you must devote to training the child. One-on-one teaching is priced higher than when several pupils are taught at the same time. Your typical training fees can range from a low of $250 for a quick review course to $1,500 for an intense several-hours-per-day preparation for a special exam of some type. Fees will also vary with the section of the country in which you run your courses.

Making Special Toys for Children

Do you have any special mechanical skills—such as woodworking, electronic design, doll-making, etc.? If you do, you may have the elements of a home-based business you never thought of. In today's world of pampered children, special toys are a big hit. Here's a good example.

A BWB we know of earns big money at home renting out large inflated whales for children's parties. These whales are a big hit with kids because they are so large—about 20 feet long, 8 feet high, and 6 feet wide—that they just amaze the children. The whales have an entrance on one side, allowing the kids to have a small room in the whale to play in. Each whale is rented for four to eight hours, depending on the planned duration of the party. A small electric-powered blower keeps the whale inflated during the party. At the end of the party the whale is deflated and carried away in a car. Each rental brings in several hundred dollars for the BWB. This is what you might call a big, big toy!

Other toys you might wish to make include specialized wooden animals, boats, cars, and so on. One BWB earns big money powering small cars with auto batteries. Kids can drive such cars at speeds up to three miles per hour in their backyard. Price? Some $1,200! Other BWBs build small boats for use on either land or sea. Again, prices exceed $1,000 per boat.

What if you don't have any mechanical skills? You can always hire someone with such skills and sell their output. When I say hire I don't mean that you put the person on a payroll. Instead, you have them work on a speculative basis, or you act as a gallery to promote their work to the public.

Your income in the toy business—which can include the ever-popular stuffed teddy bears, cats, dogs, fish, and other animals—can vary widely. Some people do little more than cut out cloth patterns, sew the cloth, and stuff the resulting "sack." The resulting stuffed animal can sell anywhere from $15 to $1,500—much depends on what's "in" this year.

For best results in the toy business, find yourself a niche. This means you should specialize—at least at the start—in one type of toy. Once you start earning money in your niche you can branch out to other kinds of toys.

How do toys help in child care? A truly good toy can occupy a child for days. This gets the child out of the parents' way. Presto—the parent has some "peace." And that's exactly what many parents seek in today's hectic world of career-minded working mothers and harassed fathers. You can earn big money at home catering to these needs.

Teach Children How to Exercise

Today's world is "crazy" for exercise. Adults want to slim down, improve their cardiac health, and extend their lives. These views are extended to their children. Parents want their children to be healthy too! So the parents seek ways to put their kids on a beneficial exercise program. You can provide such a program from home if you know the basics of exercise for children.

Your job will be to see that children get their regular exercise—be it walking, jogging, aerobics, etc. You will do this three or five days a week, depending on what program is chosen by the parents. Your exercise classes can take place in:

- **Your home's backyard** or basement, depending on weather conditions.
- **A nearby park** or recreation area having facilities of the type you need.
- **An indoor gym** that is safe and secure for kids who want to exercise (or be exercised).

You'll charge for each child you exercise, with your fee ranging from a low of $5 per child per day to a high of $50 per child per day when extensive exercises are required. Most of your exercise will be outdoors, instead of gym-type machines where an expensive investment is required.

Be sure to have a written agreement with each parent. This agreement should cover what you'll do for the child, the frequency of your services, how much you'll be paid, and the dates of your payments—1st and 15th of the month, for example. And you should cover in your agreement your legal responsibilities toward the children. Such an agreement should be prepared by an attorney that has your interests and protection in mind. For any agreement:

- **Be certain that it is in written form**—verbal agreements can rarely be enforced.
- **Be certain that the parents sign** the agreement before you allow any child to exercise under your supervision.
- **Be certain that an attorney approves** of your agreement before you show it to any client.

Your income in this business can range from a low of $6,000 a year to a high of $75,000 a year, depending on the number of children you care for and the type of service you render. Again, you relieve the parents of the chore of exercising with their children. For this they're willing to pay because it's a worthwhile service you're giving—from your own home.

Collect, and Sell, Kids' Books from Home

Some parents want their kids to enjoy the same children's books they did. You can make money from home catering to these wishes. How? By collecting and reselling popular kids books. For example, popular books include:

The Tom Swift series for boys
The Nancy Drew series for girls
The Hardy Boys series for boys

The best way to make money from such books is to acquire them from estate sales, library book sales, auctions, and book giveaways. You then advertise the books at local schools, libraries, women's clubs, supermarkets, and other outlets. Your business will build as parents get to know about the books you have available. You can even take the books back for a nominal fee after kids have outgrown them.

Other books you can promote include hobby, sports, college preparation, and similar titles. Again, you are helping parents by directing their children's reading habits into approved channels. Parents will be happy to pay you good money for doing this for their children.

Your income in this business can range from a low of $5,000 a year to a high of $50,000 a year. You'll have to build slowly because parents will require time to get to know you. And you must stay in the same area so people become aware of your services.

Run After-School Programs for Children

Some of the businesses outlined above can be operated as after-school programs for children. As such, you provide child care between the time children leave school until the parent(s) arrives home from work or other activities. Such care is worth lots of money to working parents. Here are a few after-school programs you can run. Each can be a business in itself:

1. **Arts and crafts instructions** for kids from kindergarten to post-high school teenagers.
2. **Internet surfing** for kids of any age who want to learn the art of getting on, and using, the Internet for educational and entertainment purposes.
3. **Sports training** for kids who want to become proficient in a particular sport.
4. **Cooking training** for both girls and boys whose parents want them to be well-rounded adults with many skills.
5. **Acting and stage performance skills** for children interested in the performing arts.
6. **Computer training** for kids after school. Almost every child today wants to be computer literate. You can teach kids the basics of computers and draw large enrollments in your own home business.
7. **Personal skills**—training kids in fishing, boating, kite flying, bowling, tennis, and golf, for example—to improve their self-confidence and performance.
8. **Safety awareness**—teach children procedures to protect themselves from predatory adults, fire hazards, pedestrian dangers, etc.
9. **Cheerleader training**—of both girls and boys—for middle and high schools. You can also earn money designing and making (or having made) the uniforms.
10. **Child play sessions** for children in your area after school. You will have the children play—either indoors or outdoors, depending on the weather—at useful educational activities.

The Internet Helps Child-Care Providers and Parents

Some child-care providers now use the Internet to allow parents to see their children at play, learning, napping, or being fed at their day-care center. This onscreen access from the parent's computer at work gives you—and the child-care provider—a better chance to demonstrate high-quality skills.

Seeing their child onscreen during the day gives parents much greater confidence in their day-care providers. And the people you find for this service will earn greater respect from parents. Why? Because when seen on computer screen in living color, the provider's work becomes more visible. Parents realize the key importance of their child-care workers.

This can lead to higher wages and more employment for child-care providers. The result? Your income will grow as you find, and recommend, more child-care providers whose skills are way above the average. Your future is brighter when the Internet is your partner!

Another important feature of Internet usage in child care is the protection it provides both children and parents. Knowing that the parent has Internet access every minute of the day will prevent unfair child-care providers from abusing children they supervise. This feature alone is enough to lead to widespread use of the Internet in the child-care field.

Six High-Earnings-Potential Child-Care Businesses for You

Here—in summary form—are a number of potential child-care business for you. So if such work interests you, study this summary in Table 8-1 carefully. It can help you pick the right home-based business for your future wealth!

Table 8-1. Best Child-Care Businesses for BWBs

TYPE OF BUSINESS	WHAT YOU DO	HOW TO FIND CLIENTS	MONEY REQUIRED TO START	ANNUAL EARNINGS POTENTIAL	TIME TO FIRST INCOME	EQUIPMENT NEEDED
Provides a list of local child-care facilities at companies.	Compile lists of what firms offer employees in terms of child-care benefits.	Ads in local papers, parents' newsletters, magazines.	$500 to $1,000	$7,500 to $60,000	4 to 8 weeks	Desk, phone, PC, fax, typewriter.
Child-care referral service.	Find and check out baby-sitters for parents.	Ads in local papers, religious publications, mall bulletin boards.	$500	$12,000 to $48,000	2 to 4 weeks	Desk, phone, PC, fax, typewriter.
Summer camp in your home for kids.	Provide a summer camp for kids.	Ads in local papers, religious publications.	$500 to $800	$6,000 to $48,000	8 to 12 weeks	Desk, phone, PC, fax, typewriter.
Baby-sitting in your home.	Care for children in your home.	Ads in papers, mall bulletin boards.	$250 to $600	$30,000 to $90,000	4 to 6 weeks	Desk, phone, typewriter.
Operate children's tours.	Take kids to interesting places in your area.	Ads in school papers, mall bulletin boards.	$300 to $600	$8,000 to $40,000	6 to 8 weeks	Desk, phone, PC, fax, typewriter.
Run special courses for kids.	Teach kids specialized subjects.	Ads in local papers, religious publications, mall bulletin boards.	$600 to $1,000	$12,000 to $75,000	6 to 8 weeks	Desk, phone, PC, fax, typewriter.

CHAPTER 9

SELL INFORMATION AND GROW ENORMOUSLY RICH
By S. David Hicks

YOU'RE LIVING IN the world's greatest Information Age. No matter who we are, today we all need information to live full, successful lives. And you can build a big fortune catering to this thirst for information. Remember, as was said long ago, *Knowledge is power.* Today, you can add: *Information is power and money!*

What We Mean by the Word "Sell"

When I use the word "sell" in this chapter I'm not thinking of face-to-face sales. Instead, I mean the following easy ways for you to earn money by selling information of many different kinds:

1. **Sell by mail**, Internet, telemarketing (using hired operators), dealers, or agents information products or services you buy from others. You almost never even see your customer; the entire sale is done by mail, phone, Internet, or other non-face-to-face methods.
2. **Sell, by the same means** as in step 1, information products or services you acquire and print on your own, using outside printers.
3. **Write (or have someone write)**, and sell, by the same means as in step 1, information products that you develop, based on your own ideas and beliefs.

So—to make it big in information selling—you do *not* have to be an author, do *not* have to write a single word, do *not* need any literary skills, and *never* have to make a face-to-face sale! What you *do* need, however, is:

1. **A strong desire** to become wealthy in your own information sales business.
2. **A willingness to search out** ways to sell information to anyone needing it and willing to pay your price.
3. **A creative approach** to the information market with an open mind that's ready to accept new ideas.

So if you have all—or most of—these characteristics, you can make your millions selling information. Let's get you started. I've done it. And so can you, because I'm probably not as smart as you are!

What Kinds of Information Products Can Make Me Rich?

The number of information products and services you can sell is almost endless. Typical big-profit producers include:

- **Books** of many kinds—both soft and hard cover
- **Newsletters**—for consumers and businesses
- **Software**—for games and business programs
- **Educational courses** of all kinds
- **Calculators** and estimating tools
- **Diet guides** and daily meal planners
- **Videos** that teach a skill or entertain people
- **Computer** keyboard cutouts
- **Plus thousands of other items** or services

The key idea is that you sell information that helps people in one or more aspects of:

- Their financial lives
- Their personal lives (relationships)
- Their jobs or careers

Focus on one or more of these topics and you hone in on the core interests of most people—interests on which they're willing to spend money to improve their current situation. And that money will be spent with you—the best way they could spend it! Who better to send their money to than you?

What kinds of information sells best? Any information in the three categories mentioned above will sell well. For example:

1. **Financial information sells well** to people seeking new, or expanded, careers. At my company, International Wealth Success, Inc., we've been helping people with their finances for more than thirty years. During these years we've earned millions of dollars selling financial information by mail, the Internet, and telemarketing. A number of our typical ads for these products are shown in Figures 9-1 through 9-4. Our *Financial Broker, Finder, Business Broker, Business Consultant Kit* (K-1), listed at the back of this book, has sold more than 5,000 copies at $99.50 each. Do the arithmetic on this: 5,000 × $99.50 = $497,500.

2. **Relationships occupy many people's minds** nearly twenty-four hours a day. So you'll find that information on various aspects of relationships is always popular. For example, the excellent book *1001 Ways to Be Romantic* by Greg Godek is reported to have sold more than 125,000 copies at $11.95. And its sequel, *1001 More Ways to Be Romantic* by the same author, is reported in the publishing-industry press to have had advance sales of more than 50,000 copies. These two useful and helpful books have really caught the attention of people who need help with relationships. Develop a new idea for relationship materials such as

   • **Improving** an existing relationship
   • **Quickly starting** a new relationship
   • **Rapidly ending** an unsatisfactory relationship
   • **Techniques for** beginning relationships where none exist now.

   You can become rich in a short time. Why? Because almost everyone seeks ways to make new friends, find a spouse, meet people with similar interests, or expand their network of valuable acquaintances. You can make a bundle serving these needs.

How to
MAKE EXPORT-IMPORT RICHES

GET STARTED IN YOUR OWN EXPORTING BUSINESS (and in importing, if YOU wish) for less than $250! Earn big fees without ever having to touch what YOU sell. As this user of our big Kit writes:

"Enclosed is a copy of my first commission check from my export business. The sale was for $32,000 and my commission was $4,269.50. Not bad for starting with $100 capital and your 'Import-Export Kit.' They are getting ready to order two more similar machines."

YOU CAN GET SIMILAR ORDERS! How? By using our BIG "Import-Export Kit" which gives YOU:

* 5,000 ways to earn big fees for selling needed products all over the world
* Easy steps to take to do the simple papers used in both importing and exporting
* Simple letters YOU can mail or fax to your overseas customers to make sales fast
* Ways to work from YOUR home without ever having to travel further than your mailbox
* Get BIG repeat orders which put large fees into YOUR pocket quickly and easily
* Ways to be paid through YOUR own bank with checks that will never, never bounce!
* Quick finance sources to give YOU loans or grants to operate YOUR business
* Personal help 800-number telephone line for on-the-spot answers to YOUR questions. Or if YOU can't call, an address to write or fax to get instant answers and help

ALL THESE BENEFITS CAN BE YOURS – sooner than YOU think! YOU can bring in big fees within days after making the first contact by mail or phone. One user of this Kit is making $30,000 per month profit after ALL costs after making just one phone call! YOU might be able to do the same, once YOU have this big Kit in YOUR hands.

With this Kit on hand YOU'll have 99% of what YOU need to know to get started. The other 1% YOU get by doing – while YOU're being paid to learn! Other key data YOU get in this Kit:

* How to avoid the 12 most common mistakes of potential exporters
* Directory of Federal and State export help YOU can get free of any charge
* Sources of assistance (including financing) by state – there's more money around for YOU than YOU ever have thought!
* Contacts for top overseas markets – people YOU can talk to or write or fax for big sales
* Typical forms used in export-import deals all over the world
* Easy, fast ways to get paid for the work YOU do in exporting and importing
* Building YOUR export-import business to the level that gives YOU the income you desire

DON'T WASTE ANY TIME: Get into export-import NOW! YOU'll be able to get away from nasty bosses, a slave-wage pay check, and constant threats of being fired.

BE YOUR OWN BOSS IN A BUSINESS WHERE YOU WORK only a few hours a day. Bring in big chunks of money every day of the year. Go from poverty to riches in just a few hours. Why scrimp and save to get what YOU want when YOU can make millions in just a few months in an interesting and rewarding business?

SEND FOR YOUR EXPORT-IMPORT KIT TODAY! Fill out the coupon below. YOU'll get started in just hours!

ABOUT THE AUTHOR:
Tyler G. Hicks is the president of INTERNATIONAL WEALTH SUCCESS, INC., as well as the president of a large lending organisation in New York. He is internationally recognized as the foremost expert on making money from scratch and is the best-selling author of many books, including *How to Get Rich on Other People's Money*, *How to Start a Business on a Shoestring and Make Up to $500,000 a Year*, and *How to Borrow Your Way to Real Estate Riches*. Over 2 million people (worldwide) have profited from his books. He will provide free consultation for every buyer of this kit.

FREE CONSULTATION!

Here's US $99.50. Send me my EXPORT-IMPORT KIT now! (Airmail outside North America: add $60; there is no postage cost for surface - sea mail shipment)   Credit Card Orders: 516-766-5850.

Send material to (PLEASE PRINT):   Please send your payment to

Name: _____
Street: _____
City: _____
State: _____
Country: _____
Tel/Fax: _____

INTERNATIONAL WEALTH SUCCESS INC.
P.O. BOX 186
MERRICK, NY 11566

Figure 9-1. A typical ad for one of IWS, Inc.'s, financial products.

DO YOU SINCERELY WANT TO MAKE A MILLION IN MAIL ORDER?

Today YOU have a golden opportunity to make millions in mail order! There never was a better time to make BIG money in this easy, laid-back way!

Thousands of money-making opportunities exist today for the mail-order beginner. Get rich without ever going to work! Cash in on the double-income family that has plenty of money to spend but no time to spend it! So they shop by mail – sending you buckets of cash every day!

Order your money-in-the-bank, good-as-gold Mail-Order Riches Success Kit today and start:

- **Seeing your mailbox stuffed with big, big cash orders every day**
- **Going to the bank every day to deposit money – not to take it out**
- **Building business-at-home riches free of cranky, surly bosses**
- **Racking up easy, ovenight profits in the world's best business!**

This BIG, opportunity-of-a-life Kit will deliver sizzling sales of any item YOU want to sell by mail order. You'll have a top-dollar income because the author of the Kit, Ty Hicks, has made millions in mail order himself. He shows YOU exactly:

- **How to start your mail-order business at home in just hours**
- **Where to find products that will deliver megabucks to your wallet**
- **Dozens of ways to bring money into YOUR business in just a few days**
- **How to find low-cost (and no-cost) mailing lists to use**
- **Secret ways to get the people to buy from you again and again**
- **Where to meet with Ty Hicks free of charge or how to call him on the phone!**

This BIG Kit helps YOU move ahead with little or no effort. You owe it to yourself to advance great wealth! To go for it ... to live your dreams in your own golden-opportunity business!

What's more, Ty Hicks is as close to you as your phone to help YOU unleash your greatest creative skills – which we all have. Then you may tell us, as the readers did, who bought the kit from us:

"I ordered your Kit 2 months ago. I've already made $16,400 from it and project an income of over $100,000 in the next two months. Thanks for the time you spent with me on the phone – you've been wonderful!"

"I raised $200,000 from a 20,000–name mailing in just a few weeks. Thanks for your help!"

"Not long ago I was working my head off at two jobs and not enjoying either. Now I make more money and work at home when I feel like it."

So send for the BIG Mail-Order Richess Success Kit which is guaranteed to give YOU the info YOU need to start your own riches-building mail-order business that can deliver millions to YOUR mailbox!

Priced at only $99.50, Ty Hicks tells thousands of his happy buyers: "This Kit gives YOU 99% of what YOU need to know to get started in mail order today. The other 1% you learn by doing – while you bring in the big bucks!"

To order, use the coupon below. Make a jumbo income from the wealth methods this BIG kit gives YOU! Once you have YOUR kit Ty Hicks will help you:

- **Pick moneymaking products or services to earn YOUR millions**
- **Reach your income goals quickly and easily in your own business**
- **Get any financing YOU may need to start making YOUR millions!**

ABOUT THE AUTHOR
Tyler G. Hicks is the president of INTERNATIONAL WEALTH SUCCESS, INC., as well as the president of a large lending organisation in New York. He is internationally recognized as the foremost expert on making money from scratch and is the bestselling author of many books, including *How to Get Rich on Other People's Money, How to Start a Business on a Shoestring and Make Up to $500,000 a Year,* and *How to Borrow Your Way to Real Estate Riches.* Over 2 million people (worldwide) have profited from his books.

FREE CONSULTATION!

Future Mail-Order Millionaire Response Coupon

Here's US$100. Please send me my MAIL-ORDER SUCCESS KIT now. Airmail outside North America: add US$60.

Send material to (PLEASE PRINT):

Name: ____________________
Street: ____________________
City: ____________________
State: ____________________
Country: ____________________
Tel/Fax: ____________________

Please send your payment to

INTERNATIONAL WEALTH SUCCESS INC.
P.O. BOX 186
MERRICK, N Y 11566

To order by credit card call 516-766-5850.

Figure 9-2. A typical ad for one of IWS, Inc.'s, financial products.

Figure 9-3. A typical ad for one of IWS, Inc.'s, financial products.

find VENTURE CAPITAL millions

Become an IWS VENTURE CAPITAL PROFESSIONAL and get the BIG benefits YOU can use NOW

**Nearly instant CASH FLOW to YOU!
**Start a sizeable yearly income!
**Be in business quickly--NOW!
**Fast respect from others!
**Earn by mail, by phone, or by both!
**Get money for clients or yourself!
**Go from no-cash-flow to steady cash
**Use the ONE-HOUR FINANCIAL WINNER!

Become an IWS VENTURE CAPITAL PROFESSIONAL and YOU get FOUR FAST WAYS to earn big!

**Be PAID to tell if a business idea is good!
**Be PAID to have a business plan written by others!
**Be PAID to find a venture capitalist to fund the deal!
**Be PAID for a piece of the success action--for years!

Get help ALL ALONG the way--while getting paid for getting others to do the work:

YOU get PAID while we evaluate the idea for YOU!
YOU get PAID while a business plan is written by others!
YOU get PAID while we find the venture capitalist for YOU!
YOU get PAID from future company growth--NO fees to us--ever!

GET IN ON THE BIG TIME NOW! How? By sending for the newest IWS Kit--THE VENTURE CAPITAL MILLIONS ONE-HOUR FINANCIAL WINNER! This breakthrough in venture-capital funding shows YOU how to:

- Raise venture funds fast
- Earn BIG fees sooner
- Get ongoing income for years
- Work where, and when, YOU want to
- Have others do the "nitty-gritty" for YOU
- Get started in just one hour, or less
- Be a professional, respected by all in your area
- Share in the newest deals in business and real estate
- Work without the need for a license of any kind

Anyone interested in money, business, or real estate can use THE VENTURE CAPITAL MILLIONS KIT! For someone just starting, it's the sure way to local "insider" deals of all kinds. And YOU can start in one hour, or less, if you want!

For brokers, finders, and business people it can be the source of NEW MONEY, much of which never has to be repaid! It can expand your world--go from small, puny deals to the BIG-TIME millions!

So send NOW for the Kit that could change your life! Or call IWS and put your order in by credit card. Be the first in YOUR area to offer venture capital professional services for any firm needing help from YOU!

Here's $100. Send me my VENTURE CAPITAL MILLIONS KIT. If you wish, YOU can call Ty Hicks at 516-766-5850 day or night to order by credit card. Or enter your card number below and send this coupon to IWS, Inc., 24 Canterbury Rd., Rockville Centre, NY 11570.

NAME__________ CARD NO.__________
ADDRESS__________ EXPIRES__________
CITY__________ STATE__________ ZIP__________

Buy this month and get Special Venture Capital List on self-adhesive labels updated every six months for one year!

Figure 9-4. A typical ad for one of IWS, Inc.'s, financial products.

3. **Job and career information** is important to almost every working man and woman in the world. For instance, the famous job-finding book *What Color Is Your Parachute?* has sold millions of copies to job seekers. Why? Because it is a practical, down-to-earth guide that helps its readers enormously. It is probably one of the best examples of useful job information published today. You—too—can achieve large sales if you sell job or career information that helps people get a better job sooner. For instance, books on résumé preparation sell well. Why? Because almost every job seeker must prepare a résumé. And almost every job seeker is fearful of—and abhors—preparing a résumé. Give them a book on ten-minute résumé preparation and you may never have to look for a job again! Among the many bestsellers my company, IWS, Inc., publishes are several career guides, including:

- *Credits and Collection Kit*, which shows a person how to start, and prosper in, the great business of getting people to pay what they owe. For just $29.50, a person can get started in a new career that could last them a lifetime.
- *How to Become a Second Mortgage Loan Broker* is a book that tells you what its title says. At $25, this book could help any interested person get started in a new career in this booming field.
- *How to Make a Fortune As a Licensing Agent* is a book priced at $15 that tells you what its title says. Again, an interested person can use this book to get started as a licensing agent in the industrial or entertainment fields.
- *How to Become Wealthy Publishing a Newsletter* is a $17.50 book, giving down-to-earth information on coming up with the idea for your newsletter, printing your first issue, and going on from there to multiple issues.

These, and other similar products listed at the back of this book, help people in their careers. You—too—can make a career for yourself guiding others to a more profitable career for themselves!

Several Real-Life Examples of How Information Products Can Help People

The best test of any information product or service is what it does for its users. Here are several real-life examples of results obtained with some of the above-mentioned products. We hope your customers can report similar—or better—results with your products or services:

> "Thanks for the *Financial Broker Kit,* which arrived this morning. I closed a $425,000 deal with it this afternoon. Thanks again!" This BWB works as a loan broker from his home in Tennessee.

Another BWB called from Louisiana:

> "To this date I have made nearly $1.25 million in loans (all by phone) and things are getting better every day."

This BWB from Virginia made it big in real estate:

> "I took ownership of my first investment property (with no money down and no credit check) as a result of your book *How to Make $1 Million in Real Estate in 3 Years Starting with No Cash.* Here is how the deal was structured. I got a first mortgage for $15,900; the seller took back a second mortgage for $17,500 with no interest (straight note). At closing the seller received $10,000 and I mortgaged out with $3,858.32 in cash in my pocket. Also, all my closing costs were financed in the first mortgage. Lastly, I am structuring a deal to sell this property and should net an additional $5,000 to $10,000. Thank you very much."

This subscriber to the IWS newsletter also did well in "paper" real estate:

> "I subscribed to *International Wealth Success* in November and bought my first income property with no money down the same month. I got an investor's loan from a local S&L and the seller paid all closing costs and took back a second mortgage for the balance of the purchase price. This duplex gives me about $100 per month profit after the two mortgage payments and all expenses. Not bad for no cash investment of my

own. Now this same property owner wants to sell four other properties under the same terms. I'm on my way to building my wealth in real estate. "

How, and Where, to Find Salable Products

Look Inside Your Mind

The best place to find salable products is in your own mind! Why do I say this? For several important reasons. Products you develop yourself:

- **Are often more original** and more salable than products you buy from others.
- **Usually have your personal view** of a need that's based on real experiences.
- **Can be way ahead of any copycat products** others develop after they see the great market you've found.
- **Can carve a market niche** that you alone occupy for months—or years—before the competition catches on.

So how do you develop a product or service on your own? You look at your job, your hobbies, your interests, and every other aspect of your life and ask yourself:

1. **What's needed to make my job simpler**, make me more efficient, or get rid of some of the "grunt" aspects of the work I do every day?
2. **How could I do better in my hobby**, be it a sport or an indoor activity such as model building, billiards, houseplants, sewing, crocheting, etc.?
3. **What does the world need** for better living, more recreation, greater health, etc., that I can offer?

Answers to these questions may help you come up with a new information product or service you can sell by mail, the Internet, telemarketing, and other means. Your unique approach can put you into an unchallenged position until your competitors find out and try to imitate your success.

But you'll be so far ahead of them that it will take them years to catch up—if they ever do. Here are two examples of coming up with your own products that sell well:

As a mechanical engineer doing design work early in my career, I found the need for ways to make quick calculations so we could get a job out by 4 P.M. on a Friday. Yet when I referred to my college texts, I found that they were full of good theory but lacked the practical aspects of daily design work. So I decided to develop a series of quick calculation procedures for the most common problems I, and other engineers, met in our daily work—such as sizing a pump, picking an air-conditioning unit, etc. Other engineers who saw these procedures grabbed them from me, saying "Gee, these are great! Gimme every one you have!" Soon these engineers began to say: "I'll be happy to pay you for every one of these procedures you work up." So I charged them $10 each, which they were happy to pay. Why? Because the procedures made their job easier, made them more efficient, saved them time, and gave them a feeling of security because they knew the procedures were safe and valid.

From there it was a simple step to selling these same procedures to technical magazines for $50 each. Then I gathered them all together and put them into a book titled *Standard Handbook of Mechanical Engineering Calculations*, which has earned me more than $1 million in royalties. Thus, an information need I saw on my job led to enormous help for working engineers all over the world and kept my bank account very liquid. Today these procedures are sold in both book and CD-ROM form, increasing the royalty earnings to you-know-who!

Darryl M., a BWB, saw the need for more information on black history. He read many books on the subject. Lots of these books—he noted—were out of print, having been published twenty-five to seventy-five years ago. Showing these books to his friends he got the immediate reaction—"Could I borrow these from you? I'd love to read these books. They look very interesting." After lending out a few books, Darryl suddenly thought, "Why don't I have a few of these printed and sell them?" Trying to contact the firms that published many of the older books proved difficult—they were no longer in business. Further study showed that many of the books were in the public domain. This means that anyone can reprint the book and doesn't have to pay royalties to the author because his or her address is somewhere in the wild blue yonder. And the original publisher long ago joined his or her authors in the same place of rest. Darryl reprinted six of the titles on black history and promoted them by direct mail to his friends. His first printing of 250 copies of each title sold out in just a few weeks. Reprinting the books, Darryl expanded his direct-mail campaign to lists he rented. Soon he was reprinting 2,500 copies of each book. Sales to black-owned bookstores soon followed. Today Darryl has a booming business in black-history information.

Check Out Products Offered by Others

"But I can't come up with any products or services of my own," some BWBs tell me. "How can I find anything worth selling?" That's easy.

1. **Review the offerings** from people in the information business—such as book publishers, video producers, audio studio output, CD manufacturers, software publishers, etc.
2. **Request free samples of information products** you think you can sell by mail, Internet, telemarketing, etc. Most publishers will be happy to send you free samples. If a publisher seems reluctant, just tell him or her, "I'll return it to you in good condition after I review it. I'm not trying to get it free." Hearing this, almost every publisher or supplier will send you samples for review. When you receive the sample, review it carefully. Figure out where you can sell it. Keep one fact clearly in mind at all times: It's easier to sell to niche (specialized) markets than to "everyman or everywoman." Find an information product for a niche market that you know—based on your job, lifestyle, sport, or hobby—and you have a potential millionaire-maker.

Big fortunes are being made almost every day by people selling information products or services produced by others. Here's an excellent recent example:

Tom and Ann, two BWBs, wanted to open a how-to video store. They saw a great future in selling how-to videos on any number of topics such as computer usage, speed swimming, electrical repairs, effective public speaking, boat navigation, and more. Reviewing video producer's catalogs they found nearly 7,000 videos available for sale. Instead of spending the $50,000 needed to open a store (money they did not have), Tom and Ann decided to print a catalog of videos on various how-to topics and mail it to prospects. Checking with video suppliers, they found some who would supply "mats"—printed ad pages—free of charge. This meant the catalog could be prepared for just a few hundred dollars. Tom and Ann prepared a sixteen-page 5 × 8-inch catalog and mailed it to a rented list. Their results were way beyond their expectations. For every dollar they spent on their catalog they brought back $3.04. Working carefully, they plowed some of their profits back into an expanded twenty-four-page catalog with much the same results. Today their ninety-six-page catalog continues to produce strong results every time they mail it—which is four times per year. Thus, information on video—produced by others—can generate strong income for BWBs who want to sell by mail, Internet, or telemarketing. Tom and Ann never bothered to open their store. Their profits are too high working from home selling how-to videos!

To make money selling information developed by others, look for niche-type products—that is, specialized items that appeal to a particular group of people. Thus, you might look for information products for:

- **Lovers of rare breeds** of birds, cats, dogs, fish, etc.
- **Race-car buffs** who love fast cars that race for big purses around the world.
- **Privacy supporters** who want to hide their identity from the prying eyes of everyone.
- **Get-even believers** seeking to even the score with someone they feel harmed them.
- **Environmental activists** who will do everything they can to protect the world from pollution and other environmental damage by careless earth-dwellers.
- **Computer "jocks"** who love their PCs and will buy almost any worthwhile information on getting more production from their machines.
- **Internet aficionados** who live and breathe this way of getting data and communicating with family and friends.

• **People with any other unique interest** about which you can find information products that will answer their questions.

Why do I recommend niche markets for information products? For several good, hard-money reasons. These reasons are:

1. **Niche markets are reachable**—that is, the people in a niche market belong to certain groups whose names are available to rent for direct-mail purposes; such people subscribe to, and read, magazines whose subscriber lists you can rent.
2. **Niche-market people tend to be** strong believers in (and buyers of) products in their field; you can make money from them more easily than when you try to sell to everyone.
3. **Niche-market people make it easier** for you to start—and succeed in—selling specialized information at a price that can give you a good profit while making your customer feel that he or she got good value for the money.
4. **Niche-market people are loyal**—they'll come back, again and again, to spend money for your offerings. They're so steady in their buying habits that you can accept their checks as being as good as gold—they'll never bounce! Why? Because your niche-market customers love what you sell them. So they want to be the best customer you have!

Now that you know how to earn money from products offered by others, let's look at one other way to find salable products or services. We want you to have every opportunity possible to get rich selling information from your home-based business.

Use Specialized Sales Plans

When you first start your own home-based business, you may have so much to do that you need help and guidance. One good way to get this guidance is to join a company that has specialized sales plans for beginners. Reputable companies that have such sales plans can get you started in your own home-based business for less than $300. Reliable companies:

1. **Do not require you to buy** and store any inventory of any kind.
2. **Set you up as an independent contractor** in business for yourself and not on a payroll.
3. **Give you one-on-one personal advice** for helping you succeed—at no extra cost.
4. **Have been in business for years**, during which they established a good reputation for themselves.
5. **Are members of key organizations** in their field, plus the Better Business Bureau.

Using these five points as your guide, you can start checking out companies offering specialized sales plans. For example, my firm, International Wealth Success, Inc., (IWS, Inc., for short) offers an Executive Representative Specialized Sales Plan in which you have the opportunity, and right, to:

1. **Offer for sale**—by any acceptable means—all of our newsletters, books, kits, and reports to any market you choose to serve.
2. **Receive a 40 percent commission** for the first $2,000 in total list-price sales, and 50 percent commission for life thereafter.
3. **Get personal one-on-one sales help** directly from me—in person, on the phone, by fax, or by mail—depending on your wishes.
4. **Be paid for every item your customer buys** from us— whether through you or directly from us—even ten years after you get your customer! Your sales commission is paid once a month—on the first of the month.
5. **Collect your commission in advance** on every sale you make directly to your customers. Being paid "up front" makes many BWBs feel good because they don't have to wait to get paid.
6. **Sell any of our products** with NO INVENTORY in your home, NO SHIPPING COST of any kind, NO PACKING, MAILING, OR SHIPPING CHORES of any kind—ever.

7. **Work with a firm** that has been in business more than thirty
   years, is a member of the Newsletter Publishers Association, the American Booksellers Association, and the Better
   Business Bureau. Further, our newsletter, *International
   Wealth Success,* is the longest-running business-opportunity
   newsletter published in the United States still under the
   control of its founder.

To become an Executive Representative of IWS, Inc., send
$120 to IWS, Inc., P.O. Box 186, Merrick, NY 11566-0186. You
will immediately be sent your Executive Representative Agreement, plus a five-year subscription to the IWS newsletter, which
is published twelve times a year. You can order by credit card
by calling (516) 766-5850 day or night.

There are other specialized sales plans available for selling information or books by mail. Before you join any such
plan, be sure to check it out against the points listed above.
Never join a plan that requires you to carry an inventory,
makes you ship the product, offers to sell you preprinted
catalogs, or charges you thousands of dollars for a large
number of catalogs—5,000 or more. Such plans seldom
make money for anyone but the outfit selling you the deal!

What's a Fair Price for You to Pay for Products or Services?

The more you pay for what you sell, the less you keep. And
you want to keep as much of your sales dollars as you can.
To answer the fair-price question we say this:

Never pay more than one-half the selling price of a product or
service you are selling, except at the start when there may be a
small extra charge to get you set up in the business.

In number terms this means that once you're making
sales of a product or service, your cost and list price will
look like this:

List Price	Your Maximum Cost
$10.00	$5.00
$25.00	$12.50
$50.00	$25.00
$100.00	$50.00

Remember—when I tell you that half is the *most* you should pay for any product or service, I'm assuming that:

- **You do NOT carry any inventory** of the product you're selling.
- **You do NOT ship the product** you're selling to people anywhere.
- **You are NOT buying a large number** of preprinted catalogs— say 2,000 or more.

The ideal way to earn money with specialized sales plans is to work only with paper—that is, catalogs, fliers, envelopes, and stamps. For example:

One of our Canadian Executive Representatives sells our newsletters, kits, and books all over the world by mail order, direct mail, and telemarketing. He gets orders from Canada, Indonesia, Saudi Arabia, England, and elsewhere. To pay his 50 percent (and keep his 50 percent commission), he just faxes us his credit card number and we put the charge through. His payment for the products is already in his bank, having been deposited when he was paid for them by his customers. A typical order from this Executive Rep is $800, meaning his income was $1,600 from just this one order. Yet this Rep NEVER sees what he sells, NEVER packs a single product, NEVER goes to the post office to ship any products, NEVER has to type a bill! It's all done for him by IWS, Inc.

You can sometimes get a better price for the products you sell. For example, you may be able to buy books, how-to videos, and other information products for 10 percent of their list price. See Chapter 5 for details on buying products at a high discount. The one problem with such sales is that the products are often not very salable. That's why they're being sold at a big price reduction.

One powerful way to use such high-discount products is to make them part of a larger item, such as a course. You thereby have a low-cost component, which reduces the overall cost of the product you sell. But you must make this low-cost item an integral part of the course so it does not appear to just have been thrown in to bulk up the overall product.

As an Executive Rep in our program you can advertise free of charge in the IWS newsletter. Then you might write us, as this BWB did from Pennsylvania, to say:

"Thank you for providing me with motivation to begin my home-based mail-order business. The first few years were questionable, but patience and perseverance are two key factors you encouraged. If it had not been for your newsletter, we probably would never have either started or become successful in our business. Thanks for your encouragement and ads, which continue to produce better results than many of the paid ads we've run in the last eight and a half years!"

Another reader writes from Iowa:

"I started my business in my bedroom, doing what I like, instead of working for someone else. Today we have twenty-two people working for us. Business is great!"

This BWB called from California:

"I sold 500,000 copies of my mail-order book at $10 a copy for a total income of some $5 million." This BWB then retired after his son took over the business.

Another BWB from Pennsylvania says:

"Having my ad in your newsletter is very important to us. It has produced more than forty times the cost of the subscription in the last year."

Selling with specialized sales plans can help you build wealth in your own home business. Just be sure the plan you pick is favorable to you. Why make someone else rich when you can become wealthy with the right plan?

With the right sales plan you can be a stay-at-home mom. Or you can become a kitchen-table millionaire offering useful information products by mail and on the Internet. Breakthrough thinking and creative solutions will keep your bank account full to the brim!

Where to Market Your Information Products and Services

There are many places to market your products or services. But not all these places will work for every product or service. Some will—some won't. Your task is to find those places that work for your product or service. Typical places you can market include:

- **Newspapers**—daily, weekly, monthly
- **Magazines**—weekly, monthly, quarterly
- **Internet**—with your own Web site or in a mall
- **TV**—using infomercials or spot ads
- **Radio**—with commercials of varying length
- **Telemarketing**—both outgoing and incoming
- **Books**—such as this with back-of-the-book ads
- **Fliers**—put on cars, doorsteps, in takeout orders
- **Direct mail**—every day of the year to prospects

Do such marketing outlets work for the home business? They most certainly do. Take, for example, the story of one successful home-based BWB:

He made sales of $200 to $400 a day placing fliers on cars in parking lots. His sales grew to $85,000 a week—from his one-bedroom apartment—from which he ran ads in newspapers for a variety of information products useful to large groups of people.

With actual results such as these, it *is* possible for you to achieve the income level you seek in your own home business. Let's see how you can get the best results for yourself in each of these places.

Newspapers—you can use classified ads in small-town daily and weekly newspapers to promote mass-market products or services. *Products and services that sell well* in newspapers include reports on saving money, recipes for unusual dishes, dating services, sport gadgets or memorabilia, business opportunities of various kinds, and so on. *For fastest results* use a toll-free 800/888 number for prospects to respond to your offer. At the start, answer the phone yourself; as sales build, get an answering service so you can concentrate on new products and services for your customers. *Income potential* from newspaper classified ads can be as high as $100,000 per week. However, for planning purposes, it is wise to plan on much less—say $1,000 per week within three months of starting your continuous ad campaign in a variety of newspapers. *Hot sellers today* include statues of sports figures (golf, football, and so on, with a brief write-up of the sports legend depicted by the statue), mortgage-reduction programs, weight-loss programs, unique dating services, real-estate tax-savings services. *Marketing secret:* Weekly papers often pull better results at a lower cost than dailies; small-town papers pull better than large-city papers for most information products.

Magazines—start with classified ads; expand to space ads of varying sizes (1-inch to full-page) if the response to your product or service is strong—that is, you bring in more money than it costs you to run the ad, pay for the product or service, and ship it to your customer. *Products and services that sell well* in magazine ads range from books to courses to reports on a variety of business, hobby, health, and relationship topics. Aim your information products at the largest markets—such as people with financial problems (almost everyone), young people seeking their first credit card, downsized workers wanting to start their own business so they can avoid future layoff horrors, single women seeking lasting relationships, etc. Be certain your products or services are helpful and strongly solution-oriented for troubled people. *For fastest results* try weekly magazines first. Shift to monthly magazines if weeklies don't pull strongly enough to pay their cost. Use both weeklies and monthlies if you earn a big enough return from them. *Income potential* from magazines can range from $1,000 to $10,000 per issue, depending on the price of your product or service and the response you get. *Hot sellers today* include information on home businesses, multilevel marketing, medical billing services, mailing lists, winning gambling techniques, reduced-cost telephone services, etc. *Marketing secret:* Work with the magazine's editorial staff to get some free comments on your information product that will back up your ad. Most magazines are willing to do a free write-up of your product or service when you first start advertising. The combined punch of the ad and write-up can last for months, giving you strong sales.

The Internet—this marvel of information distribution is worldwide and can get your information products into the hands of people you never thought of as a market. With it, you can turn your home-based small business into a worldwide power that collects money from millions of people needing what you produce. *Products and services that sell well* on the Internet are those that are computer- or Internet-related—that is, books, courses, and reports that help people understand, and use, their computers and the Net, as well as related software, hardware, and services. With your own Web site you can promote a full line of specialized information products. To start on the Internet for the lowest cost, consider signing a nonexclusive agreement with a mall. Most mall operators are willing to put your catalog product info pages on their mall at no charge. Then they'll take a 25 percent commission on any sales they make. While this may seem high, it is really low when you recall that your offer goes onto a medium accessible to 100 million people today—with more growth in the future. *For fastest results* get onto an Internet mall—you can do this in days. Then consider getting your own Web site. *Income potential* can range from less than $100 per month to $10,000 per month, or more. As time passes, the income potential from the Internet is expected to rise because more people will access it and use it to order information products. *Hot sellers today* in the information field include Internet and computer books, reports, and courses, data on how and where to get money for business and personal use, financial information on stock and bond investing, etc. *Marketing secret:*

Internet buyers tend to be more upscale and better educated than magazine and newspaper readers. Hence, you can offer more advanced information products to this market and expect good sales results at higher prices for each product.

Television infomercials and ads on cable TV—both local and national channels, and worldwide—are used for almost any type of information product or service you might want to sell to the general public. *Products and services that sell well* include books and courses on real estate, mail order, import–export, financial brokerage, home businesses, and related topics. *For fastest results* use the findings that show that the shorter infomercial programs—five to fifteen minutes—pull better today than the longer thirty- to sixty-minute shows that started the infomercial boom. Shorter shows cost less to produce and air, and have almost the same impact as the longer shows. *Income potential* from infomercials and TV ads can range from $100 per day to as high as $25,000 a day. Much depends on the number of shows per day, the price of your product or service, and the impact of the show on its watchers. *Hot sellers today* are books, kits, reports, and self-study programs on making money at home, real estate, import–export, and financial brokerage. Other consumer topics—such as credit cards, mortgage loans, college preparation, health, and beauty information—also sell well in either the infomercial or ad form on twenty-four-hour television. *Marketing secret:* Run your infomercials and ads twenty-four hours per day on cable TV. With the introduction of digital TV, and the dozens of analog cable channels specializing in hundreds of special interests, you have a wide-open market ready to look over, and buy, your information products. What's more, cable TV is much cheaper than the major networks and delivers a more focused audience. There are millions of day- and nighttime watchers who will order your information products or services. Be sure to offer an 800/888 toll-free number for credit-card orders. Then you may be able to top an early infomercial BWB who made $1 million in sales the first weekend he was on TV!

Radio—use short commercials for your information material. *Products that sell well* include courses, books, and help for kids studying for high school and college entrance exams. *For fastest results* sell core-interest information on jobs, scholarships, estate planning, quick mastery of school math, etc. These topics sell year-round on radio. *Income potential* can range from $5,000 a year to $100,000-plus per year, depending on the frequency of your radio commercials and the population served by the station(s) you use to carry your commercials. *Hot sellers today* are products aimed at helping students qualify for higher SAT (Scholastic Aptitude Test) scores. Nearly every parent wants his or her child to be admitted to the best school. Higher SAT scores are one way to reach this goal. *Marketing secret:* Seek out smaller radio stations in your area. They often charge less than large stations and their listeners are more loyal and much more likely to buy from you. Also, religious stations often produce great sales for educational products of all types.

Telemarketing—this method uses telephone salespeople who call and try to sell your information products to people in, and outside, your area. *Products that sell well* are those devoted to earning money in the stock market, futures markets (porkbellies, copper, silver, coal, etc.), and home businesses, plus many others. People who buy from telemarketers typically want to earn money fast. You can serve such information needs by developing or finding existing products tailored to this basic human drive. *For fastest results* sell products that are easy for buyers to use—such as video- and audiotapes and CDs. Today many buyers seek speed learning along with as little thinking as possible. *Income potential* ranges from $5,000 to $100,000-plus per year. *Hot sellers today* are keyed to current business trends—such as training for a career in computers, air conditioning, real estate, the stock market, and similar activities. *Marketing secret:* Keep tuned to the newest "turn-ons" in careers and moneymaking. Then consider promoting them via telemarketing. If such topics are being pushed by other telemarketers, there is probably room for you to jump in and earn a good income.

Books—such as the one you're reading—can be powerful marketing tools. Why? Because your readers are interested in the book's topic, and many related subjects. The reader of a book shows his or her interest just by reading the book! *Products that sell well* in back-of-the-book information sections (see the back of this book) are books, tapes, CDs, and software, on subjects related to that of the book itself. When a coupon, telephone number, street address, and credit-card purchase option are provided, you can obtain large revenues from just a few ad pages. *For fastest results* promote information products on topics related to the content of the book. You will then get orders soon after the book is published and for many years thereafter. Why? Because a good book remains on library shelves long after it may have been declared out of print by its publisher. *Income potential* can range from $4,000 to $35,000 a year per book. Thus, with several such books your annual income selling information could range from $12,000 to $105,000 from the comfort of your own home. *Hot sellers today* are information products on starting your own business, changing your career in later life, recreational and game software of all types, and instructions for starting in a variety of occupations—import–export, financial brokerage, credits and collections, child care, mail order, etc. *Marketing secret:* The more you show, the more you sell! So list as many information products at the back of your book as possible. And give a short description of each product so your reader can make a buying decision without having to ask for more information, causing a possible loss of the sale. **NOTE:** You do NOT have to write a book to get ads in the back of it. You can buy this space by arranging a deal with the publisher. Small publishers will charge less and be more willing to run your ads.

Fliers—usually single-page sheets distributed in parking lots of all types (railroad stations, airports, malls, etc.) can provide you with low-cost marketing. *Products that sell well* are usually career or sports related. Thus, fliers for courses, sports training, and so on can pull well. *For fastest results* get as wide a distribution of your fliers as possible. That is, use station, airport, mall, and other parking lots so you get a wide cross-section of local residents as potential customers. You can pay school kids the minimum wage to do the distributing for you. And you can have someone drive around the parking areas to check on the distribution while you direct the work from home. *Income potential* can range from $3,000 to $60,000 a year, depending on how many fliers you get out there and the number of parking lots in your area. *Hot sellers today* include information products on jobs, careers, instruction in specialized subjects, beauty topics for women, etc. *Marketing secret:* Use colored-stock (paper) fliers instead of plain white. Why? Because colored stock usually pulls better than plain white.

Allow the prospect to reply by phone. Why? Most people are too lazy to reply by mail to a flier solicitation.

Direct mail—given various names—is where you send out letters that sell an information product to people or companies (called business-to-business, or B-to-B). *Products that sell well* include books of all types, courses, software, instructional videos, audiotapes, CDs, and so on. Direct mail is one of the longest-running, and most successful, ways of selling information products. For example, many information-type newsletter publishers say their primary marketing method is direct mail. At IWS we've sold our highly successful newsletter, *International Wealth Success,* for more than thirty years by direct mail. These efforts have given us subscribers in nearly every country in the world. And all this direct mail has been done from home. *For fastest results* get a good information product and promote it to a list of prospects. Use a catalog and promote as many products as you can in each mailing. As we noted earlier, the more you show, the more you sell. *Income potential* can range from $5,000 to $250,000-plus per year from your home. One BWB is reported to earn more than $1 million a year out of a one-bedroom apartment selling information on small businesses, careers, and similar topics. So you have almost an unlimited income potential selling information by direct mail. *Hot sellers today* include software, how-to videos, books, courses, audiotapes, and similar products covering small business, career changes, or specialized occupations (financial brokerage, import–export, mail order, child care, the Internet). *Marketing secret:* Use postcards (see below), special "express" type envelopes, and any other attention-getting devices to get your direct mail opened—and read. Mailing year-round will pay off because if the other business person isn't mailing and you are, your mail will be opened, read, and—hopefully—acted on!

What Results Should I Expect from My Marketing?

Most of the time the income you earn from your marketing will be less than you expect! But every now and then the results will be far better than you expect. The result—in general—will be that you'll earn more in your home-based business than you would on a salary. What's more, you'll be free of demanding bosses and you can increase your income by working longer hours. In short, your life, and your future, are in your own hands!

As a real-life example of the results you can expect from your marketing, let's take a look at a new way to sell your information products by direct mail—the postcard mailing. Using this method of marketing you:

- **Use an oversize or standard-size postcard,** which you can mail for about 66 percent of the cost of a letter.
- **Give a full selling message** on the back of the card, and sometimes on the front also.
- **Get people to act on your offer** either by calling a toll-free number or writing to you.

Your postcard information offer can request payment for what you're selling, or you can offer to provide more information on your products. Typical information products sold with a postcard mailing include books, newsletters, reports, courses, videos, CDs, and audiotapes. To get started selling by postcard, take these easy steps:

1. **Decide what you want to sell by postcard.** Any of the information products mentioned above—plus many others—can be sold by postcard to a good prospect list.
2. **Get a list of prospects.** You can do this by renting names from a mailing-list broker. Select a list of people who bought similar information items from other sellers. Or you can build such a list yourself by running small classified ads in magazines and newspapers read by people interested in your type of information product. Charge a nominal amount for data about your product—say $1 to $3 to cover your ad and mailing costs.
3. **Prepare the offer** for the back (and part of the front) of your postcard. You can do this yourself or you can have someone prepare the sales message using a computer or typewriter. Since your sales message is short, the wording can be prepared quickly—in just a few minutes.
4. **Make your mailing.** Have the stamps and mailing label put on the front of the card. You can do this yourself at

home or have someone else do it for you. High school kids love to do this work after school for just a few dollars per thousand cards. You can mail at any time of the day or night—the mail is always picked up and sent on its way.

5. **Watch as the orders come in.** You can have the orders sent to your home or business address, or to a post office box. Your mailing address does not make much difference to people if your offer appeals to them!

6. **Keep track of your orders and responses.** You can expect anywhere from 0.5 percent to as high as 2 percent response to your postcards. This means you'll get from five to twenty orders per 1,000 postcards you mail. A lot depends on the mailing list you use.

What will your earnings be from your postcard mailing? Here are typical results for an information-product mailing:

Number of cards mailed = 1,000
Number of sales made = 20 (this is a 2 percent return)
Price of information product to customer = $30
Income from mailing = 20 × $30 = $600
Mailing cost = $250 (this is 25 cents per postcard)
Product cost in the mail = $7.50 each
Total costs = $250 + $150 = $400
Profit before overhead = $600 - $400 = $200

Your profit is $200 on $600 in sales, or $200 ÷ $600 = 0.33, or 33 percent. This is a high profit and is typical of well-conceived direct-mail programs run out of your home. Do twenty such mailings and your profit is $4,000; 100 mailings will give you $20,000 in your pocket! Not bad when you remember that your overhead for a home-based business is nearly zero!

How to Predict Your Sales Results

What results can you expect from other ways of marketing your information products? Here are useful numbers that will help you project your income and profit. *Note:* These numbers are based on my experience. Your results may be higher—or lower—depending on your offer and the buying public you contact:

Newspapers—sales can range from 0.1 to 0.5 percent of the paper's circulation for classified ads. Display ads can range from 0.5 to 1 percent of the paper's circulation, depending on the ad size (from quarter-page to full-page) and the type of information product or service you are selling. *Note:* With a circulation of 100,000 copies, 1 percent sales = 1,000 units; 0.1 percent = 100 units sold.

Magazines—sales can range from 0.2 to 0.8 percent of the magazine's circulation for classified ads. Display ads can range from 0.75 to 2 percent of the magazine's circulation, depending on the size of your ad. Some ads report having pulled as high as 8 percent of circulation, but this is a rare occurrence. In general, both classified and display ads pull better in niche magazines than in general newspapers.

Internet—sales depend on how you advertise on the Net. With your own Web site, your sales—in general—will be larger than when you're in an Internet mall—a Web site with several different advertisers. On the Net, advertisers talk about the number of sales per 1,000 page requests. A page request is an accessing of your page by a Net user. One sale per 1,000 page requests is currently thought to be good. If this sounds low, remember that you can have 20,000 page requests per twenty-four-hour day from all over the world. One computer maker is currently selling $1 million per day on the Net, and expects sales to grow to much more than this as time passes. So the future is bright for sales of information products and services on the Net.

TV—here you sell mostly via a toll-free telephone number, but include your address in your infomercial because some buyers dislike talking on the phone. Your sales can range from 0.1 percent of your viewers to as high as 1 percent. Much depends on the information you're selling, its appeal, the quality of your presentation, and how many other TV infomercials are selling similar materials. You will seldom start with TV infomercials; they come later in your sales cycle, after you've sold via mail order, direct mail, etc. Today's infomercials are usually on specialty cable channels. And with satellite TV dishes, the world is at your doorstep. Further, the Internet is now available via cable TV, at speeds 100 times that of an analog modem on a home computer. And with all the specialized cable channels, such as Wingspan (for airplane buffs), Animal Planet (for you know who—animal lovers), Food Network, Health Network, etc., you have a wide-open market for your information products and services of all types.

Radio—is similar to TV. For most radio commercials you'll use a toll-free number for ordering either the product or free information. Few people listening to the radio at home or in their car can get a pencil and paper quickly enough to jot down a street address. But most people can remember the last seven digits in a toll-free phone number. Radio responses will run 0.05 to 0.1 percent of your listening audience. As a test, use a thirty-second commercial. If it pays off, extend it to a sixty-second one.

Telemarketing—uses hired operators to sell your information products or services. Sales can range from 0.01 to 0.5 percent of people contacted. Your product or service should be priced at the higher level—$100 or more. Lower-priced products seldom generate sufficient sales to justify the telemarketing expense.

Books—can bring in significant sales for years because they stay around on people's shelves and in libraries. You can expect sales of 0.04 percent of your book's readers—both the initial buyers and later readers. Back-of-the-book ads are probably the lowest-cost marketing method you can use, other than word-of-mouth. Use them whenever you can—they really pay off for a long time.

Fliers—are strongest for local sales. Thus, you might sell data on local real estate sales, health foods, gardening, etc. Response rates can be 0.1 percent, but may reach 1 percent. The advantages of fliers are their quickness of delivery, their low cost, and their ability to pinpoint an area or group. Their disadvantage is the low response rate.

Direct mail—is the king of information sales because you can rent lists of almost any type of information buyer or seeker. Further, you can direct your mail advertising to exactly the person you want to sell to. With a good list you can expect to sell 1 to 2 percent of the recipients of your sales message. Direct mail works for products in all prices ranges—from the lowest to the highest. But we suggest that you avoid the lowest-priced products because it's difficult to earn a large income from them unless you do mailings in the millions. Instead, price your information products above $10 per unit. Products in the $100 price range can keep you in luxury cars, big yachts, and the best of homes in town!

Seven Steps to Information Sales Success

I want you to be a big sales success in your information business. Why do I say this? Because your success makes me happy. And your success makes the information field more lucrative for everyone in it. Since I'm in the same field, I'll ultimately earn more money if you do! So I'm gaining from your success—not losing! Here are seven steps for your sales success:

1. **Offer a unique, different product or service.** If you can develop, or find, the product or service on your own, do so. This will give it a uniqueness that others don't have. Your sales will be much easier, and stronger, when your product or service is somewhat different from what others offer. Remember: *Uniqueness sells!* So try to develop your own product or service.
2. **Make your offer to prospects—not suspects!** You can spend years trying to sell to suspects—people you think might want your product or service, with little result. Offer your same product or service to prospects and your sales can go through the roof! Why? *Because prospects want what you're offering. Suspects couldn't care less!* And who are prospects? They're people who've bought similar products or services in the past from other sellers, or yourself. So send direct mail to such people; air TV infomercials on cable stations viewed by prospects; run radio commercials to listeners who use your type of product or service. Follow this advice and your sales will boom!

3. **Provide a range of products or services to your prospects.** They want to see as many offers from you as possible. Why? Because they love what you're offering; they want to buy something from you because it proves to you their loyalty. And—of course—they get a product or service they want. Likewise, you're happy to sell them what they want. As we noted earlier—*the more you show, the more you sell!* While you may start with only one product or service, you should try to expand your line as quickly as possible. The more you show, the more you sell!

4. **Price your product or service at a level** that's similar to that of your competition. Don't think that under-pricing the competition will get you the business! Instead, it might just put you out of business! And doubling the price over your competitors because you think you can make a fast buck can have the same result. Instead, price at about the same level as your competition. People feel more comfortable—and are more likely to order—when your prices are in a generally accepted range. You don't have any competition? Price at a level of the nearest remotely similar products or services.

5. **Give personal service to your customers.** We all love attention from the people we do business with. I guarantee you that if you give personal attention to your customers, they'll give you more business! How can I say this? Because I give personal attention to all my customers and it has paid off again and again—for more than thirty years. By giving personal attention to your customers you beat your competition—again and again. There is no substitute for personal service. It works—every time! Think of your own buying habits. Don't you go back to the merchant who treats you with care and attention? We all do! So do the same in your own home-based business!

6. **Promote and advertise continuously.** Don't take time off to relax—instead run that ad, make that mailing, air that commercial! Get out there and promote seven days a week. *It will pay off for you—I guarantee it!* In our business, we even take phone calls on Sunday. And do you know what? We get lots of orders on Sunday. If we weren't open we might lose those orders forever. So—promote and advertise continuously. It will put money into your bank

account—sooner, and in greater amounts, than you ever thought possible!

7. **Cross-market every way you can.** When you *cross-market* you sell one product in another. Thus, when you use back-of-the-book ads, as discussed earlier in this chapter, to sell books other than the one in which the ad appears, you're cross-marketing. This form of selling can be the cheapest you'll ever do. And it can be the most effective. Why? Because your cross-marketing is going to prospects (see step 2, above)—not suspects. Cross-marketing can put you into the millionaire class sooner than you think!

Nine Information Businesses That Can Make You Rich

Now that I've told you how to make money selling information, I'd like to give you a number of these businesses that can make you rich—working out of your own home. Should you ever have any questions about any of these businesses, just give me a call. As a subscriber to my newsletter, I'll be glad to help you every step of the way. Full financial details are given for most of these businesses at the end of this chapter. Here are your great information home-based businesses you can start and succeed in on little cash.

PERIODICAL-TYPE INFORMATION

Newsletters on specialized topics can easily make you rich! You can publish your newsletter on a daily, weekly, semimonthly, monthly, quarterly, or annual basis. Experienced newsletter publishers suggest at least a quarterly basis. Any publishing schedule less frequent than this—say, semiannual or annual—doesn't keep your readers involved to the point where they want to renew on a regular basis. And it's in the renewals where you make your money. *Topics* for newsletters can range from acorn collecting to zebra cultivation. There's really no limitation on topics for newsletters—provided there's a large enough audience to support your costs and give you a profit. Popular (and profitable) topics include financial subjects (stocks, bonds, investing, etc.), small business (startups, finance, operations, etc.), sports of all types (insider information, predictions, discussions and interviews with star athletes, etc.), and government regulation (environmental, health, education, etc.). *Prices* of newsletters can range from a low of $12 per year for a quarterly to a high of $3,500 a year for a banker's newsletter. *Consumer newsletters* sold to the general public are usually priced lower than business newsletters. Thus, monthly consumer newsletters are often in the price range of $24 to $48 per year. *Monthly business newsletters* range in price from about $295 to $895 per year. But don't let this price difference mislead you. Consumer newsletters can have 10,000, 20,000, or 50,000 subscribers. Some higher-priced business newsletters have to grunt and groan to get 1,000 subscribers. *Your income* from newsletters in the information field can range from $50,000 to $1 million per year per newsletter.

Examples: *International Wealth Success, The Money Watch Bulletin, The Kiplinger Washington Letter*

REFERENCE INFORMATION

Nonfiction how-to books are always popular information products and have sold for more than 100 years. Such books have identifiable markets—such as airplane pilots, recreational boaters, plumbers, house electricians, accountants, lawyers, and so on. You can promote to them via direct mail—the longest-used method of bringing in money every day of the week. Today you can also use the Internet—either with your own Web site or on a mall. The critical point is that your prospects are identifiable and reachable! *Prices* for nonfiction how-to books can range from a low of $10 to a high of $150 for a single volume. Multiple-volume works will cost more—often in excess of $1,000 for a set. *Sources* of how-to books are the many publishers in the field. Look in the card catalog or electronic filing system under "Books in Print—Titles" and "Literary Marketplace" in any large public library for a list of available titles and their publishers. Contact the publisher for details of their discount schedule and payment terms. You will often be able to sell a book before you buy it. This means your cash outlay is zero! *Your income* from selling nonfiction how-to books by the various means listed earlier can range from \$5,000 to \$5 million a year, depending on the size of your selling activity and the types of books you sell. Beyond a sales level of \$1 million a year you'll probably have to move out of your home and into an office–warehouse facility. But I'm sure you won't object to this because your bank account will be nice and fat! Still, there is one publisher in the United States who refuses to move out of his home-based office even though his annual sales exceed \$300 million! I hope you beat his record for sales in your home-based business!

Examples: *101 Great Mail-Order Businesses, Success Secrets of the Motivational Superstars, 199 Great Home Businesses You Can Start (and Succeed in) for Under \$1,000*

SPOKEN-WORD REFERENCE INFORMATION

Tape-recorded books provide easy-to-listen-to information people can hear on their portable tape player or tape deck of their home or car radio. And these tapes can also provide best-seller novels and other works for easy listening while walking or driving. While videos may offer an easier learning experience, audiotapes are still highly popular because they are so lightweight and so easy to carry. Also, the audiotape was the first transportable electronic learning device and it has never lost its popularity. And, with the introduction of the portable tape player, the audiotape made a strong comeback. *Topics* for tape-recorded books can range from any how-to subject to novels, poetry, drama, business, etc. *Sources:* You can easily get the right to tape the books you want to sell by contacting the publisher of the book. Or you can buy already-recorded tapes from firms preparing them for sale to distributors like yourself or the general public. *Prices* for tapes sold to customers can range from about \$9 to as high as \$25, depending on the subject of the tape, and its availability. *Your income* from tape-recorded books can range from \$5,000 to \$100,000 a year, depending on how many tapes you sell each year.

Examples: *Foreclosures and Other Distressed Property Sales, How to Borrow Your Way to a Great Fortune, Million Dollar Marketing*

Take this real-life example, sent to me in a letter from a reader:

"I have been involved with mail order since I was seventeen years old. Over the last couple of years I have been selling two courses that I personally wrote and recorded onto cassettes. One is titled 'How to Make a Fortune Operating Your Own Mail-Order Dating Service'; the other is 'How to Make a Fortune with Your Radio Control Hobby.' Both courses have been selling well with very little advertising. The majority of sales are due to press releases and free ads. After realizing that my profits are greater on these courses than any other product I have ever sold, I decided to concentrate my efforts into this direction full time. I research, write, edit, record, and produce each course that is being sold through my catalog. I also design, write, and produce the newsletters that I sell. I average two to three days from start to finish on the production on a new course. My profit potential on each course I sell is great. Thus, the charge for shipping and handling pays for the cost of one catalog, the materials involved, packaging, and actual shipping expenses. If I sell a course for $20 and charge $4 for shipping and handling, the $20 covers advertising, minor overhead expenses, and mainly my marked-up profits."

Another BWB, who was a former worker in the construction industry, sold $1 million worth of tape-recorded information on equity sharing in real estate in just one weekend on national cable TV!

OUT-OF-PRINT INFORMATION

Out-of-print books are often sought by readers because the information in them is still useful to them. A good example of this is older engineering books sold to the developing nations. The technology in these out-of-print books often reflects what the country is working on now. So the books are valuable to people in such countries. *Topics* for out-of-print books can range from engineering to cooking to mime to acting, etc. These books provide their readers with useful information that hasn't changed much with the passage of time. *Prices* for out-of-print books can be much higher than recently published books because the out-of-print books are scarce. Typical prices can range from $25 to as high as $250 per book, depending on the scarcity of the title. *Your income* can range from $5,000 to $75,000 per year.

Examples: *General Engineering Handbook, The Loss of the S.S. Titanic, Recipes from the 1700s American Kitchen*

SHORT REPORTS ON IMPORTANT TOPICS

Reports are short discussions of important topics. A typical report can run from two to twenty—or more—pages, 8½ × 11 inches. Such reports are usually stapled—though the cover sheet may be on colored-stock paper. *Topics* for reports can range from a variety of business subjects to personal care of the body and its many parts—hair, teeth, eyes, etc. Most reports sold today, however, deal with business topics. Short reports—up to twenty pages or so—have the advantage of being mailable at first class rates at a nominal cost, giving speed of delivery, which almost everyone wants today. Further, such reports are easily printed on a photocopying machine—again at nominal cost. *Prices* for reports can range from $3 to as high as $50, depending on the topic. Business topics are priced higher than personal topics because business people usually are in greater need of the information. *Your income* selling reports can range from $3,000 to $60,000 a year, depending on the type of reports (business or personal) you're selling and the amount of marketing you do. **Examples:** *How to Make Big Money with Real Estate Options, 100 Recipes for Cajun Lunch and Dinner Dishes, Hiring Independent Contractors for Your Business*

DETAILED BUSINESS-STUDY REPORTS

Detailed study reports present an in-depth study of a particular business. Such reports can run from 100 to 300 pages in length, in the 8½ × 11-inch format, and often contain dozens of charts and tables of data related to the business. *Topics* range from agricultural businesses to zoological businesses. Each report is an in-depth study of the business it covers, giving full information on typical revenues, number of employees of various types, companies in the business, current problems faced by the business, future outlook for the business, etc. Thus, such reports are valuable to people in the business, people thinking of going into the business, and others who deal with the business as part of their activities. *Prices* for such reports can range from $850 to $6,000 each, depending on the business covered, the length of the report, the importance of the information, etc. Some information publishers dealing in such reports have several hundred on their list. Others have just one or two such reports that they sell. *Your income:* You can earn from $12,000 to $300,000 a year selling such reports, depending on the number of reports you market and their average prices. Getting such reports written takes dealing with authors who know the business inside and out.

Example: *Economics and Future of the Software Business, The Container Shipping Business, The Internet Marketing Business*

COMPUTER SOFTWARE

Computer software is one of the newest information businesses. It did not come into being until the popular adoption of the personal computer by people worldwide. Software is considered an information-type product because it shows people how to achieve certain desired results. *Topics* can range from simple business tasks such as budgeting, inventory control, and long-range planning to game and recreational software used by children or adults, or both. Popular topics are business, word-processing, planning, forecasting, etc. Likewise, games of all kinds sell well. However, their prices are usually less than that of business software. *Prices* can range from a low of $10 to a high of $3,000, or more, depending on the topic, the capacity (power) of the software, and how strongly it is needed in the field of its sales. *Your income* can range from $8,000 to $500,000 a year in the software business, depending on the type of software you sell, and its market.

Examples: *Bulk Mailer—Mail List Power!, Constructor (a real estate game), Pipe Stress Analysis*

CD-ROMs

CD-ROMs are among the newer information products for use on computers, although compact discs have been around for years in the music world. CD-ROMs have the advantage of high-density storage of information. A whole set of thick books can be stored on one small, thin CD-ROM. *Topics* on CD-ROM range from business information—such as the entire telephone book for all of the United States—to geographic data, maps, charts, photos, etc., plus games, instructions for boating, flying, chess, computers, and more. Zip code information for every address in the United States, plus bar-coding for reduced mailing charges are important business topics that help home-based businesses succeed. *Prices* for CD-ROMs can range from a low of $10 to as high as $895 for certain business information. Users of CD-ROMs often regard the prices as low—based on the enormous amount of information one CD contains. *Your income* can range from $6,000 to $250,000 per year selling information on CD-ROM by mail, on the Internet, and with magazine ads. But your income level will depend on the field you sell your CD-ROMs in—business gives the highest income; recreational provides the lowest income. **Examples:** *Zip Code List for the United States, National Telephone Directory, Boating Guide and Trainer*

VIDEOS FOR EDUCATION AND RECREATION

Videos are one of the most popular forms of information for education and recreation. Thus, the renting of movie videos is probably one of most common activities of American—and worldwide—families on a Saturday evening. Educational videos are also popular. *Topics* covered by educational videos range from instructions for using a powerboat or sailboat to fishing, electrical wiring, home building and repair, typing, computer usage, software applications, etc. Entertainment videos provide the latest movies, along with help in mastering popular games—checkers, chess, bridge, etc. *Prices* for videos range from a low of $4.95 to a high of $69.50, depending on the topic. Older videos can be bought at large discounts—see the *Directory of High Discount Merchandise Sources*, at the back of this book. *Your income* selling, or renting, videos can range from $4,000 to $300,000 per year, depending on the types of videos you handle. Some specialty video sellers use a catalog of their products and sell entirely by mail. Most such dealers only sell their videos; they do not rent them because the paperwork is too cumbersome. **Examples:** *Your Guide to SBA Loans and Programs, Ty Hicks Mailbox Millionaire Course, 38 Proven Ways to Close That Sale!*

To show you how the selling of information can change your life, take a look at this recent fax message from one of our Associate Publishers:

"The following person is ordering your video *Your Guide to SBA Loans and Programs.* Thanks again for offering this Associate Publisher Program. I am finally, after the longest time, actually making money in my own home-based business!"

Sell Information to Multiple Users

There are many places you can sell your information products to multiple users. These places include:

- **Libraries** of all types—public, private, university, school, etc.
- **Schools** of many types—public, private, vocational, colleges, universities
- **Bookstores**—small and large, chain and independent, college and university
- **Military posts**, ships, camps, forts, garrisons, air fields, etc.
- **Newsletters** which promote your items with reviews and comments on the contents

At my firm, IWS, Inc., we sell hundreds of books each year to city, state, school, and college libraries. Our books are in libraries in the largest cities in the United States—New York, Los Angeles, San Francisco, etc.—as well as in many overseas libraries. These institutions are great customers who buy again and again, year after year. And—as a final proof of why information publishing and sales is such a great business—I want to cite a few statistics from a recent survey by the Publishers Marketing Association. The survey showed:

- **The average annual revenue** of home-based book publishers in the year of this writing was $325,000.
- **Highest reported income** of a home-based book publisher exceeded $300 million per year.
- **Nonfiction titles** comprised 81 percent of the books published by the firms surveyed; self-help led the nonfiction field, with business next.

So you see—the information business really is a great one for home-based BWBs!

Summary of Home-Based Wealth Building Information Products

Here's information on ways for you to build great home-based wealth in your own information business. If you have any questions on these businesses in Table 9-1, give me a call.

Table 9-1. Information Businesses for BWBs

TYPE OF BUSINESS	WHAT YOU DO	HOW TO FIND CUSTOMERS	MONEY REQUIRED TO START	ANNUAL EARNINGS POTENTIAL	TIME TO START	EQUIPMENT NEEDED
Newsletter publishing and sales.	Publish helpful newsletter(s).	Direct mail, classified ads.	$600	$1 million	6 weeks	Desk, PC, fax, phone.
How-to nonfiction book sales.	Sell how-to books (and possibly write them too).	Direct mail, classified ads, space ads.	$500	$1 million	8 weeks	Desk, PC, fax, phone.
Sales of short reports on helpful topics.	Sell reports to people and companies.	Direct mail, classified ads, space ads.	$600	$60,000	4 weeks	Desk, PC, fax, phone.
Computer software.	Sell new and older software to computer users.	Direct mail, classified ads, space ads.	$800	$500,000	6 weeks	Desk, PC, fax, phone.
CD-ROM sales.	Sell CD-ROMs to people who seek specialized information or entertainment.	Direct mail, classified ads, space ads.	$700	$250,000	6 weeks	Desk, PC, fax, phone.
How-to videos.	Sell how-to videos to people and companies.	Direct mail, classified ads, space ads.	$600	$300,000	8 weeks	Desk, PC, fax, phone.
Tape-recorded information.	Sell audiotapes to people and companies.	Direct mail, classified ads, space ads.	$800	$100,000	6 weeks	Desk, PC, fax, phone.
Write success materials.	Help people succeed in life.	Direct mail, classified ads, space ads.	$500	$1 million+	12 weeks	Desk, PC, fax, phone.

CHAPTER 10

DO GOOD WORKS AND GET MONEY THAT NEVER NEED BE REPAID

By S. David Hicks

YOU CAN GET money for worthwhile purposes. And this money never need be repaid! You might call such money the ultimate purpose of a home-based business—that is, work that helps people in their everyday lives. What kind of money am I talking about?

I'm talking about *grants*. A grant is money given to you, or your business, to perform a particular activity. Grant-funded activities are projects or services that aid social, educational, religious, cultural, or other functions in a community or other area. The grant covers work for a given period of time—typically one or two years. Some grants are repeated—or "renewed"—year after year. Grants might be made to:

- **Run** a summer concert series or community art group.
- **Weatherproof** aging homes in a low-income community.
- **Run** recreational programs for local youths.
- **Analyze** traffic patterns on a given highway or freeway.

Grants Are Everywhere

Hundreds of thousands of grants go out to those who seek them (called *grant seekers* or *grantees*) each year. In the year of this writing, grants given out in the United States alone included:

- **$6 billion in grants** given by medium- and large-size corporations to groups doing useful work.
- **$10 billion in grants** given by private foundations.
- **More than $200 million in government grants** for arts and cultural projects of many kinds.
- **More than $10 billion in environmental grants** by the U.S. government. (There are more than twenty categories in which the government gives grants!)

Can grant seeking be a home-based business? You bet it can! Many thousands of men and women get grants successfully from home. As a grant seeker, you can work at home, if you wish. Or you can get involved in outside meetings and project activities, if you prefer.

What will you do as a grant seeker? If you like the idea of being a leader, or if you already have your own company or organization, you might wish to *direct* the grant getting for your company or organization. In a small organization of one to ten people, this might mean that you find out what grants are available, write letters or make calls to foundations, and help prepare short proposals.

In a larger company or organization of 10 to 100 people, your role might be more like that of a "traffic cop," where you simply "direct traffic," making sure that people are assigned to look for grants, to contact the grantors, and so on. Still another possible role is to work as a consultant from home, providing grant-seeking services to various companies or organizations for a fee.

Whichever role you choose, you are an important person in charge of helping people. Grant makers (called *grantors*) are among the wealthiest organizations on earth and they are willing to pay you (the grantee) handsomely for this. Shouldn't you get some of the grant money, if you wish to? Let's see how you might do so—starting right now.

Who Makes Grants?

Grants are made by many different organizations and agencies. Here's a list of the most frequent kinds of grantors:

- U.S. government, through its various agencies and departments
- State governments
- City and county governments
- Corporations of medium and large size
- Foundations of many types, including corporate foundations
- Public charities, such as the Red Cross or American Heart Association

Who Gets Grants?

A wide variety of individuals and organizations get grants. Grantees include:

- Nonprofit organizations
- Schools
- State and local agencies
- Churches
- Businesses

Types of Grantors and How They Differ

To win grants effectively in your home-based business, you should know what kinds of grants are given by the main grant makers. This will make your life easier when "shopping" for grants. Keep the following in mind:

1. **Grants to individuals** are given mostly for academic purposes (such as scholarships) or for scientific research projects. So if you want to get a grant for yourself as an individual, you will apply for those types of grants. The majority of the grants made today are given to companies or organizations. So we will focus on how you, as the head of your own home-based company or organization, can win grants.

2. **Grants to businesses** come from certain grantors. *Commercial* or *for-profit businesses* can get certain grants. But the conditions under which they may do so are highly specific. The number of grants given to *nonprofit* organizations is much higher. Grants to businesses come almost entirely from government agencies, such as the U.S. Small Business Administration (SBA) or from your state's Community Development Office. These agencies are charged with helping businesses start up and become profitable.

3. **Foundations** and corporate grantors generally cannot give grants to a business. By law, foundations and corporate grantors are not allowed to make grants to for-profit businesses. Why? Because these grantors get special tax exemptions from the government in return for doing what they do best—giving "free money" to nonprofit organizations. This arrangement helps to ensure that needed work for the public good gets done, even if the government can't afford to do the work and businesses have no interest in it. Thus, a foundation might fund a program to restore a decaying historic building, provide special job training for disadvantaged youth, or even to sponsor free lunchtime jazz concerts at a busy downtown mall. Wealthy foundations (there are more than 45,000 in the United States alone) appreciate having their tax-exempt status and are eager to give grants to nonprofit organizations that can do the needed work. By law, each foundation is required to give out a certain dollar amount in grants every year.

4. **Corporate grantors** and foundations give grants to nonprofit organizations. Since foundations and corporate foundations are *nonprofit, tax-exempt* organizations themselves, they give grants almost exclusively to other nonprofit organizations.

Now let's summarize what you just learned about various grant-making organizations and how you can work with them to get free money:

- **If you want to get a grant** for a profit-making business or to help an existing profit-making business, apply to the federal or state government.
- **Form a nonprofit home-based organization** to get grants from foundations. Remember—nonprofit organizations and their

people (you) often enjoy a very pleasant (and lucrative) life doing good works for other people from their home base.

In this chapter we give you the basic steps in preparing a winning grant proposal. These steps are much the same for each type of grantor. So you can use these secrets for almost any proposal, whether it's going to a government agency or to a foundation.

Also, we tell you where to find government and other kinds of grants. But we focus the discussion on grants from foundations and corporations, since that is where you will most likely find the grant you need. If you have not already formed a home-based nonprofit organization, don't worry. We give you steps for forming a nonprofit organization later in this chapter.

For What Purposes Are Grants Made?

As you'll recall, the ultimate purpose of grants is to help the health, education, culture, history, and community well-being in national, regional, and local areas. If you can perform one of these tasks, you and your home-based organization have a good chance of getting a grant. The most common purposes of grants are for:

- **Improvement of education** at a university, college, or in a school system.
- **Delivery of human services,** such as senior citizens' care, child care, etc.
- **Betterment of health** of the general public.
- **Arts and humanities** advancement, including courses, concerts, and exhibits.
- **Improvement of the environment** and animal welfare.
- **Scientific and technological** research.
- **International affairs.**
- **Social science** research.
- **Religion.**

Then there are *favorites* (often called *priorities*) in the area of grants. Such favorites are grants made by foundations set up for highly specialized purposes. Examples might be grants for projects designed to:

- **Study the feeding habits** of polar bears.
- **Analyze workloads** in the garment industry.
- **Improve cockpit crew** coordination in commercial aircraft.

Why might favorites be important to you? Because one of the favorites might tie in exactly with the type of work you and your home-based firm are capable of doing. You might be the only person in your state—or in the entire country— who can do the work for a favored or high-priority grant subject! Whenever you look for funders, a key to winning grants will be to try to learn the grantors' priorities.

For you and your home-based organization, grants have a more immediate purpose. Grants are made to your organization to:

- **Reimburse you** and your firm for work done, or to be done in the future.
- **Cover expenses** such as salary costs, rent, light, heat, and other utilities.
- **Pay for supplies**, travel, research, and the like.

Any grant money you receive is to pay for estimated expenses you'll have in your home-based business accomplishing the purpose of the grant. Grants are *not* made to earn a profit for you or your organization. However, it is generally acceptable today for a nonprofit organization to make a profit, as long as any profit is put back into improving the organization. But don't turn away from grants thinking they're a waste of time. Many successful grantees are just as successful as their friends in commercial business. Grants can get you many beneficial results in your home-based business.

What Types of Grants Should You Seek?

When talking about types of grants, people sometimes mean the type of grantor that gives the grant: There are *government* grants, *foundation* grants, and *corporate* grants. When writing your proposal or making plans for a grant, it is wise to be specific, describing the type of grant in terms of *how the grant will be used*. In this way, we have *emergency* grants to cover emergency situations, *conference* grants to fund conferences, *department* grants for university or hospital departments, *project* grants for projects, *research* grants for research, *general support* grants, and so on. You don't need to remember these, but you should know the *subject* of your grant (say, *polar bear habitats*), and the type of grant (say, *research*) so you can describe the grant you seek for your home-based business in one or two sentences.

You certainly should not apply for every grant in sight just because it offers a chance for "free" money. Nor should you pin all your hopes on one grantor, even when that grantor seems likely to approve your grant request. Grant experts agree that a few well-thought-out grant proposals, sent to carefully picked grantors, serve you much better than a flood of blind requests.

In deciding what types of grants to seek, take the following steps:

1. **Analyze** your interests and the capabilities of your home based-organization.
2. **Decide** what types of projects would be best handled by your firm. (I'll call this your subject area to make it easy to refer to.)
3. **Assemble** information on your capabilities—such as your education and experience. (The saying "Know thyself" is wise advice here.)
4. **Get** to know the "who, what, where, why, and when" of grants being offered in the subject area you've identified (see the "Five W's of Grant Getting" below).
5. **Look** for grantors that provide the kinds of grants you're interested in. For the best results, don't stop there.

6. **Seek** the "best matches" between the grantors and their grant requirements and your home-based organization and its skills. As a guide, use the Five W's below to see how well your organization matches up with each grantor.
7. **Develop** a plan for getting the grant(s) you seek by tailoring your proposals to your list of best matches and by making certain you can do outstanding work based on each grantor's priorities.

The Five W's of Grant Getting

You probably remember the five W's. Most of us learned the importance of these five words in school: **WHO, WHAT, WHERE, WHY,** and **WHEN.** No news story can exist without them, and no good grant proposal can either. To succeed at grants in a home-based business, know the following:

- **WHO** you'll have working on your project and **WHO** you'll be submitting your proposal to.
- **WHAT** each grantor wants to have done on a project and **WHAT** your home-based organization can offer that sets you apart from others.
- **WHERE** each grantor gives grants (city, state, or region) and **WHERE** you can reasonably perform grant work.
- **WHY** you and your home-based organization are the best choice for the grant and **WHY** the grantor will be interested in you.
- **WHEN** proposals must be submitted by (deadline) and **WHEN** the grantor wants the project work to begin.

Knowing these five W's can go a long way to helping you win grants. Let's look at an example of how this information might help you get a grant.

Choosing the "Right" Grantors

Let's say you and your home-based organization specialize in landscaping, tree-planting, and the growing of ornamental plants to beautify your community. As a plant expert, you have long been interested in *bonsai* plants—those miniature trees from Japan—as a hobby. One day it occurs to you that it would be great if you could find a way to combine your interest in bonsai trees with a grant on that same subject. Bonsai has been a popular fad in the area of the country where you live—Florida—for quite a while.

So you decide to seek a grant for setting up and running a home-based evening educational program teaching adults how to grow bonsai trees. You don't have to be the one who teaches the classes—one of your part-time staff can do that—but you want to see if you can get such a grant.

You learn from a book at the local library that only two organizations in the country, the ABC Foundation in Atlanta and the XYZ Trust in San Francisco, give grants for plant-growing classes (actually, there are many foundations that give such grants, but for this example we assume there are only two). Knowing this, would you spend time calling or mailing to any organizations other than these two? No, that would be a waste of your time. By narrowing down your "target" grantors quickly, you've saved yourself a lot of work. Thus, you've identified ABC Foundation and XYZ Trust as the organizations you'll send your grant proposal to.

Once you have the names of these two foundations, you try to learn more. You want to get information on where they've given grants in the past and whether they have any special requirements for grant seekers. A telephone call to the grantors gives you the information you need, but unfortunately it cancels out one of the two grantors as a possible funder. A representative for the XYZ Trust in San Francisco tells you that XYZ Trust was set up to give grants only on the West Coast.

Since you live in Florida, you now know that it's not worth your time to send a proposal to XYZ Trust. Instead, in a call to ABC Foundation, you confirm that ABC does give grants in your area.

In addition, the representative at ABC Foundation gives you three important pieces of new information:

1. **ABC Foundation** wants proposals to be "no more than three pages in length."
2. **The next due date** for proposals is March 31.
3. **The successful grant** applicant will provide a Spanish-language speaker so that Spanish-speaking residents may benefit fully from these classes.

This gives you and your home-based organization plenty of time to put together a three-page proposal and even to recruit—on a preliminary basis—a Spanish-language speaker for the project. By adding these details to your proposal, you show the grantor that your home-based business will do exactly the kind of job the grantor wants, and you win the grant. As a rough estimate, such a project might get you a grant of $100,000 to $200,000 for a twelve-month period.

The "Business" of Grants

To do your best home-based work on a grant assignment, you or your staff should have solid experience in the field in which you'll work. Some education in the field will also lend greater credibility to your application and efforts.

Are personal contacts important in getting grants? The grants field is often said to be a "people business" in that a good deal of communication may occur between the foundation and grantee prior to a grant being awarded. So if you know someone who is familiar with a grantor, that contact might help speed your proposal to the grantor. But this does not mean you are at a disadvantage if you don't have such connections. Most grantees are in the same situation. So don't let this be a big concern.

Whatever you do, don't try to "wing it" when applying for grant money. Instead, look around until you find a grantor making grants for the type of home-based work you like and do well. Why? One grant that's successfully accomplished can lead to others with much less work in the application process. And even if you are turned down for a grant, many grantors will be happy to show you how to improve your proposal to make it a winner next time. (Remember, many grant projects are repeated yearly, giving you multiple chances to get the grant you seek.)

So go for what you (or your staff) know. Do the best job you can; finish it on schedule and on budget. Grant seeking is a task that must be approached with a complete "business" attitude. Any other view of grants wastes your time!

Where Do You Find Grantors?

Grants are easy to find. Just do some research at your local library and you'll come up with hundreds (or even thousands) of names and addresses of grantors. Look at these sources:

- **Directories of foundations**—there are many available that list foundations throughout the country.
- **Corporate directories** and corporate giving directories list corporations that make grants for various purposes.
- **Federal government data** lists thousands of grants that are available.
- **State, city, and county directories** list regional grants you can get.
- **The yellow pages** of your local large-city telephone book lists grantors under "Foundations."
- **There are also magazines**, newspapers, and newsletters published for grant seekers and grantors. For government grants, look for *Commerce Business Daily* or *The Federal Register*, for nonprofit grants, try *The Chronicle of Philanthropy*, *The Nonprofit Times*, or *Foundation News*.
- **The World Wide Web** has lots of free information for grant seekers. Just do a search for *foundations*, *grants*, and your subject area to find lots of useful data.
- **A lot of good, detailed information** can be obtained directly from each grantor once you decide which ones seem interesting. Materials you can (and should) request by phone or mail are: *application form and submission guidelines, sample grants list*, and *funding priorities*. Also, foundations are required by law to show their annual reports (called Form 990-PF) to

anyone who requests them. So you can feel free to ask for this document.

• **Grantors** may seek you out as a potential grantee once your group becomes known for its work in the field.

To become known in the field of your skill(s) use the IWS *Raising Money from Grants and Other Sources Kit* (K-8) and the *Phone-In/Mail-In Grants Kit* (K-18), listed at the back of this book. The first kit, K-8, gets you started in this great field. The second kit, K-18, focuses on the short proposals that today's grantors prefer.

Like any other search effort, you must use your head and your ingenuity when looking for grantors. Sometimes there is competition for a grant, but sometimes you may find you're the only applicant a grantor has been approached by in years.

Why? Either your home-based team (which may be only you) is the only one capable of doing the grant work, or other people have not done their "homework" in looking for a grant. If you do your homework and use the five W's above you'll be surprised at the amount of grant money you can tap into for your home-based business!

How to Apply for a Grant

There is a simple process that is commonly used in applying for most grants. Follow these steps and don't try to take short-cuts. Using these simple steps, a two-page, single-spaced letter may get you several hundred thousand dollars in grants! So why try to take shortcuts when the effort required is so small and the possible rewards are so big?

Some grantors have specific guidelines (the *application guidelines* mentioned above) and an application form that they ask you to fill out. Be certain to read these guidelines and be sure to fill out the form. (A sample grant application form is shown in Figure 10-1.) Have the foundation mail the guidelines to you or even read them to you over the phone, if necessary. If you're pressed for time, you might find that a friend or colleague at another nonprofit organization has a copy he or she can fax to you.

Oftentimes the grantor's written guidelines will be much the same as the steps we give you here. But there may be times when the grantor's guidelines include very specific requirements that you must follow if you want to get the grant. Always follow the grantor's guidelines, unless you are prepared to explain why you haven't done so. The home-based grant seeker who's done his or her homework is the one who usually wins. If you can't, or don't, follow the grantor's guidelines, you haven't done your homework.

The basic steps that are winners for home-based people seeking grants of all kinds are:

1. **Identify** the grant program and type of grants you have in mind.
2. **Organize** yourself and get any official approvals needed.
3. **Research** potential grantors thoroughly.
4. **Contact** potential grantors—ask for their grant guidelines.
5. **Prepare** your grant proposal. Be clear, be concise, and be accurate.
6. **Submit** your proposal to the grantors you've chosen as prospects.
7. **Follow up** with grantors approximately six weeks after submitting your proposal.

Don't let these steps frighten you; they are simple. Some people can prepare a grant proposal in just a few hours. The hourly pay for home-based people who write proposals for a fee can be enormous, especially when you're aiming at big bucks!

Let's take a look at each of these steps and see how it's done. You'll see that getting grants is much easier than you might think.

Identify the Grant Program and Grant Type

As we said earlier, you must know something about the field in which you're applying for grants. For example, let's say

GRANT APPLICATION FORM

ORGANIZATION INFORMATION
Date of Application: _____
Legal Name of Organization: _____
Address: _____
City, State, Zip: _____
Telephone: _____ Fax: _____
Individuals Responsible: _____
Name of top paid staff: _____
Title: _____
Direct-dial Phone #: _____
Contact person: _____
Title: _____
Direct-dial Phone #: _____
Organization Description (2–3 sentences): _____
_____
_____

Is your organization an IRS 501(c)(3) not-for-profit? ❏ Yes ❏ No
If no, is your organization a public agency/unit of government or religious
institution? ❏ Yes ❏ No
If no, name of fiscal agent (fiscal sponsor): _____

AMOUNT AND TYPE OF SUPPORT REQUESTED: $ _____
Check type of support requested:
❏ general ❏ operating support ❏ capital ❏ project support ❏ endowment
❏ start-up costs ❏ technical assistance ❏ other _____

If a project, give project duration:_____Month____Year to _____Month____Year
If operating support, fiscal year:_____Month____Year to _____Month____Year

BUDGET
Total annual organization budget: $ _____
Total project budget (for support other than general operating): $ _____

PROPOSAL SUMMARY
(If operating or startup support, relate to the organization. If project and other
support, relate to the project.)
Project name (if applying for project support): _____
Please give a 2 to 3 sentence summary of the request: _____
_____
_____

Geographic area served: _____
Population served: _____

AUTHORIZATION
Name of top paid staff and/or Board Chair (type): _____
Signature: _____

Figure 10-1. Sample grant application form.

you're applying for a grant to teach local high school students how to help fix up and weatherproof decaying houses in low-income areas in their city. To get a grant for this purpose, you must:

- **Know something about home repairs** and weatherproofing.
- **Know local housing conditions** in your area.
- **Know the basics of teaching people** the elements of home repair and weatherproofing.

Of course, you can have a staff of home-repair teachers who will do the teaching for you. But to prepare the proposal you do need to know something about home repair. You probably wouldn't even pick such a topic for your grant if you didn't know anything about the housing situation in your area.

You can, if you wish, hire people and then "wrap a grant proposal around them." Thus, if you know a little about home repair and weatherproofing and you learn that grants are being offered for repairing and weatherproofing homes in your own, or in a nearby city, you can hire capable builders and get them to help you prepare your proposal. The only drawback is that your home-based staff may leave you after the grant work is done because they see how easy it is to get a grant with the right staff!

If you're an expert in some area of information, you can almost certainly get a home-based grant on your own: All you need do is find a grantor that wants your type of expertise to fund a study or activity. Write your proposal (or have someone write it for you) and send it to the grantors you've picked. A good proposal is almost certain to get the funds you seek.

Lastly, recall the examples we gave earlier to show how you can set your sights on the right grantors: If you seek grants for a home-based commercial business, you automatically rule out foundation grants as something you'll be seeking, because foundations give only to nonprofit organizations.

If, on the other hand, you want to study polar bears, you should look for foundations that fund polar-bear studies. (You can also check to see if the federal government has any grant programs for polar-bear studies.)

It is also necessary to know the dollar amount and length of the home-based grant you seek. Thus, if you want a $300,000, three-year grant, rather than a $20,000, six-month grant, you should look for grantors that give (or that have given in the past) $300,000, three-year grants, or some similar grants. To summarize:

- **Know the field** in which you want to work.
- **Get to know the grantors** in this field.
- **Tailor your proposal** to your grantors.
- **Keep applying** until you get your grant.

Organize Your Effort

If you plan to get grants amounting to more than $25,000 per year from foundations, you *must* be a tax-exempt, non-profit organization. You can easily get nonprofit status by filling out a few forms available from your state government and from the Internal Revenue Service (IRS). You only have to do this once.

Start by filing for tax-exempt status with your state or the IRS. (Both are required and the application forms are free. It does not make a big difference which filing you do first.) Call your state Charitable Registration Office (names of the office vary among states) and request copies of forms for applying for nonprofit, tax-exempt status. Figure 10-2 shows an example of a state nonprofit registration form. The kind of organization you will be applying to form is sometimes called a *public charity* or "501(c)(3) organization" because of the laws that govern it.

Along with the form, state governments and the IRS require that you send several additional items. These include articles of incorporation and copies of annual reports (or, if your organization is brand new, a budget and balance-sheet statements). Most states charge a small fee for processing your application.

Next, call your local IRS office and request a copy of the free instruction booklet, Publication 557, *Tax-exempt Status*

REGISTRATION STATEMENT FOR CHARITABLE ORGANIZATIONS

Office of the Secretary of State, State House
Telephone: (555) 555-1212; e-mail: state@xxx.tax

Fee Submitted: _____
Month Fiscal Year Ends: _____
County: _____
Name: _____
If name under which solicitation is made is different from above, indicate here:
_____

Mailing Address of Charity: _____
Address of Physical Location: _____
Telephone: _____ Fax: _____
Federal ID No.: _____
Names and addresses of any chapters, branches, or affiliates in state: _____
_____
_____

Names and addresses of officers, including principal salaried executive officers:
_____
_____

Names and addresses of persons who have final responsibility for the custody and
final distribution of the contributions: _____
_____
_____

Purpose or purposes for which contributions are to be used: _____
_____
_____

Does your organization engage or have a contract with a professional solicitor or
counsel? ❑ Yes ❑ No
Professional solicitor: _____
If YES, attach a copy of the contract(s) and give name and address of firm(s).

Does applicant or any officer, director, partner, or employee of applicant, or any
person holding any financial interest in the applicant, have any interest in any
mail house, cashiering, professional solicitor, fund-raising counsel, or other business with which applicant does business pursuant to or in conjunction with a
contract between the applicant and a professional solicitor, fund-raising counsel,
or solicitor? ❑ Yes ❑ No
If YES, provide details. _____

Is any officer, director, partner, or employee of the applicant, or any person holding
any financial interest in the applicant, also an officer, director, partner, or employee
of a professional solicitor, fund-raising counsel, or solicitor with which the applicant
does business? ❑ Yes ❑ No
If YES, provide details. _____

I solemnly affirm under the penalties of perjury and upon personal knowledge that
the contents of the foregoing COR-342 and each supporting document are true.

_____
Signature of the President, Chairman or Principal Officer

Figure 10-2. Example of a state form for requesting
nonprofit organization status.

for Your Organization, and a free copy of Form 1023, *Application for Recognition of Exemption.* You must pay a nominal fee when you file your application, based on the amount of grant money your organization earns, or plans to earn.

Answer all the questions and send in the forms. After about six weeks you should have your response. If your request is approved you'll be given a tax-exempt number. Use this on all your proposals and correspondence with foundations.

It's hard to get grants from foundations if you don't have your tax-exempt status. Don't let this requirement "throw you." It's easy to satisfy. And you can, of course, go on applying for grants from corporations, governments, and other grantors where home-based tax-exempt status is *not* required. You do *not* need to be a 501(c)(3) organization to get grants from such grantors for your home-based business.

Research Potential Grantors

Research is the "homework" part of grant seeking that we've been emphasizing. Let's go look at the research steps.

1. **Make a list of grantors** that seem most likely to support your organization or your program.
2. **Choose potential grantors** by reviewing their descriptions and recent grant histories in the sources listed earlier. Grantors that are good prospects are:

    • **Grantors** that gave grants similar to yours in the last few years.
    • **Grantors** that have given grants for the type of support you seek.
    • **Grantors** located in your city, state, or region.

3. **Once you have a good list** of potential grantors, the next step is to research carefully the grantors you've listed. Here the directories and databases available through your library, and listed above, will be very valuable. But at this point you might want to look into the kinds of information you can get straight from the grantors: sample grants

lists, application guidelines, and so on. Remember, research is work; it takes time, but it always pays off.
4. **Before you contact a grantor,** make sure you'll use the
right approach. Many foundations prefer a phone call or
a short letter as the first step. Others want a full proposal.
You can often find this information in a foundation directory or in the grantor's publications. But there's
nothing wrong with making a quick phone call to a
grantor, as we'll see.

Contact Potential Grantors

In the *Phone-In/Mail-In Grants Kit* (K-18) listed at the back
of this book, I recommend that you approach your potential grantors by:

- **Phoning** to find if the grant you seek is of interest to the
grantors.
- **Writing** the grantor, asking the same questions.
- **Saving time** for yourself and the grantor because you won't
send unwanted proposals.

By using the phone-in/mail-in technique, you can find
dozens of interested grantors in a day or so. Once you've
found them, you can concentrate on getting the grant money
you seek from one or more of these grantors.

So don't waste anyone's time. Go right to the target! Find
out if the work you're proposing to do under a grant is really
wanted by any grantors. There's no sense trying to make a
grantor want to do the work that interests *you*. It is better to
do the work the *grantor* is interested in doing! That's where
the money is and where it will continue to be.

Prepare Your Grant Proposal

Many BWBs seeking grants think that a proposal must be 6
inches thick to win a grant. Not so! When questioned, most
people in charge of approving grants say:

- **The shorter** the proposal, the faster its approval.
- **Short proposals** are read first, long proposals last.
- **A two-page** proposal letter is enough to get a tentative "yes" answer.
- **Grantees** who save grantors' time are always popular and they're remembered!
- **Long proposals** don't convince as strongly as short proposals do.

So recognize, here and now, that conciseness pays off! Make your proposal short, and you may win those big-buck grants sooner. Since you can get a quick answer on the possibility of getting a specific grant that interests you with just one phone call or a short letter:

- **Prepare your proposal** in summary form to start.
- **Use this summary** as your letter or phone script.
- **Get a quick answer** first from the grantor.
- **Then expand your proposal** to include more data.

To show what I mean, let's say you've decided to apply for a grant as detailed earlier to teach high school students home repair and weatherproofing for aging houses in low-income areas in your city. Your summary proposal might read like this:

We seek a $150,000 grant to teach 1,500 local high school students the basics of home repair and weatherproofing in the Central City area of the state. Included will be tours of declining areas, visits to local homes needing repairs, and lectures on the basics of home rehabilitation.

Once you get a grantor interested in making this grant, you can fill in the other topics of your proposal, namely:

- **The need**—why the grant work is needed.
- **What will be done**—a description of the work you'll do.
- **Who will do the work**—information on your home-based staff.
- **How results will be measured**—tests or other measures you'll use.
- **How much money is needed** and how it will be used.

- **The future**—what other grants might be used to continue this work.

You have your targeted grantors, and you now have a brief outline of your proposal. Your next step is to call or write all target grantors, asking if they're interested. If you call targeted grantors, you'll get faster answers. Don't be afraid to call! Grantors *need* your business to stay in business. If you call, use a working script like the following:

> Good morning (or afternoon). We're seeking a $150,000 grant to teach home repair and weatherproofing to local high school students in the state, especially those in the Central City area. The grant will be for one year. Would you (or your organization) be interested in making such a grant?

You'll get an immediate "yes" or "no" answer. If the answer is "yes," say, "Would a two-page proposal be enough for you to make your decision?" The answer to this question will probably be "yes." If it is, say, "Thanks. We'll get the proposal to you within the next three days. To whom should I address it?" Make notes of everything you're told, including the name of the person to whom you're told to send your proposal.

When you first ask your question about the grant and the answer is "no," ask, "Do you have any information on the foundation's priorities or recent grants that you could send me?" Note the answer! Why? You may be able to qualify for one of the grants the organization *is* making. So your phone call won't be wasted. If you'd rather write to grantors to learn if they'd be interested in your grant request, use a short letter like that shown in Figure 10-3. Call in advance to get the name of the person to whom you should address your letter.

Finish Your Proposal Sections

Your proposal will have six brief sections following the initial statement covering the grant amount and time period,

YOUR LETTERHEAD

Date
Contact Name
Grantor Organization Name
Address
City, State, Zip

Dear Contact Name:

We are seeking a $150,000 grant to teach home repair and weatherproofing to local high school students in the state of _____, especially those in the low-income areas of Central City. The grant will be for one year.

Your organization has been chosen as a possible grantor.

Those who would benefit from this grant include the high school students, their teachers, owners of homes in low-income areas, members of local government, and state building societies.

We look forward to your response concerning your interest in this grant request. A full proposal is available if the grant request interests you.

Very truly yours,

Your name
Your title

Figure 10-3. Sample grant request letter.

along with the purpose of the grant. This information is in the first paragraph of the letter in Figure 10-3. This will be followed by the six sections:

- **The Need:** High school students in the Central City area are not familiar with the repairs needed by decaying homes in their area. Ignorance of the important needs of homeowners in low-income sections in the area leaves these students at a disadvantage in their lives. Further, the area suffers because its residents are not as well-housed as they should be.
- **What Will Be Done:** This grant will furnish funds to teach these students how to perform home repairs and weatherproofing to upgrade low-income residences in the Central City area. The students will be taught how to do carpentry, electrical, weatherproofing, roofing, and plumbing work. The grant will provide teaching facilities for 1,500 local students. Programs funded by this grant will supplement the students' regular science courses, which do not give enough attention to practical skills.
- **Who Will Do the Work:** A staff of four competent home mechanics will conduct the studies on a part-time basis, including the instructions and lectures onsite. This staff will give the students hands-on training in the skills they need to develop to become competent mechanics.
- **Measuring Results:** Students will be tested at two-week intervals to determine their comprehension and understanding of the topics presented. The grantor will be sent the results of these tests at two-week intervals. A final examination will rate each student on his or her understanding of the work of home repair.
- **Money Needed:** A total of $150,000 is needed for one year to cover salaries, office expenses, travel, group transportation, and miscellaneous costs. Detailed breakdowns of each expense category are available and will be sent to the grantor on request.
- **The Future:** If this program is successful, as the grantee expects it will be, future high school classes can be taught in the same way. Further, other areas of the state can be served with similar programs.

That's it. The above simple proposal could get you $150,000 for one year to do the work described. And if the grantor likes the work you do, you may get many other grants from the same organization!

Submit Your Proposal

Be sure to send your proposal to the person whose name you were given as the contact at the foundation. You don't want your proposal to be delayed. And check your package carefully to make sure you include any items the grantor may have requested.

Follow Up

Most grant seekers consider it acceptable to call or write a grantor about six weeks after submitting a proposal, if they haven't already heard from the foundation. The follow-up should be brief and should simply state your firm's continuing interest in the grant. If you get a positive response on the grant award, you'll be ready to start the grant work. If you're turned down, this will be a good opportunity to get free advice on what you can do to make your proposal a winner in the future.

Take the Grants Road to Success

Many people have no idea that a big, rich, and exciting world exists all around them in grants. And grants help people. You can help people by getting grants for home-based work that's important in your area or in the nation. You'll be joining a great group of people who "do well by doing good." But what's more important, you will benefit in many ways by getting and working on grants in your home-based business. These ways include the following:

- **You'll learn how** to manage people.
- **You will become** a known figure in your bank because you'll deposit grant funds and write checks.
- **People will look** up to you when they learn that you're doing important work for humanity and for your community.
- **You'll meet** important people in the area—people who may later help you in profit-making work.
- **You will become** an expert in putting together business proposals and plans, all of which can benefit you enormously in your own home-based business.
- **You'll have** operating funds in the meanwhile for your grants work—perhaps more than you've ever seen in one check at one time.

So if you can do something for people or for an area, or if you can get people who can do this, consider grants. They could be your first step to great riches—your route from being laid off or downsized to great wealth in your own home-based business.

CHAPTER 11

HOW, AND WHERE, TO GET MONEY FOR YOUR BUSINESS

No MATTER WHAT kind of a home-based business you start, you'll need money to pay for your initial expenses. Some BWBs have more trouble finding the money for their new business than from any other challenge they meet. Yet if you approach the money-raising chore sensibly, you should be able to get all the money you need. Let's see how *you* can get the money you need—quickly and easily.

Seventeen Sources of Money for Your Home-Based Business

Here are tried—and proven—sources of money for every home-based business. Look these over and see which ones you might use in your new business:

1. **Credit card line of credit**—can range from a low of $100 to a high of $100,000 for yourself or for your business, depending on whose name the card is in.
2. **Unsecured line of credit** from your commercial (business) bank extended to your business for keeping your checking and savings account with the bank.
3. **Personal line of credit** with a bank, credit union, savings and loan association, or other lender; you use some of the funds for the business.

4. **SBA-guaranteed loan** from your own commercial bank or from one of the Small Business Administration's preferred lender banks in your area or a distant location.
5. **Loan from a local development company** or agency specializing in loans to small businesses, women, minorities, startups, etc., in your city, county, or state. Such loans can range up to $100,000.
6. **Micro-loan from lenders** specializing in such small loans, which typically go up to $25,000. A one- or two-page simple application is an important part of these small loans, allowing them to be made quickly.
7. **Loan from a relative, friend, or business associate** made on the basis of full repayment, with interest, on a stated time schedule.
8. **Inventory, startup, or other type of loan** made by a lender known to your supplier or customer.
9. **Accounts receivable financing** on work you've already completed for a known organization—such as a large company, a hospital, university, city, state, etc.
10. **Home equity loan** on your, or a relative's, home, which you use to finance your business needs.
11. **Private-lender loan** from an individual or organization that specializes in funding new and small businesses showing promise of generating strong profits.
12. **Venture-capital money** from government or private venture-capital funders targeting small businesses. There are many such funders operating today. But you must search them out locally because they often do not seek wide publicity for themselves.
13. **Grants** from foundations, corporations, or governments can provide much-needed funding for startup home-based businesses; see Chapter 10 of this book for full details on getting grants for your home business.
14. **Export-business loans** are available from both state and federal government sources. To learn which agencies in your state make such loans, check your local phone books. Federal government loans for exporters can be checked at (800) USA-TRADE (800-872-8723).
15. **Small business development center** (SBDC) loans are available in almost every state. See your state phone book listing for the phone number. Or call me—your author—

and I'll give you the number for your state, if you're a subscriber to one of my business opportunity newsletters.

16. **Small Business Investment Company loans** may be available for your business if you plan to enlarge it to a level where you employ fifty or more people.

17. **Go public using new small-company offers** known as ULOR—Uniform Limited Offering Registration—or SCOR—Small Corporation Offering Registration. Using this way of going public, you can raise up to $1 million per year. Most small home-based businesses get their initial funding using a loan; then they go public after they've grown to a suitable size and operate from a rented office or industrial building.

Now that you have seventeen ways to raise money for your business, you're ready to take a closer look at them. So let's get started getting you the money you need for your home-based business!

Just remember that there are millions of dollars available to you today for your home-based business. This money is available quickly, easily—without yards and yards of paperwork.

How can I say this? I can say it because for the last thirty years I've helped Beginning Wealth Builders raise millions of dollars for all kinds of business and real estate deals. During that same time I've been (and still am) president and chairman of the board of a lending group with assets of more than $100 million. So I speak from long—and highly successful—experience in getting money for BWBs.

Understanding the Borrowing Process

In years of encouraging people to borrow money to build a home-based fortune, I've tried to explain to them the borrowing process. Just so you're on the same wavelength that I am, Figure 11-1 illustrates the way the borrowing process works for any home-based business.

As you see in Figure 11-1, the lender puts money into *your* hands in the form of a loan. You use this money to buy

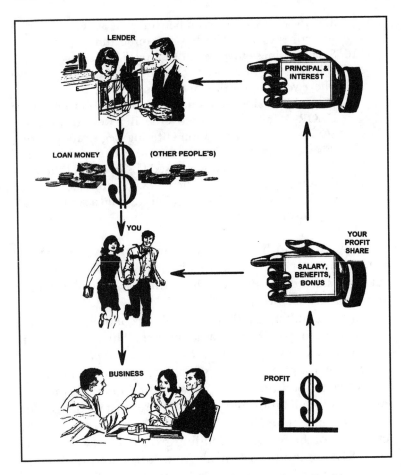

Figure 11-1. How borrowing works in any home business.

or start a home-based business or real estate venture. This venture earns money, part of which is a profit. From this profit you take a share for yourself. Part of the remaining profit you use to repay the loan that allowed you to buy or start the venture. *Remember:* It is this venture that is earning the profit to repay the loan! You're using the power of Other People's Money—OPM. (*Note:* With venture capital or a grant, you do *not* have to repay the money you received, if you did the work for which the money was advanced.)

Is this magic? No! It's the way smart home-based BWBs have built wealth for centuries. Why isn't the method better known? Because the people who use it are so busy counting their money that they don't have time to tell others about the enormous power of borrowed money to build great wealth for anyone willing to work at using it! But this book tells *you* all you need to get started in your own home-based business.

Proof by the Thousands

My office files bulge with thousands of letters from BWBs telling of the power of borrowed money in their home-based business lives. (I regard real estate investments as a business because the purpose of any business investment is to earn money for the owners.) These thousands of letters tell of what BWBs are doing *today* to use the incredible wealth-building power of borrowed money. Here are parts of two recent letters. Read them with the open mind all home-based BWBs have. And know that you *can* do the same—or better! The first reader writes:

"Thanks for the inspiration your books have provided me in my development as a real estate investment entrepreneur. To this day, when I feel overwhelmed by demands of property management and development, I refer to the commentaries and passages in your books to recapture the spirit and zeal they evoke inside me. I am very proud and happy to report that my property holdings now produce sufficient cash flow to live on comfortably. I am therefore leaving my banking career as an assistant vice president to pursue property purchase and management on a full-time basis. I specialize in three- and five-family buildings. Here's an approximate income statement for four of them":

	BLDG. 1	BLDG. 2
Rent	$20,000 *	$44,300
Expenses	- 6,000	- 5,500
Mortgage payments	- 10,250	- 19,800
Net profit	$3,750	$19,000
	BLDG. 3	BLDG. 4
Rent	$44,500	$41,800
Expenses	-8,000	- 7,500
Mortgage payments	- 19,500	- 18,500
Net profit	$17,000	$15,800

*My family and I occupy one apartment rent-free.

Another successful BWB writes:

> "Recently I read your book *How to Make One Million Dollars in Real Estate Starting With No Cash*. I began buying real estate one year ago when I was twenty-one and had no credit. Now I have a lovely home and two co-op apartments—a five-family and a six-family—all for no down payment. They appraise for just under $800,000. It still amazes me that I own real estate."

There you have two home-based BWBs building their wealth *today*. Not ten years ago, not even five years ago. But today!

And *you* can do the same—today! Using borrowed money—fast hard cash I call it. I'm so certain that you *can* do what these BWBs are doing in your own home-based business that I stand ready to help you, as a friend, day or night. So let's get you a loan—*now!*

Loans by the Dozen—Take Your Pick

Some of the most creative businesspeople in the world work for lenders. Why do I say this? Because today's lenders are constantly coming up with new ways to get people to borrow their money.

And why do lenders spend sleepless nights trying to find new ways to entice customers to borrow? Because the competition between lenders is so intense that the only way to survive is to come up with new ways to "throw money into people's faces"—other people's money!

For example, my financial institution is—as we say—so liquid (money on hand) that we slosh! What does this mean? It means that we—like many other lenders today—have more cash on hand than we can find borrowers for. So we have to spend much of our time looking for qualified "takers" who will borrow our money.

To show you a few of the ways lenders get people to borrow their money, here are some recent ad headlines advertising money available for business and/or real estate deals:

- No Income-Verification Loans
- Fast-Turnaround Fixed-Rate Mortgages
- Private Mortgage Money Available
- 100% Insider Financing
- How to Take the Hassle Out of Business Loans
- Jumbo Money Available—Now
- Need Commercial Financing Fast?
- Cash-out Refinancing
- 125% Home Equity Loans
- SOHO Loans (that is, Small Office/Home Office Loans)
- Bankruptcy, Late-Pays No Problem

I could go on and on with other interesting headlines designed to get a borrower to take the lender's money. So if you're thinking, "Oh, I can't qualify for a loan, my credit is no good," stop right now. There *are* plenty of lenders who say:

- Bad Credit? *NO* Problem!
- Bankruptcy—*NO* Problem!
- No Income Check, Ever
- No Job Verification Needed

Yes, there *are* dozens of new offers from lenders every week. And there are thousands of lenders just waiting to make you that loan you need. The keys to getting that loan are so simple that anyone can use them. And I mean *you!*

Isn't it clear that if lenders dreamed up SOHO (small office/home office) loans that they're desperate to put loans out? I know that my lending organizations are desperate to do so!

Keys to Getting Your Loan Quickly

Many home-based BWBs don't think through their loan needs before applying and find that getting a loan takes longer than planned. You can cut such delays by using the following keys to getting any home-based business or real estate loan:

1. **Apply to the right type of lender.** Some BWBs apply for a real estate loan at a business lender's office. They don't get a loan because the lender makes only other kinds of loans. So know your lender first!
2. **Seek a loan in the lender's range.** Some lenders won't lend more than $500,000; others won't lend less than $500,000. So be sure the amount of money you're seeking is within the lender's range.
3. **Type your loan application.** Don't submit a handwritten loan application for a home-based business or real estate loan. It will almost never be approved. Typed and computer-generated loan applications are the accepted means of communication in business today. Use them!
4. **Don't tell the lender "Time is of the essence."** Nearly every BWB borrower thinks this sentence will produce the money tomorrow—or even today. Not so! "If time is so important," thinks the lender, "why did the borrower wait this long to apply? Can't the borrower plan his or her time better?"
5. **Don't "bug" the lender with constant phone calls asking when you'll get your money.** The lender is likely to say "Never!" just to get rid of you. Wait for the lender to evaluate your application and give you an answer.

6. **Keep "hunger" out of the application.** Sure, you may be on your last legs, the sheriff may be knocking on the door, your kids may have to wear hand-me-downs, and you don't know where your next meal is coming from. But do *not* let this show in your application! Lenders turn away from "hungry" borrowers because such borrowers frighten them. Be relaxed, cool, competent, polite—and you'll get a loan.

Although you may not agree with the above keys, let me say they *do* work! And that—to me—is the measure of any method. Does it work? Some of my readers happily report:

"Tell Ty Hicks his methods of borrowing really work. Using his borrowing techniques, and starting with nothing, I now have an $80,000-a-year business. That's my first year's gross!"

"I have been reading and studying your books for some time. I opened accounts at four different banks and applied for a loan at each. So far I received $10,000 in loans. All are nonsecured personal signature loans."

Be Ready to Get Your Loan

You can use a loan to do many things that will zoom your home-based wealth. For example, you can:

- **Buy** a going home-based business.
- **Start** a new home-based business.
- **Expand** an existing home-based business.
- **Save** a nearly failed home-based business.

A loan gives you great power to build your future wealth. Knowing this, you should take every positive step you can to get the loan you need.

To be ready to get the loan you want, see the loan from the lender's view. In my lending activities where we're lending some $25 million or more each year, we look for three characteristics in each loan deal. These are the "go signals" we and all other lenders look for:

- **Capacity** is your ability to repay the loan on the terms acceptable to yourself and your lender. This means that if you agree to repay the loan at the rate of $1,000 per month for seven years that you *can* meet these payments without too much stress on your budget. So be sure to indicate in your loan application that you *will* have a large enough cash flow from your home-based business to make the agreed-on periodic payments on your loan.
- **Collateral** is hard assets your lender can attach if you can't repay your loan. Because a lender uses profits from his or her business to make a loan to you, the lender wants to be certain the loan will be repaid. Why? Because each dollar of profit represents many hours of work. If any of these dollars are lost because you can't, or won't, repay the loan, the lender is hurt badly. But if there's some type of collateral (for example, real estate, machinery, stocks, or bonds) that the lender can take over, it's a lot easier to make the loan. And remember, good friend, a cosigner with a steady income is good collateral for every home-based business loan.
- **Character** covers your desire and intention to repay the lender. Though it may surprise you, there are some people who take out loans with little intention of repaying in a timely manner. To show a possible lender that you have a strong desire and intention to repay the home-based loan on time, include in your application or cover letter a budget showing the monthly loan payment and how it will be made each month until the loan is repaid in full.

So, good friend, if you should come to me for a business or real estate loan, your chances for a **"YES"** answer are excellent if:

- Your loan application is typewritten.
- We make the type of loan you're looking for.
- The amount of your loan is in our range.
- You're willing to give me a few days to answer you.
- You have the ability to repay the loan.
- You have suitable collateral to pledge.
- You show me in a letter that you *will* repay us.

Now that you have some idea of how to impress any lender favorably, let's take a look at the many ways for you to get business money *today*. And be sure to remember that I am here to help you every step of the way! Stick with me, and you'll build a fortune on other people's money in your own home-based business.

Use the Power of the Printed Word

Some of you who've read some of my earlier books know that I publish a monthly newsletter—*International Wealth Success*—which gives many details and tips on borrowing money. Each month my newsletter lists dozens of lenders seeking borrowers. And each month there are dozens of people who run free ads looking for money. And, as one reader told me on the phone: "My ads really get results for me. I found a lender for my $50,000 loan. Ty, I'm on my way!" You'll find full information on the newsletter at the back of this book.

You can advertise for lenders. Believe it or not, lenders *do* read ads run by people seeking home-based business or real estate loans. In advertising for a loan, you're using the power of the printed word. And believe me, good friend, the power of the printed word is beyond belief! I'm the author of more than 100 published books, and people keep writing me—day and night—for help.

What kind of an ad might you run to get a loan for your home-based business? That's easy. Just sit down with pencil and paper and write out what you need. Here are a few examples of ads that pull well for home-based BWBs:

LOAN NEEDED to buy successful auto-repair business. Monthly repayment will return your $35,000 loan in three years at 12% interest. Call 123-4567.

$50,000 LOAN NEEDED to start home-based wedding-dress business. Collateral available. Call 123-4567.

I NEED $250,000 to expand my growing home-based business.
Good collateral offered. Call 123-4567.

What if you don't have any collateral, may have a "slow-pay" credit history, or may have gone bankrupt in the past? You're in—as we say—a "weak-credit" situation. (Please don't be offended—I'm just trying to paint the worst possible picture to show how you can still get a loan.) If you have any or all of these conditions, you need help.

Help from a *cosigner, comaker,* or *guarantor.* Each does the same job—helping you get your loan—but in a different way.

- A *cosigner* agrees to repay your home-based business loan in the event you are unable or unwilling to do so.
- A *comaker* is really a coborrower. That is, the comaker is equally liable to repay your home-based business loan.
- A *guarantor* guarantees that the loan will be repaid. But a guarantor is *not* a borrower as a comaker is. Instead, the guarantor pledges some collateral or asset that assures the lender the loan will be repaid.

For most BWBs, getting a cosigner is the fastest and easiest way to get a loan if their credit isn't the strongest. To get a cosigner, use the power of the printed word and run an ad in your local paper saying:

COSIGNER NEEDED for $50,000 home-based business loan.
Will pay liberal fee to cosigner after loan is obtained.
Call 123-4567.

CAN SHOW BIG PROFIT on $100,000 home-based business loan. Will share with cosigner who helps get loan.
Call 123-4567.

How much will you have to pay a cosigner, comaker, or guarantor? That depends on whom you're dealing with. But the top fee is a *one-time* amount of 5 percent of the loan after *you* obtain the money—*not* before. *Never pay front money of any kind for a loan.* You *can* get OPM without paying front money!

As the amount of your loan increases, the fee percentage decreases. Thus, on a $1 million loan the fee might be 2.5 percent, *after* you get the loan. Again, note that this is a one-time fee—not an annual fee.

You can use the power of the printed word even further by joining the Global Cosigner and Money Finders Association. This organization, described at the back of this book, publicizes your need for a cosigner under a code number so your identity is kept confidential. GCMFA does *guarantee* to circulate your need widely. But GCMFA *cannot,* and *does not,* guarantee that you'll get the loan you need because business conditions vary so widely.

And if you're a do-it-yourselfer, you may want to get the *Guaranteed Loan Money Kit* (K-16) described at the back of this book. It gives you specific detailed, step-by-step instructions for finding cosigners, comakers, and guarantors for home-based business loans. We don't have space here to duplicate all the great and tested ideas in that kit.

When looking for cosigners, take time to prepare a simple list of all your relatives, friends, business, associates, and/or friends of friends and business associates who might cosign.

Although none of these may cosign for you, some might recommend people who *will* cosign. Because the exercise won't cost you anything except some time, it's really worth trying. Why don't you start right now, right here for your home-based business loan? Fill in as many lines as you can on a sheet of paper listing friends, relatives, and others who might cosign—the longer the list, the better.

Put Your Telephone to Work

There are thousands of lenders around the world who make home-based business loans by phone. While the actual loan doesn't go through phone wires, the information needed for the loan and a temporary approval does. What's more, many of these lenders have an 800 phone number. This means your long-distance calls to these lenders are free!

How do loans by phone work? They depend on the following information:

- **Type of loan** you seek
- **Amount of money** you need
- **Length of time** for which you need the money
- **Your income** and expenses

Many lenders making home-based business loans by phone will overlook a poor job or business history, bankruptcy, or other financial problems if you own your own home and have some equity in it.

In helping BWBs get loans by phone, I tell them that with just thirty-two words and fifteen seconds of time they can get a "yes" or "no" answer from a lender. So you really need not put too much time into finding out if you can get a loan for your deal.

And—if you want—you can become a Loan-by-Phone Broker to help others get loans this way, working from your own home. You'll earn a good commission on each loan you place. Of course, if you place a loan for yourself, you'll have to skip the commission. You can get full information on being a Loan-by-Phone Broker from the kit of the same name, detailed in Figure 11-2.

Make the Mail Bring Your Money

Some people don't like to use the phone. While I really can't understand this view because I'm on the phone day and night helping readers of my newsletter, I respect people's views. So I say, use the next best way—the United States Postal Service—the best in the world! You *can* get loans by mail—it's done every day of the week. And the money you get by mail is just as good and just as powerful as the money you get in a bank or from another lender.

LOANS-BY-PHONE

Collect BIG fees for getting people loans over the telephone. Many 800 numbers for your toll-free calls to get money faster

- ✖ Immediate funding
- ✖ NO fees; NO points
- ✖ NO credit check
- ✖ NO appraisal fees
- ✖ Instant approvals
- ✖ Worldwide low rates
- ✖ One-hour approvals

- ✖ All types of business loans available
- ✖ Mortgages for real estate—1st, 2nds, 3rds, where needed
- ✖ Letter of credit—all types—by phone
- ✖ Apply by phone, toll-free; save time
- ✖ Anyone can apply; everone eligible
- ✖ Problem cases our specialty

Today, almost everyone needing money for business or real estate is in a hurry. You can serve their needs (and your own if you're looking for a loan) by using the newest way to raise money–LOANS-BY-PHONE.

Even if you don't like to make phone calls, and even if you can't make a phone call, LOANS-BY-PHONE can help you. How? By speeding up the process of loan approval—saving you and your client time.

There are dozens of ways you can use this new approach to raising money for any kind of business or real estate deal. In a matter of moments you can learn 1) if a loan can be made 2) what the interest rate will be 3) when a closing can be held for the loan.

Get the new, never-offered-before LOANS-BY-PHONE KIT. It could get you $1,500 to $25 million or more.

 BE A LOAN-BY-PHONE BROKER

- ♦ GET names and phone numbers (some toll-free) of more than 200 lenders who work by phone. (Your cost is less than 50¢ per name.)Updated weekly.
- ♦ GET "The Art of Making Loan-Getting Phone Calls"—tips on making each phone call work for you by having others make the calls for you.
- ♦ GET typical application forms, client agreements, time-zone map for planning your phone calls, interest-rate tables.
- ♦ GET monthly updates on LOANS-BY-PHONE LENDERS for three months, at no cost to you when you become our Loan-by-Phone Broker.
- ♦ GET step-by-step LOANS-BY-PHONE procedures for yourself and your client–the methods you can use now today to earn big fees from clients or to get big loans for yourself.
- ♦ GET fast loan decisions—don't wait around for weeks–get your answer–YES or NO in just minutes. If the answer is NO, move on to the next lender by just punching in a few numbers. Stop losing time and money–now.
- ♦ GET rich from loan fees faster. Make just a few calls each day and earn your money in an hour or less—take more time off. Work less–earn more.

Become a LOANS-BY-PHONE BROKER and get started in under 2 hours. You will get the complete kit plus 3 updates of LOANS-BY-PHONE LENDERS (10 or more per month) for just $100.

Enclosed is $100.00. Send me the *LOANS-BY-PHONE PROGRAM* plus my 3 monthly updates of lenders.

NAME	SIGNATURE	
ADDRESS		PHONE #
CITY	STATE	ZIP

To order by Credit Card please include: Credit Card #   Expiration Date
(Send Check or Money Order or charge by phone—516-766-5850.)
Send order to IWS., Inc.,24 Canterbury Rd.,Rockville Centre, NY 11570.

✖ = what some lenders say about the loans they make

Figure 11-2. How to be a Loan-by-Phone Broker.

To get loans by mail, you take these easy steps:

- **Get** the names and addresses of mail-order lenders.
- **Find** out what kinds of loans they make.
- **Tailor** your loan application to meet their requirements.
- **Fill out** the lender's loan application.
- **Send** the application in by mail.
- **Watch** the mail for a response.

Most mail-order lenders will get you your answer in seven days or less. In my lending organization we try to give the borrower an answer in twenty-four hours. Sometimes it takes us less time; once in a while, it's a bit longer—thirty-six hours. But at least 95 percent of our borrowers get their money within twenty-four hours after their loan applications are approved. We call it the fastest OPM around!

So don't look on mail-order loans for home-based businesses as slow because they take longer than loans by phone. I tell our borrowers, "Any loan money is welcome! Because you didn't have to work for loan money, you save enormous amounts of time and energy. This helps you reach your financial and life goals much faster."

You can become an expert in mail-order loans by using the *Loans-by-Mail Success Kit*, detailed in Figure 11-3. It helps *you* get your mail-order loan. And it also shows you how to help others—for a nice commission—get loans by mail from the comfort of your home. You really should have this kit if you want to get lots of home-based business loans by mail.

Get Credit Card Loans Fast

Today we all live in a world of instant gratification. People don't want to wait weeks and weeks to get something they need. You'll find plenty of people getting money they need for home-based business or real estate by using the credit lines on their credit cards. Although the interest rate may be higher than with a signature loan, the money you get

How to Get Rich in
MAIL ORDER
CA$H LOAN DOLLARS.

°<u>Overcome</u> BAD CREDIT for yourself and others!

°<u>Get CASH in a flash</u>--maybe one day, or less!

°Find an "Angel" for your cash needs!

°Develop signature-loan MONEY POWER!

°Rate <u>YOUR</u> loan chances in minutes!

°Wipe out <u>ALL DEBTS</u> with just one loan!

°Deal by mail--<u>NO</u> interviews; <u>NO</u> pain!

°Get liquid assets for any personal need!

°Get <u>INTEREST-ONLY</u> mail-order loans!

°Be the "fastest loan broker" around!

°Get <u>DOZENS</u> of different kinds of loans!

°Be a <u>MAIL-ORDER UNSECURED SIGNATURE LOAN</u> wheeler-dealer!

°Make friends with money lenders forever!

°Get <u>MAIL-ORDER LOAN</u> convenience, speed, efficiency, confidentiality!

°Earn <u>BIG FEES</u> helping others get quick unsecured signature loans!

°Know who's lending for what use!

°Laugh "all the way to the bank" <u>NOW!</u>

°Deal by mail and avoid face-to-face hassles and arguments!

<u>GET UNSECURED PERSONAL SIGNATURE LOANS FOR YOUR CLIENTS OR YOURSELF</u> using the IWS MAIL-ORDER LOAN SUCCESS SYSTEM--the fastest way to get a signature loan today! Learn how to deal with lenders--prepare winning loan applications--help yourself or others to the <u>BILLIONS</u> available for unsecured loans! Build your own, or your clients' loan rating fast! It's <u>ALL</u> here--plus much, much more in this <u>NEW</u> powerful <u>SYSTEM!</u>

Written by Ty Hicks, a man who has supervised the lending of some $50 million in all types of unsecured signature loans, this <u>SYSTEM</u> is just what's needed to get people the money they seek! And <u>YOU</u> can use the <u>SYSTEM</u> for your clients, or for yourself. It works, works, works for <u>YOU!</u> And it works for anyone you're helping get a loan. The <u>SYSTEM</u> gives you thousands of lenders to contact--shows <u>YOU</u> how to build your own list of willing and interested lenders! Send your check or money order for your <u>SYSTEM</u> today! Get loans <u>SOON!</u>

THIS IS THE ORDER BLANK

$$

$ Here's $100. Send me my MAIL-ORDER LOAN SUCCESS SYSTEM. If you wish, you can call Ty $
$ Hicks with your credit-card (Mastercard or Visa) order at 516-766-5850 9am to 10 pm. $
$ Have your credit card ready? Ask Ty any questions you may have! $

$ NAME_____Apt/Suite #_____$

$ ADDRESS_____CITY_____STATE_____ZIP_____$

$ Send check or money order to: IWS, Inc., 24 Canterbury Rd., Rockville Centre, NY 11570 $

$ Credit Card #_____Expiration_____Signature_____$

Figure 11-3. How you can get a loan by mail order.

from a credit card loan is just as useful and powerful as any other borrowed money. You can put it to work quickly and easily in your home-based business.

Most credit cards offer a line of credit allowing you to write checks up to a certain amount, say $5,000 to $100,000. So you just use these checks to invest in the home-based business or real estate that interests you. And the interesting aspects of credit cards are:

- Credit card issuers don't care how many cards you own.
- Issuers' views are the more cards out there, the better!
- You can have a line of credit on each card without other issuers caring.

You can become—as some have—a "plastic millionaire" with your credit cards! Just multiply the number of cards you have by your line of credit on each (if it's the same), and you may be a millionaire! For example, just 200 credit cards (not a very large number these days), each with a $5,000 line of credit, will make you a "plastic millionaire" (200 × $5,000 = $1 million). Or ten cards at $100,000 each also add up to $1 million!

To get a credit card, you must apply for it. If you've been bankrupt or a very slow payer of your bills, you may find it hard to get your first card. Not to worry, as the British say. There are ways to get that credit card, which is the first of many. Here's how to do it:

1. **Apply for a *secured credit card*** at a bank that issues such cards.
2. **Deposit enough** in a savings account to get your credit card. This is usually $300 or $500, though you can, if you wish, deposit more if you have it.
3. **Use your credit card** to make a purchase as soon as you get the card. Why? Because it gets you into the credit stream of the world.
4. **Pay your bill** for the purchase as soon as it comes in. Don't wait even a day. Establish a "quick-pay" reputation. This will save you on interest cost and make you a "thirty-day wonder"—one of those people who pay in thirty days or less.

Most banks issuing secured credit cards will allow you to use half of the amount you have on deposit for charges on your card.

Amount on Deposit	Your Usable Credit
$300	$150
$500	$250
$750	$375
$1,000	$500

Once you've had your secured card for a few months and have made some timely payments on your charges, your bank will probably increase the amount of usable credit you have from one-half to three-quarters, as shown here:

Amount on Deposit	Your Usable Credit
$300	$225
$500	$375
$750	$562
$1,000	$750

After a year or so of timely payments on your card, you may find that your bank removes the deposit requirements on your card and allows a modest line of credit. Thus, you may get a line of credit of $500, plus freedom from any deposit requirement.

Again, *use your card immediately.* Then, *make your payments as soon as you receive your bill.* Your credit report will improve, and you'll have more money for your home-based business. And, best of all, other card issuers will be after *you* to accept and use their credit cards!

Once you have a card with one bank that's *unsecured*—that is, doesn't need a backup deposit—you'll be swamped with offers of other cards. And by keeping your credit clean by making timely payments on every bill, you can become a credit card millionaire! On OPM, yet.

One of the best sources of information on banks issuing credit cards and their specific requirements is the excellent book *Money Raiser's Directory of Bank Credit Card Programs—The Directory of MASTERCARD and VISA Credit Card Sources.* You'll find full details about this book in Figure 11-4.

Use the "Reverse Flip" Method

When you use the money you borrow in your home-based business to buy something of value, you might wish to consider using a "reverse flip" to reward your cosigner or guarantor. With a reverse flip, you assign to your cosigner or guarantor the item (such as real estate or machinery) you bought with the borrowed money. Then, any payments you make on the item will be credited to your cosigner or guarantor when (and if) the item you bought reverts to him or her because you stopped making payments on the loan you used to buy the item.

By assigning to your cosigner the item you buy, you prove several important points to him or her:

- **You are sincere** in your efforts to build home-based wealth; otherwise you wouldn't assign the asset.
- **Much of the risk for the cosigner is removed.** Many assets go *up* in value while you're paying off the loan; your cosigner or guarantor is protected by the asset's value increase and the paydown on the loan.
- **Your willingness** to let the full asset go back to (called *reverting to*) the cosigner or guarantor shows your intense desire to protect your helper while building home-based wealth for yourself.

Figure 11-4. How to order the **Money Raiser's Directory of Bank Credit Card Programs.**

You will, of course, pay a nominal fee to your cosigner or guarantor for his or her help. If you don't have the money for the fee, you can offer a percentage of the income from your home-based business, or a percentage of the profit you realize on the sale of the business, or a combination of the two. With any of these plans, you avoid an immediate outlay of money for the fee.

As an example of how your cosigner or guarantor might profit from a percentage of the gain when the home-based business is sold, here's a recent letter:

> "I bought *How to Borrow Your Way to a Great Fortune*, believed it, went out and borrowed $10,000, and bought a business brokerage. Never in my life had I sold anything; by profession I'm a dental technician. But reading your book and following the instructions made me make a decision, and today I'm doing well. I was recently offered $25,000 for half my brokerage."

So consider the reverse flip. It may be just the answer *you* need to get the loan that will build *your* riches quickly!

Aim for "Big" Signature Loans

People call me on my business phone day and night (8:30 A.M. to 4 P.M. and 8 P.M. to 10 P.M. EST) to tell me about the great home-based deals they're swinging. Some talk about really big financing—"$10B"—that is, ten *billion* dollars. And just recently they've starting talking "10T"—ten *trillion* dollars!

My answer to all these dreamers is, "We're just small potatoes back East here. But we have Wall Street and the Statue of Liberty, plus a few other attractions. If you're interested in a signature loan up to $50,000, we'll be delighted to talk. But the Bs and Ts are out of our world!"

Some—the smart ones—listen. The dreamers, however, go off on their own, chasing the Bs and Ts. The smart ones often wind up with a "big" signature loan.

And what do I mean by a big signature loan? By "big" I mean: any home-based business loan you get by simply signing an application and a promissory note for an amount of $35,000 or more. No collateral is pledged for the loan.

Now I know the people looking for the Bs and Ts won't think a $35,000 loan is big. Yet the lenders who are making such loans (banks and finance companies) *do* think that a $35,000 *unsecured* loan is big. Why? To free up $35,000 in funds for just one loan, the lender must do at least $350,000 in business, if the lender has an after-tax profit of 10 percent. Because $350,000 in business means lots of work, hours, and risk overcome, the lender is extremely cautious about making the loan. Remember: A signature loan means that all the lender has as collateral is some ink on a piece of paper! A lot less ink than in a new ballpoint pen.

Yet, big signature home-based business loans *are* available. Just check with your commercial bank. One well-known bank currently makes personal loans up to $50,000 on the following:

- **Secured** *only* by your signature.
- **In the form** of a line of credit that doesn't cost a penny until you start using it.
- **With your money** just a phone call away once your line of credit is approved.
- **With your check mailed** to you the same day you request it on the phone.
- **And** *no* **personal interviews** are needed; you can fill out the application in the privacy of your own home, at your leisure.

Other lenders offer more flexible terms on their big signature loans for home-based businesses. For instance, a lender that goes to $20,000 on such personal loans:

- **Has** fixed or variable interest rates.
- **Offers** flexible monthly repayments.
- **Lends** for a variety of purposes—repairs, vacation, travel, education, or business, for example.
- **Gives** a 3 percent cash refund on the interest, *after* you repay the loan in full.

- **Has** no hidden charges (for example, fees, points, or pre-payment penalty) of any kind.
- **Provides** fast loan service with an 800 number for toll-free calls to the lenders.

Although these "big" loans using a signature as collateral may not seem large to some people, others put them to effective and profitable use in their home-based business. An example is from this BWB, who writes:

> "I read several of your books and used many of your ideas to improve my financial status. In the last year I bought two eight-unit apartment buildings at a time when I had *no* money. I used 100 percent borrowed money. In just one year I increased my net worth from $8,000 to $50,000."

So don't scoff at these "small" loans! They can make *you* rich in your own home-based business. Start getting your personal signature loan at your local commercial bank. Just drop in, give them a call, or write a short note. Then you may write me a letter telling me how successful you've been getting OPM for yourself—fast!

Explore Credit Union Loans

There are some 15,000 federal credit unions in the United States today, plus thousands of state-chartered credit unions. These lending institutions are giving the banks plenty of competition in the areas of personal, business, and real estate loans. You should check credit unions in your area to see:

1. **If you're eligible** to join.
2. **What types of loans** they're making.
3. **How large a loan** you might get.

Some credit unions limit their membership to employees of one company. Other credit unions are associated with religious groups, fraternal organizations, governments, and the like. If you can't qualify with any such background, consider a "central" credit union—that is, one that's open to any and all residents of a state or city. To find such a credit union in your area, just check your local yellow pages under the heading "Credit Unions." You can join a credit union free of charge and can get many benefits, including:

- **High-interest** savings accounts and certificates of deposit (CDs).
- **Low-interest** loans for many purposes, including a home-based business.
- **Kind,** attentive, understanding service.
- **Fast** loan approval.
- **Long** repayment period.
- **No points,** fees, or other charges.

To get a home-based business loan from your credit union, follow these easy, fast steps:

1. **Find** out what types of loans they like.
2. **Get** a copy of the loan application(s) used.
3. **Fill out** the application for your loan, *typing* it throughout.
4. **Comply** with *all* the credit union's regulations.
5. **Submit** your application; wait for an answer.

Most credit unions today are interested in making good business loans, so you'll find the welcome mat is out for you. To ensure getting the loan you seek, remember to:

- *Be professional* in all your dealings; this will win respect and loan approval.
- *Stand out above the crowd* by typing your loan application and meeting *all* the rules of the credit union's loan committee.
- *Never threaten* or otherwise try to force the credit union into doing what you want. Instead, do what the credit union asks; you'll get many more loans that way!

Remember that credit unions *want* to make loans. Why? Because their whole objective is to help people improve their financial condition. Don't turn away from a credit union loan—it could be the answer to *your* home-based wealth-building start!

See If an Annuity Will Help You Get a Loan

Life insurance companies, along with real estate lenders, are among the most creative firms around. Their recently introduced "whole-life annuity" might get you the loan you seek. There are other names for this type of annuity. But they all get the same results, namely:

- **The annuity acts as collateral** for a loan you get from a lender other than the insurance company.
- **It grows in amount** for seven or ten years until the annuity equals the amount you borrowed.
- **The lender is ensured** that the principal (the amount you borrowed) will be repaid whether you live, die, or fail to repay the loan.

To buy such an annuity, the borrower must put up about one-third of the amount of money borrowed. Some borrowers try to borrow the cost of the annuity, giving them the loan free and clear. This *can* work; the only tough part is finding a lender who will finance the annuity. Although this is possible, it usually takes a little longer than finding a direct lender for a home-based business project.

To see how an annuity works—in very brief detail and without the many legal wheres and wherefores—let's take a $100,000 ten-year loan as an example:

Amount of annuity at full value: $100,000
Loan amount needed: $100,000
Cost of annuity today: $33,300
Length of annuity: Ten years
Net to you if annuity is taken out of loan: $100,000 - $33,300
  = $66,700
Net to insurance company: $33,300

There *are* lenders who will advance money to you with an annuity as their collateral. The best way to find such lenders is to read my book *Business Capital Sources*, described at the back of this book. Or, you can look in the yellow pages under "Loans," "Banks," or "Finance."

You can get the borrowed money you need for your home-based business. And that money can grow in the form of an investment you make. One reader writes:

> "I started using your techniques and built $2,000 of borrowed money into $120,000 net worth in just two years. I have a real estate firm, a trout farm, and a sports store."

So ask your insurance broker about a single-premium life annuity. Then study the information carefully. It just may give you the loan you seek.

Look for Over-Appraised Assets

When you go out to buy an asset such as an income-producing building, a cargo airplane, or a printing press, it usually will be appraised by a professional. This person will say in a written report, "This asset is worth $300,000 in today's market."

Now, when you want to buy that asset using OPM, a lender will usually loan 75 percent of the appraised value. So on the $300,000 asset mentioned above, you could borrow $0.75 \times \$300,000 = \$225,000$ on a long-term loan—defined as twelve years or longer. The balance, $300,000 - $225,000 = $75,000, would have to come from your savings or from another loan.

But what would happen if the seller were willing to sell this asset for $225,000? Then you'd be able to get the asset with *zero* cash. This is called 100 percent financing and is an excellent example of using OPM to build your wealth. Why might someone be willing to sell an asset at less than the appraised price? There are any number of reasons, such as:

- **A strong desire** to unload a burdensome asset.
- **An asset is owned** by an estate that wants quick cash.
- **Family problems** make the seller want a quick sale.
- **The owner "wants out"** so badly that any price is acceptable.

Although you may not have run into such reasons yet, I assure you that they occur every day, somewhere. How do I know? Because my reading public keeps me informed through visits, phone calls, and letters as to what they're doing now, today. These readers say:

> "In the last six months I bought $500,000 worth of income real estate with *no* money down. Each of these properties gives me a positive cash flow, every month! Now I'm looking for more real estate to expand my holdings and income."

Another reader says:

> "I took over three buildings for *no* money down. One is an office building; the other two are rental homes."

So be on the lookout for over-appraisals. They could be your source of great wealth on OPM.

Apply with Many Different Lenders

You *can* get more than one home-based business loan at a time. This can give you multiples of OPM. At my lending institution we have plenty of people with two, three, and even four loans—all at the same time. For example, a person might have a long-term mortgage for, say, $475,000, an auto loan for $20,000, and a signature loan for $5,000.

And do you know what? We're *happy* this person took all these loans from us. Why? Because if he or she didn't take them from us, I'm sure they would have gone elsewhere. We'd have lost the business—namely the interest income we earn on each of these good, solid loans.

And I'm also willing to bet you—though I haven't checked the actual record—that this person has other loans with other lenders. Just as long as the payments can be made in a timely fashion, we lenders are happy!

I've urged BWBs for years to use OPM in the form of multiple loans for their home-based business. Why? Because with multiple loans:

- Each loan is smaller, meaning that it's easier to get the money.
- The more loans you get, the more money you'll have to build your home-based business wealth.
- Having several loans will make you a more ambitious business person—you have to be, if you wish to pay your loans off!
- Managing the payments on several loans at once will train you to be a much better manager.

Readers *do* build home-based wealth using multiple loans. They write me nearly *every* day of the year telling me how multiple loans *are* working for them. This reader from Washington state wrote:

"I followed your advice in your book and applied at seven different lenders for a $6,000 signature loan from each lender. Five said 'yes,' and I got $30,000. I used this money as the down payment on a video rental store, which is doing $120,000 a year with a net of about $24,000 a year after paying my wife's salary (she runs the store). Thanks so much for your methods, which really work!"

"I read your book *How to Borrow Your Way to a Great Fortune* about three and a half years ago. I put some of your principles to work and have gone from a net worth of $12,000 to a net worth of over $333,000."

"I bought my present business, a tavern, using the Ty Hicks method. I took out three loans of $5,000 each and have since paid back a third of each. Or, I should say, my business paid them back and will continue to do so. I also took out an auto loan, which my business pays back, too. My business also pays all notes ($47,000 per year). The three loans above were for the $10,000 down payment and other fees (legal, inventory, and so on). My net—after the business pays all bills and loans—is about $800 a week; this gives me about $40,000 per year. But when all notes are paid off, I'll have another $47,000 a year income!"

There you have three modern-day proofs that multiple loans *do* work for home-based businesses. And they *can* work for you! Just convince yourself—if I haven't already done so—that OPM:

- **Can be** the most powerful force in your business life.
- **Offers you** salvation from a dull, dead-end job with surly, unappreciative bosses.
- **Gives you** the opportunity to build a home-based fortune, even if you don't have a spare thin dime to your name at this time.

When I started looking for work as a teenager, my family was so poor they couldn't afford to have my shoes resoled. So I cut out pieces of newspaper and put them in the bottom of my shoes so my socks wouldn't touch the ground. But in the rain and snow, the water soaked through the paper, making my feet freeze. Yet by using the power of OPM, I was able to rise above such humble beginnings. Today I loan my excess money to BWBs so they won't have to stuff newspapers into their shoes to plug the holes!

What's more, I've heard the stories of all the doomers and gloomers who say it can't be done. It *can* be done! It *is* being done! And you—I'm convinced—*can* get multiple loans today for your home-based business, just as the BWBs whose stories we've heard did.

Sure, it's true that your credit will be checked by most lenders. But you can get around poor credit—as I showed you earlier in this chapter. And some lenders may not even bother to check your credit if you show them that you're a sincere, hard-working borrower who *will* repay the loan.

To get multiple loans quickly and easily, take these steps:

1. **Decide on the types** of lenders with whom you want to work (banks, finance companies, mortgage brokers, savings and loan associations, and credit unions).
2. **Get the names** of a number of such institutions in your area. I recommend that you work locally at first because lenders will have a greater sympathy for you and your plan.

3. **Contact each lender** by phone, by mail, or in person. Ask for several copies of their loan applications. At the same time, ask for any printed information that they have on their loans.

4. **Tailor your loan application** so it meets the interests of your target lender. Type every application as recommended earlier. Ask only for the type of loan the lender makes.

5. **Submit your application** with a brief letter telling the lender about your sincerity and your desire to repay the loan fully in a timely manner using the profits from your home-based business.

6. **Continue submitting applications** to other lenders, using the same procedure. Keep sending out your applications until you have submitted one to every lender on your list. *Never give up!*

7. **Wait for a response** from each lender. Don't call, asking for a response. Wait—the response will come when the lender is ready to contact you.

One last thought: If any lender asks why you sent applications to five or ten different lenders, reply in full truth: "I'm looking for the best deal. So I sent applications to all lenders who appear to be qualified to handle my needs and whose reputations are excellent."

Find Loans Close to Home

Many BWBs almost go bonkers when I tell them they might be able to get business loans locally at 0, 3, or 4 percent interest. "That's impossible!" they say. "Who would give a loan at 0 percent interest? I never heard of such a thing."

That's when I have to tell these "smart" BWBs, "Just because *you* never heard of something, doesn't mean it can't be! Close your mouth and start listening. You just might learn something! Remember: You're not learning when you're talking."

You can find very low-cost home-based business loans close to home in the following places:

- **Your state** Job Development Agency (or an agency that serves this function under a different name)
- **Your state** Business Development Agency (or an agency that serves this function under a different name)
- **Your city** Job or Business Development Agency (or an agency that serves this function under a different name)
- **Your county** Job or Business Development Agency

These agencies, which you can find in your local telephone book under "Government" (usually the colored pages in the front of the white pages), are delighted to make loans to local business people to create new jobs, build factories, train workers, and expand existing businesses. Note that these are *not* personal loans. Instead, they are business or income real estate loans. Such loans are made to businesses providing local jobs, real estate operations for business, training activities for local workers, and other business or real estate use.

To encourage business and real estate people to accept this readily available money, interest rates are held *very* low. Also, rates are held low so that the company accepting the money can still earn a profit, even though it's paying off one or more business loans.

How can you latch onto some of these zero-interest or very-low-interest funds quickly and easily? Here's what you can do:

1. **Find out which agency** in your state, city, or county makes the type of loan you need.
2. **Do this by calling** (faxing or writing) the information office for your state, city, or county, as listed in the colored pages of your local telephone book.
3. **Ask for information** on the various business loans, grants, and other forms of assistance available to you and your firm. You will be quickly sent this data free of charge because most agencies are actively seeking to make new loans, grants, or other types of advances to stimulate business and jobs.
4. **Fill out the application** or other forms required to get the funding you seek. *Be certain to type every application!* Never fill out such applications in longhand—you are almost certain to be rejected.

5. **Provide all information requested,** even if some of it seems to be unnecessary. When you're dealing with a government agency, you do as requested. If you don't, you'll find that your time is wasted because you won't get the money you seek. Government personnel have *their* way of doing things. If you go along with these ways, your chances of getting the funds you seek will be much better!

6. **Wait until you are told of the decision** of the agency—don't "bug" your contact for an answer. It will come soon enough.

Don't Overlook Industrial Development Agencies

Many cities, states, and counties have quasi-official industrial development agencies that make loans, grants, and other monetary advances to local business and real estate activities. These development agencies often have private sources of funds and may have state sources.

You can apply for money from industrial development agencies in the same way you can apply for loans from job and business development agencies. Just remember that all these agencies want to improve business and jobs in their area. So be certain that the funds you're seeking *do* exactly that— that is, build your home-based business and jobs locally. Then you're almost certain to get the money you seek and need!

Go to Uncle Sam—He'll Help

Many BWBs I talk to shun the Small Business Administration (SBA) of our federal government, saying, "Those loans take too long." Yet I have letters in my files saying, "We took your advice and sent to the SBA. The money was in our hands in fifteen days." While that may seem like a long time to some people, I've known others who waited eighty days, ninety days, and longer for a business loan from a conventional source such as a bank or commercial finance company.

The SBA doesn't always *make* loans these days. More often the SBA will *guarantee* a loan. This speeds the entire process and gets you your money sooner. Additionally, you can get an SBA loan faster if you have someone ready to buy the guaranteed portion of your loan. Further, many lenders, such as my financial organization, who want greater security in the loans they make, will gladly buy the guaranteed portion of an SBA loan because it is guaranteed by the full faith and credit of the U.S. government.

A recent development by the SBA is the micro-loan—defined as a small loan up to $25,000. Such loans are made with minimum paperwork—just two pages. And the loans are made quickly—in a week or so. Check with your local SBA office for full details on micro-loans.

To get an SBA loan for your home-based business or the real estate related to your business, take these steps:

1. **Call the local SBA** office in your area. It is listed in the colored pages in your local phone book under "U.S. Government."
2. **Ask for a business loan application.** You will be sent this completely free of charge along with information on the loans the SBA is currently making or guaranteeing.
3. **Fill out the loan application completely,** typing every entry. Be certain to answer *all* questions. Where a question does not apply to your business, mark it "not applicable."
4. **Send the application to the SBA,** including a letter explaining any points needing extra information. If you know someone interested in buying the guaranteed portion of the loan, include this information in your letter. It is *not* necessary to give the name of the person who will buy the guaranteed portion of your loan.
5. **Wait for a reply.** These days it should come quickly under the revamped SBA procedures. I hope you get a "yes" response!

To understand how the SBA guarantee works, let's say that you need a $200,000 loan for your home-based business. After you send your application to the SBA, you get a response stating that the SBA will guarantee your $200,000 loan from a local SBA-approved lender such as a bank. You follow these steps:

1. **You apply for a $200,000 loan** at your local bank, presenting your loan approval and guarantee offer.
2. **The bank, after reviewing your application,** approves your $200,000 loan and advances this amount of money to you in the form of a check or line of credit.
3. **Of the $200,000,** 90 percent of it, or $0.9 \times \$200,000 = \$180,000$ is guaranteed by the United States government. Thus, the bank is "at risk" for just $\$200,000 - \$180,000 = \$20,000$. And because you'll be repaying principal and interest monthly on this loan, the $20,000 will soon be repaid.
4. **The bank turns around and "sells"** the guaranteed $180,000 of your loan to someone like myself. Then the bank has its $180,000 back, which it can lend out to other borrowers, while still collecting on your loan.
5. **Meanwhile, a buyer like myself** gets monthly payments from the bank at an interest rate higher than I could get elsewhere. And if the borrower fails to repay the loan in full, the U.S. government will make good on any missing money within sixty days after the borrower's default (failure to repay). Besides, I have the fun of knowing that I'm helping a small business and the government make our great capitalistic system work better! To me, I might as well put my money to such use instead of letting it sit idly in some bank or money market account earning pennies in interest.

The key to an SBA loan is a well-prepared application for a home-based business that's useful to the economy. And if you can find a loan buyer, your chances of getting the loan you seek are much improved.

Don't Forget the "Little FHA"

Another branch of our great government, the Farmers Home Administration (often called the "little FHA"), makes many loans outside agricultural business. You might be able to obtain such a loan if you have a home-based business that will help people in a farming area. These loans are in good U.S. dollars and are just as powerful as any other type of loan.

Because the Farmers Home Administration (FmHA) is less well-known than the SBA, it is often easier to obtain a loan from the FmHA. You must, of course, qualify for the loan, and it must meet FmHA requirements. To get the latest requirements and loan ranges, call the FmHA in your area. Or write them if you prefer. Again, the FmHA is listed in the colored pages of your local phone book. Follow the same procedure as detailed above for SBA loans, remembering that the FmHA works in agricultural areas instead of general business area.

Get Your Loan Now

There *is* money—millions and millions of dollars—available for you in the form of many different types of loans for your home-based business. And this money—OPM—is very powerful because it can help:

- **Save time** in starting or buying a home-based business.
- **Get you** instant recognition by suppliers you work with.
- **Give you** negotiating power you don't have when money is scarce.
- **Put you** on the road to home-based wealth quickly and easily.

As I said earlier, thousands of my readers write me and tell me what they've done. This reader wrote:

> "I'm so glad I bought your book. It must have been destiny that I chose this one. Your instructions alone helped my partner acquire a line of credit of $10,000 from a bank that turned him down two weeks earlier."

To show readers the power of borrowed money, I've loaned them thousands of dollars through my company, IWS, Inc. And in the more than twenty years I've been making these loans, *every* reader has repaid in full! The reason why these reader–borrowers repaid in full is because the money they borrowed was so powerful they were able to pay off their loans out of their home-based business or real estate profits.

You now know more about borrowing than when you started this chapter. And you're ready to get your loan—*now!* Follow the steps given here. Just remember to be businesslike in all dealings with lenders. Remember: You will *never* go wrong in being businesslike—it can't hurt you! And if all else fails, remember that you have a friend in Ty Hicks. Call, fax, or write, and I'll try to help. Go get that loan *now!*

And in the event you really don't need money for your business, here are a number of ways to make money from money—at home.

Ten Ways to Make Money from Money

You *can* make money from money—at home! Here are ten good ways, with their earnings potential, for you to make money from money—in the convenience of your own home. All you need are a phone, a mailing address, a desk or table to write on, and a typewriter. With these you can:

1. **Become a financial (money) broker** and find loans for companies and individuals. *Earnings potential* can reach $100,000 per year for finding company loans.
2. **Become a factor finder/broker** and get loans for firms doing work with strong-credit companies, colleges, cities, states, or the federal government. *Earnings potential* can be in the $100,000 per year range.
3. **Cash people out of mortgages** they're holding by finding buyers for the mortgages. You earn a fee for bringing the buyer and seller together. *Earnings potential* can range up to $75,000 per year.
4. **Help professionals get loans**—doctors, dentists, or other health personnel, for example. Or specialize in engineers, lawyers, accountants, etc. *Earnings potential* can reach $75,000 per year.
5. **Find mortgages for sale and sell them.** You are a middle person, acting as a finder/seller without putting up any cash of your own, except for ads and phone calls. *Earnings potential* can go to $150,000 per year.

6. **Be a grant consultant or guide** to help organizations and individuals obtain grants for a variety of worthwhile purposes. *Earnings potential* can reach $100,000 per year.

7. **Guide small companies into going public** and earn a fee based on the amount of money raised. With the greater activity in IPOs (initial public offerings) there are plenty of businesses around. *Earnings potential* can be in the $500,000 a year range.

8. **Get financing for consumer items**—autos, home appliances, boats, personal aircraft, etc. *Earnings potential* is $100,000 per year once you're established.

9. **Find collateral;** enhance (improve) a borrower's loan collateral for a fee. The official term for this is *collateral enhancement* and it has an important place in the world of money today. *Earnings potential* is $150,000 per year.

10. **Specialize in international finance** for companies all over the world. You get loans, government funding, and other financing for small and large corporations. This work takes experience; language skills are also a big help. *Earnings potential* can range up to $1 million per year for highly successful operators in this field.

There you have ten great home-based businesses in which you can make money from money. Take your pick—I'll help you in every way I can—if you're a subscriber to one of my newsletters.

CHAPTER 12

Run Your Home Business for Highest Profits and Longest Vacations

Your home-based business can put more money in your bank than any paycheck you're ever likely to get. What's more, you will be so free of money worries that you'll "soar like a bird" in your new-found freedom.

I wish you could spend a day with me visiting BWBs I know to see the effects of financial freedom provided by a home-based business. You'd be delighted—I'm sure. And your first question might be: "How can I do the same for myself?"

Why would you ask such a question? Because I would show you—in just a few hours—the results of a home-based business for these BWBs. For most of them you'd see that some—or all—of these BWBs have:

- **A beautiful home** in the best area of town.
- **A magnificent boat** (sail or power) in spotless condition.
- **Brand-new cars** in tip-top shape and running order.
- **A debt-free financial situation**—no mortgages or loans.
- **A happy family** enjoying life fully with no money worries.
- **Satisfied customers** who buy and buy—again and again.

You *can* do the same for yourself once you start your home-based business—and then run it sensibly to earn the highest profit possible.

Eleven Sure Steps to Home-Based Wealth

To ensure the growth and prosperity of your home-based business, take these easy, low-cost steps:

1. **Set income goals for your business** based on your ideas of the sales you can make each week, month, and year. Make these "stretch" income goals that make you strive to achieve them, giving greater growth to your business.
2. **Watch every penny of spending** you do for the business. Don't over-spend to buy equipment for your business. Instead, lease the equipment (with an option to buy) when you're first starting. Putting large amounts of money into equipment (such as photocopying machines, printing presses, mailing meters, and fax machines) takes cash away from your operating funds. Result? You feel strapped (and probably are) for cash. This colors your whole outlook, making you feel poor. Such an outlook isn't good for you, or your business. So, *lease, don't buy— at the start.*
3. **Keep a daily, weekly, or monthly income record.** You need such a record for tax purposes anyway. But if you do as I suggest, you'll use your income record as a control for your:

   - **Advertising spending**—when your income record shows that your sales are down, you'll advertise more to improve sales.
   - **Scheduling other expenses**—you'll delay buying general supplies until you have the cash to pay for them.
   - **Hiring part-timers**—you'll do without such help until you have the money to pay them for the work they do.

4. **Get good accounting advice from a CPA**—a certified public accountant. This will keep you up-to-date on all your tax filings and payments. It's easy to forget needed payments and wind up with penalties and all sorts of worry. So save money and reduce your worry—use a CPA. To help yourself understand the tax cycle better, prepare a simple tax calendar on a single sheet of paper showing the twelve months of the year and each tax return or payment due in that month. Thus, you'll have entries for estimated tax payments, 1099 filings, Schedule C filings,

etc. Hang this sheet over your desk and look at it every day. Then you won't miss a single tax deadline! Remember: Taxes are always with us. If you're in business, you must pay your taxes on time—and in full.

5. **Have a competent attorney available for advice.** We hope you don't have any legal problems in your business. You won't have many—if you follow the steps in this chapter. But in case you do have a problem, your attorney can advise you how to get out of it—quickly and easily.

6. **Make each day as productive as possible.** In your own business, you're the person who's in charge; you're the person who makes the sales; you're the person who makes the difference between success and failure. So you must make each day as productive as possible—if you expect your business to grow and prosper. Do this by:

   • **Answering** your mail (both conventional and electronic) and phone/fax calls quickly and reliably. Think how happy you are when an important person in your life returns your phone call. You make someone else just as happy when you return his or her phone call. What's more, it's good for business!

   • **Doing** what must be done NOW, instead of delaying or putting off important work or decisions.

   • **Improving** your output and relations with customers every time you deal with either.

   • **Trying**—every moment of the day—to increase your income from your business. Remember: The goal of every for-profit business is to earn the maximum income possible!

7. **Work the needed hours** to satisfy customer needs and wishes. Your customers may be demanding and lacking understanding of the problems of running a business. That's part of having your own home-based business and enjoying the rewards from it. Try to give every customer what he or she wants. You'll see the rewards in your business checking account. And that—after all—is why you're in business anyway!

8. **Add new products on a planned basis.** Don't let your business wither! New products add excitement and income to your business. So look for, find, and introduce new

products on a regular basis. You'll see the results in your sales income as it rises sky high!

9. **Keep improving your relations with your customers** by avoiding fights and other disagreements. The more friends you have amongst your customers, the stronger your business will be. Today is the era of "customer bonding," "relationship marketing," and serving customers on their terms instead of your terms! Look at the lifetime value of a typical customer and you'll see that it's really worth being pleasant and helpful to every one of your customers! Today's customers make many of their buying decisions based on their perception of you, your company, your level of service, the speed with which you answer the phone, whether you return phone calls, etc. The better you treat your customers, the better they'll treat you—by sending money into your bank account.

10. **Keep up-to-date with the latest developments in marketing** and customer relations. You're working in the era of selling on the Internet using cybermarketing. If you don't keep up with developments your competitors will leave you behind in the dust. So pay attention to every advance and see how you can use it to increase your sales revenue.

11. **Market to your strengths.** If you see one group or one area of the country or world in which your sales are strong, push to develop that outlet to the fullest. Such a push can build your business to levels you never thought possible. Keep an eye out for the "easy sales"—those that come quickly with little work. Then go after more of these sales—by mail, face-to-face, telemarketing, Internet, or catalog. Your business will boom. Just remember that Ty Hicks told you how to do it!

More Than 200 Quick and Sure Ways to Get Rich in Your Home-Based Business

Throughout this book you've been given many ideas for lucrative home-based businesses. But as my reader, I want you to be happy because you received more than you expected when you started to read this book. So here are more than 200 great home businesses you can start and succeed in.

To give you the maximum number of businesses in the space available we use some abbreviations to make your reading quicker. Here they are:

For Successful Sales Methods:
M = Mail-order/direct-mail sales
F = Face-to-face sales
T = Telemarketing sales
I = Internet sales/cybermarketing
C = Catalog sales

For Business Equipment You'll Need:
D = Desk
t = Telephone
f = Fax machine
PC = Personal computer

For Startup Time:
S = Short (4 weeks or less)
L = Long (more than 4 weeks)

For Startup Cost:
U = Under $1,000
O = Over $1,000

Now here's your list. I'm almost certain you'll find a golden home-based business in it for yourself. If you can't, give me a call and I'll try to guide your thinking into the right kind of business for you! My business phone number is (516) 766-5850; my business fax number is (516) 766-5919.

Products	Successful Sales Methods	Equipment You'll Use	Startup Time/Cost
1. Accessories for aviators, yachtsmen, drivers	F, M, C	D, t	L/O
2. Aircraft equipment	F, M, C	D, f, PC, t	L/O

(continued)

Products	Successful Sales Methods	Equipment You'll Use	Startup Time/Cost
3. American Indian arts and crafts	F, M, C	D, t	L/U
4. Artist supplies and instructions	F, M	D, t	L/U
5. Astrological charts	F, M	D, f, t	S/U
6. Audio compact discs	F, M, C	D, f, t, PC	L/U
7. Auto parts	F, M, C	D, f, t, PC	L/O
8. Auto tools	F, M	D, t, f	L/U
9. Boating supplies	F, M, T, C	D, t, f	L/O
10. Body-slimming products	F, I, M, T	D, t, f	S/U
11. Books of all types	I, M, T, C	D, t, f	S/U
12. Candles of all types	F, I, M	D, t, f	S/U
13. Chocolates and other candies	I, M, T	D, t, f	S/U
14. Clothing and gear for hunters	F, I, M, C	D, t, f	S/O
15. Clothing of all types	F, I, M	D, t, f	S/U
16. Collectibles	F, I, M	D, t, f	S/U
17. Commercial software products	F, I, M, T	D, t, f, PC	S/U
18. Computers	F, I, M, T, C	D, t, f, PC	L/O
19. Contact lenses	F, M	D, t, f, PC	S/U
20. Cooking utensils, containers, etc.	F, I, M, T	D, t, f	S/U
21. Cosmetics and skincare products	F, I, M	D, t, f	L/U
22. Crime-prevention devices	F, I, M	D, t, f	L/O
23. Customized balloons and arrangements	F, M	D, t, f	S/U
24. Decorations for home/office	F, I, M, T, C	D, t, f	S/U
25. Diet and fitness information	F, I, M	D, t, f, PC	S/U
26. Dolls, especially handmade	F, I, M, T	D, t, f	S/U

Products	Successful Sales Methods	Equipment You'll Use	Startup Time/Cost
27. Educational courses	F, I, M, T, C	D, t, f	L/U
28. Electronic equipment	F, I, M	D, t, f, PC	L/O
29. Electronic greeting cards	F, I, M	D, t, f, PC	S/U
30. Exercise equipment	F, I, M	D, t, f, PC	L/O
31. Exotic animals, e.g., ostrich, llama, ferret	F	D, t, f	L/O
32. Exotic beers	F, M	D, t, f	S/U
33. Fax machines	F, I, M, T, C	D, t, f	S/U
34. Fine lace for curtains, dresses, etc.	F, I, M	D, t, f	S/U
35. Fishing equipment	F, I, M, C	D, t, f	L/U
36. Flags of all kinds	F, I, M, T	D, t, f	L/U
37. Flowers of all types	F, I, M, T	D, t, f	S/U
38. Flying clothes for pilots	F, M, C	D, t, f	L/O
39. Frozen fish	F, M	D, t, f	S/U
40. Frozen lobsters	F, M	D, t, f	S/U
41. Furniture	F, I, M, T	D, t, f	L/O
42. Gadgets for home, hobby, or business	F, I, M, T, C	D, t, f	L/U
43. Gambling equipment	F, M	D, t, f	L/O
44. Gifts/novelties associated with a particular country	F, I, M	D, t, f	L/U
45. Gourmet coffees and teas	F, I, M, T	D, t, f	S/U
46. Gourmet mozzarella, olive oil, pastas	F, I, M, T	D, t, f	S/U
47. Guides to the Internet, subject-specific	F, M, I	D, t, f, PC	L/U
48. Guides to using the Internet	F, I, M, C	D, t, f, PC	L/U
49. Guns, rifles, and supplies	F, I, C	D, t, f, PC	L/O
50. Gym outfits, leotards, jerseys	F, I, M, T	D, t, f	L/U

(continued)

Products	Successful Sales Methods	Equipment You'll Use	Startup Time/Cost
51. Health foods	F, I, M, T, C	D, t, f	L/U
52. Herbs	F, I, M	D, t, f	L/U
53. Home and garden tools and supplies	F, I, M, T	D, t, f	L/O
54. Home brewing kits, instructions	F, I, M	D, t, f	L/U
55. Home health tests	F, I, M, T	D, t, f	L/U
56. Home security and privacy products	F, I, M, T	D, t, f	L/O
57. Horse- and dog-racing publications	F, I, M	D, t, f	S/U
58. House plans	F, I, M, C	D, t, f	L/U
59. Hunting supplies	F, I, C	D, t, f	L/O
60. Ice creams and sherbets	F, I, M, T	D, t, f	S/U
61. Imported specialty cheeses	F, I, M	D, t, f	L/U
62. Incense	F, M	D, t, f	S/U
63. Intelligence-gathering equipment	F, M	D, t, f, PC	L/O
64. Internet advertising	F, I, M, F	D, t, f, PC	L/U
65. Jogging clothes	F, I, M, T	D, t, f	L/U
66. Legal guides and kits	F, I, M, T	D, t, f, PC	L/U
67. Low-maintenance, live indoor and outdoor plants	F, I, M, T	D, t, f	L/U
68. Magazines	F, I, M, T	D, t, f	L/U
69. Market research reports	F, I, M, T, C	D, t, f, PC	L/O
70. Military figurines and models	F, I, M, T, C	D, t, f	S/U
71. Miniature lighthouses	F, I, M, T	D, t, f	S/U
72. Model plans	F, I, M, C	D, t, f	S/U
73. New Age products	F, I, M	D, t, f	L/U
74. New and used airplanes	F, M, C	D, t, f, PC	L/O
75. Newsletters	M, I, T	D, t, f, PC	L/U
76. Nuts	F, I, M	D, t, f	S/U
77. Paints and varnishes	F, I, M	D, t, f	S/U

PRODUCTS	SUCCESSFUL SALES METHODS	EQUIPMENT YOU'LL USE	STARTUP TIME/COST
78. Patterns for clothing	F, I, M, C	D, t, f	S/U
79. Patterns used in making toys	F, I, M	D, t, f, PC	S/U
80. Personalized key chains and other gifts for car buffs and others	F, I, M	D, t, f	S/U
81. Personalized picture holders for pocket and purse	F, I, M	D, t, f	S/U
82. Pet supplies and foods	F, I, M	D, t, f	S/U
83. Popcorn in unusual flavors and colors	F	D, t, f	S/U
84. Products used in white-water rafting and hiking	F, I, M	D, t, f	L/U
85. Professional ballooning gear	F, I, M, C	D, t, f	L/O
86. Recipes	F, I, M, T	D, t, f	S/U
87. Religious items— jewelry, figures, books	F, I, M, C	D, t, f	L/U
88. Remote-controlled model airplanes, cars, etc.	F, I, M, C	D, t, f	L/U
89. Scale-model replicas of historic items	F, I, M, T	D, t, f	L/U
90. School uniforms for athletics, band, etc.	F, I, M, T	D, t, f	L/O
91. Seeds for ornamental and medicinal plants	F, I, M	D, t, f, PC	L/U
92. Self-defense products	F, I, M, T	D, t, f	L/U
93. Shareware and freeware software collections	F, I, M, T	D, t, f, PC	L/U
94. Sleep products and information	F, I, M	D, t, f	L/U
95. Southwestern wear	F, I, M	D, t, f	L/U

(continued)

Products	Successful Sales Methods	Equipment You'll Use	Startup Time/Cost
96. Space-saving racks and shelving for home/office	F, I, M, T	D, t, f	S/U
97. Special organic soaps, personal care items	F, I, M	D, t, f, PC	S/U
98. Specialized calculators	F, I, M, C	D, t, f	L/U
99. Specialized Internet search services	F, I, M	D, t, f, PC	L/U
100. Sporting events on tape	F, I, M, T	D, t, f	L/U
101. Sports equipment	F, I, M, C	D, t, f	L/O
102. Stationery, customized and stock	F, I, M, T	D, t, f	S/U
103. Steaks, prepared meats	F, I, M, T	D, t, f	L/U
104. Stock photography for graphic artists	F, I, M, T	D, t, f, PC	L/U
105. T-shirt design and sales	F, I, M	D, t, f, PC	S/U
106. Teddy bears (handcrafted)	F, I, M	D, t, f	L/U
107. Telephones, cellular phones	F, I, M, T, C	D, t, f, PC	L/U
108. Travel guides	F, I, M, T, C	D, t, f, PC	L/U
109. Turquoise arts and crafts	F, I, M	D, t, f	L/U
110. Vegetarian foods	F, I, M	D, t, f	L/U
111. Videos of all types	F, I, M, T	D, t, f	L/U
112. Vitamins	F, I, M, T	D, t, f, PC	L/U
113. Wines (high quality, rare)	F, M	D, t, f	L/U
114. Wood and coal stoves	F, I, M, T	D, t, f	L/U
115. World Wide Web home pages	I, M	D, t, f	L/U

SERVICES	SUCCESSFUL SALES METHODS	EQUIPMENT YOU'LL USE	STARTUP TIME/COST
1. 900-number rental	F, T	D, t	L/O
2. Acting lessons	F, M	D, t, f	L/O
3. Air cleaning, deodorizing, and testing service	F, M	D, t	L/U
4. Assist businesses with getting/using merchant accounts	F, M, T	D, t	L/U
5. Athletic talent scout	F, I	D, t, f	L/U
6. Automobile detailer	F, M, T	D, t, f	L/O
7. Ballet teacher	F, M	D, t, f	L/U
8. Beauty makeovers and products	F, M, T	D, t, f	L/O
9. Become a real estate salesperson for your area	F, I, M, T	D, t, f	S/U
10. Become a "suspect artist" for police investigators	F, I, M, T	D, t, f	S/U
11. Bicycle repair business	F, M	t	S/U
12. Boat oar maker	F, I	t, f	S/U
13. Book repairer	F, I, M	D, t, f	S/U
14. Bonbon dipper	F, M	t	S/U
15. Bow maker (gift wrapping)	F, I, M,T	D, t, f	S/U
16. Bowling ball engraver	F, I, M	D, t, f	S/U
17. Chauffeur	I, M, T	D, t, f	S/U
18. Charter-boat operator	F, T	D, t	L/O
19. Clothing designer	F, I, M	D, t, f	S/O
20. Computer consultant, hardware or software	F, I, M	D, t, f	S/U
21. Computer programmer	F, I, M	D, t, f	S/U
22. Credit repair advisor	F, I, M, T	D, t, f, PC	S/U
23. Data entry from home	F, I, M, T	D, t, f, PC	S/U
24. Database designer	F, I, M, T	D, t, f, PC	L/U
25. Dating service provider	F, I, M, T	D, t, f, PC	L/O

(continued)

Services	Successful Sales Methods	Equipment You'll Use	Startup Time/Cost
26. Desktop publisher	F, M	D, t, f, PC	S/U
27. Digital artist	F, I, M, T	D, t, f	S/U
28. Dog walker and/or pet sitter	F, I, M	D, t, f	L/U
29. Family tree researcher	F, I, M	D, t, f	L/O
30. Fashion consultant	F, M	D, t	S/U
31. Fiction/nonfiction/ poetry writing instructor	F, M	D, t, f	S/U
32. Financial broker/ business advisor	F, I, M, T	D, t, f	S/U
33. Fitness trainer	F, I, M	D, t, f, PC	S/U
34. Food preparation/ catering from home	F, I, M, T	D, t, f	S/U
35. Foreclosure avoidance advisor	F, I, M, T	D, t, f	L/U
36. Fundraiser/research for nonprofit groups	F, I, M	D, t, f, PC	L/O
37. Furniture refinishing	F, I, M	D, t, f, PC	S/U
38. Get grants for people and companies	F, I, M	D, t, f, PC	L/O
39. Give cooking, sewing, or other lessons	F	D, t, f	L/O
40. Grow gourmet mushrooms	F, M	D, t, f	S/U
41. Hairpiece stylist	F, I, M	D, t, f	S/U
42. Home appliance and power tool repair	F, I, M, T	D, t, f	S/U
43. Home energy consultant	F, I, M	D, t, f	L/U
44. Home mortgage reduction service	F, I, M	D, t, f	S/U
45. Homemade ice cream maker	F, M	D, t	S/U
46. HTML (hypertext markup language) checker	F, I, M, T	D, t, f, PC	S/U
47. Hydroponic gardening	F, I, M	D, t, f	L/U

SERVICES	SUCCESSFUL SALES METHODS	EQUIPMENT YOU'LL USE	STARTUP TIME/COST
48. Import/export assistance	F, I, M, T	D, t, f	L/U
49. Income tax preparation	F, I, M, T	D, t, f	S/U
50. Instruct people in landscape design	F, M	D, t, f	L/O
51. Investment advice	F, M	D, t, f	S/U
52. Lawn and garden consultant	F, I, M, T	D, f, t	S/U
53. Locksmithing	F, M	D, t, f	S/U
54. Manage apartments, collect rents, get repairs done, etc.	F, I, M, T	D, t, f	L/O
55. Mortgage cash-out guidance	F, I, M, T	D, t, f	L/U
56. Moving assistance— address changes, van rental, etc.	F, M, T	D, t, f	S/U
57. News and magazine article clipping service	F, M	D, t, f	L/O
58. Newsletter editor	F, M, I	D, t, f, PC	S/U
59. Obtaining credit cards	F, I, M, T	D, t, f	S/U
60. Online catalog consultant	F, I, M, T	D, f, t, PC	S/U
61. Operate a bed and breakfast inn	F, I, M, T	D, t, f	S/U
62. People and business finder	F, M, I	D, t, f, PC	L/U
63. Personalized gifts and vanity items finder	F, I, M	D, t, f, PC	L/U
64. Philatelic (stamp collecting) consultant	F, I, M	D, t, f	S/U
65. Photographer	F, I	D, t, f, PC	L/O
66. Picture framing	F, I, M, T	D, t, f	L/U
67. Pool-cleaning and upkeep	F, I, M, T	D, f, t	L/U

(continued)

Services	Successful Sales Methods	Equipment You'll Use	Startup Time/Cost
68. Prepare and pack appetizers for parties	F, I, M	D, t, f	L/U
69. Prepare résumés for a fee	F, I, M, T	D, t, f	L/O
70. Prepare smoked meats, fish, and other foods for sale	F, I, M, T	t	S/U
71. Private investigator	F, I, M, T	D, t, f, PC	L/U
72. Promote and/or organize arts and craft shows	F, I, M	D, t, f	L/U
73. Provide mailing & packing services	F, I, M, T	D, t, f	L/U
74. Provide silver and gold and jewelry cleaner	F, I, M, T	D, t, f	L/O
75. Provide training programs by mail, e-mail, or on the Web	F, I, M, T	D, t, f	S/U
76. Raise money for businesses	F, I, M	D, t, f	S/U
77. Raise money for religious or fraternal organizations for a fee	F, I, M	D, t, f	L/U
78. Reminder service for birthdays, anniversaries, license renewals	F, I	D, t, f	L/O
79. Repair jewelry, shoes, clothing for people in your area	F, I, M, T	D, t, f	S/U
80. Run a print or online subscription information service	F, I, M	D, t, f	L/U
81. Run a school at home for children	F, I, M	D, t, f	L/U
82. Sell products by mail order/direct mail	F, M	D, t, f	S/U
83. Shop for others, for a fee, as a shopping specialist	F, M	D, t, f, PC	L/O

Services	Successful Sales Methods	Equipment You'll Use	Startup Time/Cost
84. Start a BBS or Internet service for hobbyists	F, I, M, F	D, t, f, PC	L/U
85. Tailor/seamstress	F, I, M	D, t	S/U
86. Teach locksmithing by mail	F, I, M, T	D, t, f	L/U
87. Teach reading	F, I, M, T	D, t, f, PC	L/U
88. Teach real estate financing techniques	F, I, M, T	D, t, f	L/U
89. Telephone answering service at home	F, I, M, T	D, t, f	L/U
90. Training dogs for the blind	F, I, M, T	D, t, f, PC	L/O
91. Travel services, including research into foreign laws and customs	F, I, M, T	D, t, f	S/U
92. Tutor	F, I, M, T	D, t, f	L/U
93. Typing service for local businesses, authors, students, etc.	F, I, M	D, t, f	S/U
94. Venture capital raising	F, I, M	D, t, f	L/U
95. Wake-up or date-reminder service	F, M	D, t, f, PC	L/O
96. Web site to help people with their insurance needs	M, I, T	D, t, f, PC	L/U
97. Wild animal trapper	F, I, M	D, t, f	S/U
98. Work-at-home advice	F, I, M	D, t, f	S/U
99. World Wide Web site designer	F, I, M	D, t, f	S/U
100. Write short articles for newspapers and newsletters	F, I, M	D, t, f, PC	S/U

PROFIT-BUILDING TOOLS FROM TYLER HICKS'S INTERNATIONAL WEALTH SUCCESS LIBRARY

As THE PUBLISHER of the famous *International Wealth Success* newsletter, Ty Hicks has put together a remarkable library of dynamic books, each geared to help the opportunity-seeking individual—the kind of person who is ready and eager to achieve the financial freedom that comes from being a successful entrepreneur. Financial experts agree that only those who own their own businesses or invest their money wisely can truly control their future wealth. And yet, far too many who start a business or an investment program of their own do not have the kind of information that can make the difference between success and failure.

Here, then, is a list of publications hand-picked by Ty Hicks, written especially to give you, the enterprising wealth builder, the critical edge that belongs solely to those who have the *inside* track. So take advantage of this unique opportunity to order this confidential information. (These books are *not* available in bookstores.) Choose the publications that can help you the most and send the order form with your remittance. Your order will be processed as quickly as possible to expedite your success. (Please note: If, when placing an order, you prefer not to cut out the form, simply photocopy the order page and send in the duplicate.)

IWS-1   **BUSINESS CAPITAL SOURCES.** Lists more than 1,500 lenders of various types—banks, insurance companies, commercial finance firms, factors, leasing firms, overseas lenders, venture capital firms, mortgage companies, and others. $15. 150 pgs.

IWS-2   ***SMALL BUSINESS INVESTMENT COMPANY DIRECTORY AND HAND-BOOK.*** Lists more than 400 small business investment companies that invest in small businesses to help them prosper. Also gives tips on financial management in businesses. $15. 135 pgs.

IWS-3   ***WORLDWIDE RICHES OPPORTUNITIES,*** Vol. 1. Lists more than 2,500 overseas firms seeking products to import. Gives name of product(s) sought, or service(s) sought, and other important data needed by exporters and importers. $25. 283 pgs.

IWS-4   ***WORLDWIDE RICHES OPPORTUNITIES,*** Vol. 2. Lists more than 2,500 overseas firms selling products to import. (Does NOT duplicate Volume 1.) Lists loan sources for some exporters in England. $25. 223 pgs.

IWS-5   ***HOW TO PREPARE AND PROCESS EXPORT-IMPORT DOCUMENTS.*** Gives data and documents for exporters and importers, including licenses, declarations, free-trade zones abroad, bills of lading, custom duty rulings. $25. 170 pgs.

IWS-6   ***SUPPLEMENT TO HOW TO BORROW YOUR WAY TO REAL ESTATE RICHES.*** Using government sources compiled by Ty Hicks, lists numerous mortgage loans and guarantees, loan purposes, amounts, terms, financing charge, types of structures financed, loan-value ratio, special factors. $15. 87 pgs.

IWS-7   ***THE RADICAL NEW ROAD TO WEALTH*** by A. David Silver. Covers criteria for success, raising venture capital, steps in conceiving a new firm, the business plan, how much do you have to give up, economic justification. $15. 128 pgs.

IWS-8   ***60-DAY FULLY FINANCED FORTUNE*** is a short BUSINESS KIT covering what the business is, how it works, naming the business, interest amortization tables, state securities agencies, typical flyer used to advertise, typical applications. $29.50. 136 pgs.

IWS-9   ***CREDITS AND COLLECTION BUSINESS KIT*** is a 2-book kit covering fundamentals of credit, businesses using credits and collection methods, applications for credit, setting credit limits, Fair Credit Reporting Act, collection percentages, etc. Gives 10 small businesses in this field. $29.50. 147 pgs.

IWS-10   ***MIDEAST AND NORTH AFRICAN BANKS AND FINANCIAL INSTITU-TIONS.*** Lists more than 350 such organizations. Gives name, address, telephone, and telex number for most. $15. 30 pgs.

IWS-11   ***EXPORT MAIL-ORDER.*** Covers deciding on products to export, finding suppliers, locating overseas firms selling exports, form letters, listing of firms serving as export management companies, shipping orders, and more. $17.50. 50 pgs.

IWS-12   ***PRODUCT EXPORT RICHES OPPORTUNITIES.*** Lists over 1,500 firms offering products for export—includes agricultural, auto, aviation, electronic, computers, energy, food, health care, mining, printing, and robotics. $21.50. 219 pgs.

IWS-13 **DIRECTORY OF HIGH-DISCOUNT MERCHANDISE SOURCES.** Lists more than 1,000 sources of products with full name, address, and telephone number for items such as auto products, swings, stuffed toys, puzzles, oils and lubricants, CB radios, and belt buckles. $17.50. 97 pgs.

IWS-14 *HOW TO FINANCE REAL ESTATE INVESTMENTS* by Roger Johnson. Covers basics, the lending environment, value, maximum financing, rental unit groups, buying mobile home parks, and conversions. $18.50. 265 pgs.

IWS-15 *DIRECTORY OF FREIGHT FORWARDERS AND CUSTOM HOUSE BROKERS.* Lists hundreds of these firms throughout the United States which help in the import-export business. $17.50. 106 pgs.

IWS-16 *CAN YOU AFFORD NOT TO BE A MILLIONAIRE?* by Marc Schlecter. Covers international trade, base of operations, stationery, worksheet, starting an overseas company, metric measures, profit structure. $15. 202 pgs.

IWS-17 *HOW TO FIND HIDDEN WEALTH IN LOCAL REAL ESTATE* by R. H. Jorgensen. Covers financial tips, self-education, how to analyze property for renovation, the successful renovator is a "cheapskate," property management, and getting the rents paid. $17.50. 133 pgs.

IWS-18 *HOW TO CREATE YOUR OWN REAL ESTATE FORTUNE* by Jens Nielsen. Covers investment opportunities in real estate, leveraging, depreciation, remodeling your deal, buy- and lease-back, understanding your financing. $17.50. 117 pgs.

IWS-19 *REAL ESTATE SECOND MORTGAGES* by Ty Hicks. Covers second mortgages, how a second mortgage finder works, naming the business, registering the firm, running ads, expanding the business, and limited partnerships. $17.50. 100 pgs.

IWS-20 *GUIDE TO BUSINESS AND REAL ESTATE LOAN SOURCES.* Lists hundreds of business and real estate lenders, giving their lending data in very brief form. $25. 201 pgs.

IWS-21 *DIRECTORY OF 2,500 ACTIVE REAL ESTATE LENDERS.* Lists 2,500 names and addresses of direct lenders or sources of information on possible lenders for real estate. $25. 197 pgs.

IWS-22 *IDEAS FOR FINDING BUSINESS AND REAL ESTATE CAPITAL TODAY.* Covers raising public money, real estate financing, borrowing methods, government loan sources, and venture money. $24.50. 62 pgs.

IWS-23 *HOW TO BECOME WEALTHY PUBLISHING A NEWSLETTER* by E. J. Mall. Covers who will want your newsletter, planning your newsletter, preparing the first issue, direct mail promotions, keeping the books, building your career. $17.50. 102 pgs.

IWS-24 *NATIONAL DIRECTORY OF MANUFACTURERS' REPRESENTATIVES.* Lists 5,000 mfrs. reps. from all over the United States, both in alphabetical form and state by state; gives markets classifications by SIC. $28.80. 782 pgs., hardcover.

IWS-25 *BUSINESS PLAN KIT.* Shows how to prepare a business plan to raise money for any business. Gives several examples of successful business plans. $29.50. 150 pgs.

IWS-26 **MONEY RAISER'S DIRECTORY OF BANK CREDIT CARD PROGRAMS.** Shows the requirements of each bank listed for obtaining a credit card from the bank. Nearly 1,000 card programs at 500 of the largest U.S. banks are listed. Gives income requirements, job history, specifications, etc. $19.95. 150 pgs.

IWS-27 **GLOBAL COSIGNERS AND MONEY FINDERS ASSOCIATION.** Publicize your need for a cosigner to get a business or real estate loan. Your need is advertised widely under a Code Number so your identity is kept confidential. $50.

IWS-28 **WALL STREET SYNDICATORS.** Lists 250 active brokerage houses who might take your company public. Gives numerous examples of actual, recent, and new stock offerings of startup companies. $15. 36 pgs.

IWS-29 **COMPREHENSIVE LOAN SOURCES FOR BUSINESS AND REAL ESTATE LOANS.** Gives hundreds of lenders' names and addresses and lending guidelines for business and real estate loans of many different types. $25. 136 pgs., 8½ × 11 in.

IWS-30 **DIVERSIFIED LOAN SOURCES FOR BUSINESS AND REAL ESTATE LOANS.** Gives hundreds of lenders' names and addresses and lending guidelines for business and real estate loans of many different types. Does not duplicate IWS-29. $25. 136 pgs., 8½ × 11 in.

IWS-31 **CREDIT POWER REPORTS.** Five helpful reports to improve your credit rating and credit line. Report No. 1: *How to Get a Visa and/or Mastercard Credit Card.* $19.95. 192 pgs., 5 × 8 in. Report No. 2: *How to Increase Your Credit Limits, Plus Sophisticated Credit Power Strategies.* $19.95. 208 pgs., 5 × 8 in. Report No. 3: *How to Repair Your Credit.* $19.95. 256 pgs., 5 × 8 in. Report No. 4: *How to Reduce Your Monthly Payments.* $19.95. 192 pgs., 5 × 8 in. Report No. 5: *How to Wipe Out Your Debts Without Bankruptcy.* $19.95. 152 pgs. Each book is also available on a cassette tape which duplicates the entire content of the report. The tapes are priced at $19.95 each and run 60 minutes. Please specify which tape you want when ordering; the tape title duplicates the report title.

IWS-32 **GOOD MONTHLY INCOME** gives you a way to earn money every month via mail order selling books and kits to people seeking a business of their own. With this plan the money comes to you and you keep a large share of it for yourself. $15. 36 pgs., 8½ × 11 in.

IWS-33 **HOW TO BUY A BUSINESS WITH NO MONEY DOWN** by Jeryn W. Calhoun. Gives step-by-step guidance on how to figure the value of a business; negotiating with the seller; no-money-down strategies; dozens of sample forms to help you buy right; startups vs. existing businesses; rules of thumb for pricing a business; understanding the P & L statement; making an offer that's right for you; financing the business you buy; effective closes when buying; legal considerations for you; closing checklist for any business. 110 pgs., 8½ × 11 in., paperback, $19.50; First Class Shipping $4 extra.

IWS-34 **HOW TO MAKE A FORTUNE AS A LICENSING AGENT** by Tyler G. Hicks. Shows the reader how to earn big fees bringing together one company wanting to license its industrial or entertainment products and another seeking to use these products. Gives examples of typical products licensed, agreements covering the license, plus where to find suitable items to license. 66 pgs., 8½ × 11 in., paperback, $15.00; First Class Shipping $4 extra.

IWS-35   *HOW TO RUN A PROFITABLE CHILD-CARE REFERRAL SERVICE* by William Frederick. Gives a comprehensive coverage of this much-needed business in today's working-mother world. Topics include starting your child-care referral center, assessing your community's child-care needs, recruiting child-care providers, marketing your services, day-to-day operations, child-care resource directory, sample letters, forms, and a prewritten news release. $22.95. 64 pgs.

IWS-36   *SUCCESSFUL FINANCING TECHNIQUES FOR BUSINESS AND REAL ESTATE* by Tyler G. Hicks. This comprehensive book covers how, and where, to get loans for any business; getting venture capital today; finding free-money grants; going public to get money that never need be repaid; making big money in your own business; proven money-making results for real estate; mail-order success secrets; building riches in exporting. $24.95. 96 pgs. Includes three bonus items related to the book's topics.

IWS-37   *HOW TO BE A SECOND MORTGAGE LOAN BROKER* by Richard Brisky. Shows the reader how to make money as a second mortgage loan broker. Covers these important topics—why second mortgages; how to get started; starting on a part-time basis; the money broker/finder business; glossary of real estate and mortgage terms; how to get clients; how to handle loan inquiries; advance fees; commissions; loan presentation; think like a lender; what a difference a point makes; the truth in lending law; the Fair Credit Reporting Act; the Equal Credit Opportunity Act; the Fair Debt Collection Practices Act; how to help financially distressed people when you can't get their loan approved; you will learn many things in dealing with lenders; other prime loan projects; other types of loans; mortgage payment tables; it's almost time to get started; second mortgage money sources; 90 pgs., 8½ × 11 in., paperback, $25; First Class Shipping $4 extra.

IWS-38   *HOW TO START AND FINANCE A BUSINESS THAT WORKS FOR YOU* by Tyler G. Hicks. This big book covers turning your wealth-building dreams into reality; making a business of your own work for you; smart ways to get loans for your business or others; building your wealth in exporting; keys to mail-order business success; making riches in real estate like a professional; great ways to get venture capital today; getting the credit you deserve; how to get money that does not need to be repaid. $24.75. 96 pgs. Includes three bonus items related to the book's topics.

IWS-39   *YOU CAN GET THE MONEY! How to Finance Your Small Business Startup or Expansion* by Robert Highman. Big, useful book covers many topics including: how to borrow $90,000 from a stranger in 5 days; earn $15,000 a month buying and selling assets you don't own; invest $500 to raise $329,000 to make $108,000 in one year; go from near-bankruptcy to $117,000 in credit cards; free advertising for your offer in over 100 trade journals; from zero to 100,000 letters per week in mail order; how to increase your business 62% in 2 years; how 100% was borrowed to buy a building for retirement; raise enough money in 17 hours to buy 3 brand new Cadillacs; includes nearly 1,000 lenders, with over 300 microloan lenders; plus much more. $59.50. 348 pgs.

IWS-40   ***OPTIONS REPORT*** covers real estate options, explaining what an option is, using an option, getting the option, locating properties to option, and how to use options to build your wealth in non-real-estate real estate. $20. 16 pgs., 8½ × 11 in.

NEWSLETTERS

IWSN-1   ***INTERNATIONAL WEALTH SUCCESS.*** Ty Hicks' monthly newsletter published 12 times a year. This 16-page newsletter covers loan and grant sources, real estate opportunities, business opportunities, import-export, mail order, and a variety of other topics on making money in your own business. Every subscriber can run one free classified advertisement of 40 words, or less, each month, covering business or real estate needs or opportunities. The newsletter has a worldwide circulation, giving readers and advertisers very broad coverage. Started in January 1967, the newsletter has been published continuously since that date. $24.00 per year. 16 pgs. plus additional inserts, 8½ × 11 in., monthly.

IWSN-2   ***MONEY WATCH BULLETIN,*** a monthly coverage of 100 or more active lenders for real estate and business purposes. The newsletter gives the lender's name, address, telephone number, lending guidelines, loan ranges, and other helpful information. All lender names were obtained within the last week; the data is therefore right up to date. Lenders' names and addresses are also provided on self-stick labels on an occasional basis. Also covers venture capital and grants. $95.00. 20 pgs., 8½ × 11 in., monthly, 12 times per year.

SUCCESS KITS

K-1   ***FINANCIAL BROKER/FINDER/BUSINESS BROKER/CONSULTANT SUCCESS KIT*** shows YOU how to start your PRIVATE business as a financial broker/finder/business broker/consultant! As a financial broker YOU find money for firms seeking capital and YOU are paid a fee. As a finder YOU are paid a fee for finding things (real estate, raw materials, money, etc.) for people and firms. As a business broker YOU help in the buying or selling of a business—again for a fee. See how to collect BIG fees. Kit includes typical agreement YOU can use, plus four colorful membership cards (each 8 × 10 in.). Only $99.50. 12 Speed-Read books, 485 pgs., 8½ × 11 in., 4 membership cards.

K-2   ***STARTING MILLIONAIRE SUCCESS KIT*** shows YOU how to get started in a number of businesses which might make YOU a millionaire sooner than YOU think! Businesses covered in this big kit include mail order, real estate, export-import, limited partnerships, etc. This big kit includes four colorful membership cards (each 8 × 10 in.). These are

NOT the same ones as in the Financial Broker kit. So ORDER your STARTING MILLIONAIRE KIT now—only $99.50. 12 Speed-Read books, 361 pgs., 8½ × 11 in., 4 membership cards.

K-3   ***FRANCHISE RICHES SUCCESS KIT*** is the only one of its kind in the world (we believe). What this big kit does is show YOU how to collect BIG franchise fees for YOUR business ideas which can help others make money! So instead of paying to use ideas, people PAY YOU to use YOUR ideas! Franchising is one of the biggest businesses in the world today. Why don't YOU get in on the BILLIONS of dollars being grossed in this business today? Send $99.50 for your FRANCHISE KIT now. 7 Speed-Read books, 876 pgs., 6 × 9 & 8½ × 11 in. & 5 × 8 in.

K-4   ***MAIL-ORDER RICHES SUCCESS KIT*** shows YOU how YOU can make a million in mail order/direct mail, using the known and proven methods of the experts. This is a kit which is different (we think) from any other—and BETTER than any other! It gives YOU the experience of known experts who've made millions in their own mail order businesses, or who've shown others how to do that. This big kit also includes the Ty Hicks' book *How I Grossed More Than One Million Dollars in Mail Order/Direct Mail Starting with NO CASH and Less Knowhow.* So send $99.50 TODAY for your MAIL-ORDER SUCCESS KIT. 9 Speed-Read books, 927 pgs., 6 × 9 & 8½ × 11 in.

K-5   ***ZERO CASH SUCCESS TECHNIQUES KIT*** shows YOU how to get started in YOUR own going business or real estate venture with NO CASH! Sound impossible? It really IS possible—as thousands of folks have shown. This big kit, which includes a special book by Ty Hicks on *Zero Cash Takeovers of Business and Real Estate,* also includes a 58-minute cassette tape by Ty on "Small Business Financing." On this tape, Ty talks to YOU! See how YOU can get started in YOUR own business without cash and with few credit checks. To get your ZERO CASH SUCCESS KIT, send $99.50 NOW. 7 Speed-Read books, 876 pgs., 8½ × 11 in. for most, 58-minute cassette tape.

K-6   ***REAL ESTATE RICHES SUCCESS KIT*** shows YOU how to make BIG money in real estate as an income property owner, a mortgage broker, mortgage banker, real estate investment trust operator, mortgage money broker, raw land speculator, and industrial property owner. This is a general kit, covering all these aspects of real estate, plus many, many more. Includes many financing sources for YOUR real estate fortune. But this big kit also covers how to buy real estate for the lowest price (down payments of NO CASH can sometimes be set up), and how to run YOUR real estate for biggest profits. Send $99.50 NOW for your REAL ESTATE SUCCESS KIT. 6 Speed-Read books, 466 pgs., 8½ × 11 in.

K-7   ***BUSINESS BORROWERS COMPLETE SUCCESS KIT*** shows YOU how and where to BORROW money for any business which interests YOU. See how to borrow money like the professionals do! Get YOUR loans faster, easier because YOU know YOUR way around the loan world! This big kit includes many practice forms so YOU can become an expert in preparing acceptable loan applications. Also includes hundreds of loan sources YOU might wish to check for YOUR loans. Send $99.50 NOW for your BUSINESS BORROWERS KIT. 7 Speed-Read books, 596 pgs., 8½ × 11 in.

K-8   ***RAISING MONEY FROM GRANTS AND OTHER SOURCES SUCCESS KIT*** shows YOU how to GET MONEY THAT DOES NOT HAVE TO BE REPAID if YOU do the task for which the money was advanced. This big kit shows YOU how and where to raise money for a skill YOU have which can help others live a better life. And, as an added feature, this big kit shows YOU how to make a fortune as a fund raiser—that great business in which YOU get paid for collecting money for others or for yourself. This kit shows YOU how you can collect money to fund deals YOU set up. To get your GRANTS KIT, send $99.50 NOW. 7 Speed-Read books, 496 pgs., 8½ × 11 in. for most.

K-9   ***FAST FINANCING OF YOUR REAL ESTATE FORTUNE SUCCESS KIT*** shows YOU how to raise money for real estate deals. YOU can move ahead faster if YOU can finance your real estate quickly and easily. This is NOT the same kit as the R.E. RICHES KIT listed above. Instead, the FAST FINANCING KIT concentrates on GETTING THE MONEY YOU NEED for YOUR real estate deals. This big kit gives YOU more than 2,500 sources of real estate money all over the U.S. It also shows YOU how to find deals which return BIG income to YOU but are easier to finance than YOU might think! To get started in FAST FINANCING, send $99.50 today. 7 Speed-Read books, 523 pgs., 8½ × 11 in. for most.

K-10   ***LOANS BY PHONE KIT*** shows YOU how and where to get business, real estate, and personal loans by telephone. With just 32 words and 15 seconds of time YOU can determine if a lender is interested in the loan you seek for yourself or for someone who is your client—if you're working as a loan broker or finder. This kit gives you hundreds of telephone lenders. About half have 800 phone numbers, meaning that your call is free of long-distance charges. Necessary agreement forms are also included. This blockbuster kit has more than 150 pgs. 8½ × 11 in. Send $100 now and get started in one hour.

K-11   ***LOANS BY MAIL KIT*** shows YOU how and where to get business, real estate, and personal loans for yourself and others by mail. Lists hundreds of lenders who loan by mail. No need to appear in person—just fill out the loan application and send it in by mail. Many of these lenders give unsecured signature loans to qualified applicants. Use this kit to get a loan by mail yourself. Or become a loan broker and use the kit to get started. Unsecured signature loans by mail can go as high as $50,000 and this kit lists such lenders. The kit has more than 150 pgs. 8½ × 11 in. Send $100 now to get started in just a few minutes.

K-12   ***REAL ESTATE LOAN GETTERS SERVICE KIT*** shows the user how to get real estate loans for either a client or the user. Lists hundreds of active real estate lenders seeking first and junior mortgage loans for a variety of property types. Loan amounts range from a few thousand dollars to many millions, depending on the property, its location, and value. Presents typical application and agreement forms for use in securing real estate loans. *No* license is required to obtain such loans for oneself or others. Kit contains more than 150 pages., 8½ × 11 in. Send $100 now to get started.

K-13   ***CASH CREDIT RICHES SYSTEM KIT*** shows the user three ways to make money from credit cards: (1) as a merchant account, (2) helping others get credit cards of their choice, and (3) getting loans through lines of credit offered to credit card holders. Some people handling merchant account orders report an income as high as $10,000 a day. While this kit does not, and will not, guarantee such an income level, it *does* show the user how to get started making money from credit cards easily and quickly. The kit has more than 150 pgs., 8½ × 11 in. Send $100 now to get started soon.

K-14   ***PROFESSIONAL PRACTICE BUILDERS KIT*** shows YOU how to make up to $1,000 a week part time, over $5,000 a week full time, according to the author, Dr. Alan Weisman. What YOU do is show professionals—such as doctors, dentists, architects, accountants, lawyers—how to bring more clients into the office and thereby increase their income. Step-by-step procedure gets you started. Provides forms, sample letters, brochures, and fliers YOU can use to get an income flowing into your bank in less than one week. The kit has more than 150 pgs., 8½ × 11 in. Send $100 now! Start within just a few hours in your local area.

K-15   ***VENTURE CAPITAL MILLIONS KITS.*** Shows how to raise venture capital for yourself or for others. Gives steps for preparing an Executive Summary, business plan, etc. You can use the kit to earn large fees raising money for new or established firms. $100. 200 pgs.

K-16   ***GUARANTEED LOAN MONEY.*** Shows how to get loans of all types—unsecured signature, business, real estate, etc.—when your credit is not the strongest. Gives full directions on getting cosigners, comakers, and guarantors. $100. 250 pgs.

K-17   ***IMPORT-EXPORT RICHES KIT*** shows you how to get rich in import-export in today's product-hungry world. This big kit takes you from your first day in the business to great success. It gives you 5,000 products wanted by overseas firms, the name and address of each firm, procedures for preparing export-import documents, how to correspond in four different languages with complete sentences and letters, names and addresses of freight forwarders you can use, plus much more. Includes more than 6 books of over 1,000 pages of useful information. $99.50.

K-18   ***PHONE-IN/MAIL-IN GRANTS KIT.*** This concise kit shows the reader how to jump on the grants bandwagon and get small or large money grants quickly and easily. Gives typical grant proposals and shows how to write each so you win the grant you seek. Takes the reader by the hand and shows how to make telephone calls to grantors to find if they're interested in your grant request. You are given the actual words to use in your call and in your proposal. Also includes a list of foundations that might consider your grant application. $100. 200 pgs., 8½ × 11 in.

K-19   ***MEGA MONEY METHODS*** covers the raising of large amounts of money—multimillions and up—for business and real estate projects of all types. Shows how to prepare loan packages for very large loans, where to get financing for such loans, what fees to charge after the loan is obtained, plus much more. Using this kit, the BWB should be able to prepare effective loan requests for large amounts of money for suitable projects. The kit also gives the user a list of offshore lenders for big projects. $100. 200 pgs., 8½ × 11 in.

K-20   *FORECLOSURES AND OTHER DISTRESSED PROPERTY SALES* shows how and where to make money from foreclosures, trustee sales, IRS sales, bankruptcies, and sheriff sales of real estate. The kit contains six cassette tapes plus a workbook containing many of the forms you need in foreclosure and trustee sales. Addresses of various agencies handling such sales are also given. $51.95. 80 pgs. and 6 cassette tapes, 8½ × 11 in.

K-21   *SMALL BUSINESS LOAN PROGRAM* is designed to obtain loans for small and minority-owned businesses doing work for government agencies, large corporations, hospitals, universities, and similar organizations. The small business loan program pays up to 80 percent on accounts receivable within 48 hours to manufacturers, distributors, janitorial services, building contractors, etc. Startups acceptable. You earn a good commission getting these loans funded, and receive an ongoing payment when the company places future accounts receivable with the lender. $100. 200 pgs., 8½ × 11 in.

K-22   *PHONE-IN MINI-LEASE PROGRAM* helps you earn commissions getting leases for a variety of business equipment—personal computers, copy machines, typewriters, laser printers, telephone systems, office furniture, satellite antennas, store fixtures, etc. You earn direct commissions of 3 percent to 10 percent of the cost of the equipment up to $10,000. You get immediate approval of the lease by phone and the lender finances the equipment for the company needing it. Your commission is paid by the lender directly to you. $100. 150 pgs., 8½ × 11 in.

K-23   *THE FORTUNE BUILDERS PROGRAM KIT* shows you how to get rich in your spare time at home in mail order/direct mail, rental real estate, specialized consulting, venture capital, export-import, finder's fees, financial brokerage, projects using 100% financing, and many unusual businesses. You get personal, on-the-phone, step-by-step supervision from IWS on selecting, starting, and getting rich in your own business. And—if you wish—you can visit IWS to get face-to-face help for your new business. This kit will help you get started in any—or all—of these businesses. $300.00. 1000 pgs.

K-24   *MERCHANT ACCOUNT KIT* shows you how and where a new or long-established business can obtain merchant status so it can accept credit card charges for its sales of products or services to customers. This big kit features typical applications for merchant accounts and shows the user how to fill out the forms for maximum chance of success. It gives sources of merchant accounts for all types of businesses—such as storefront, home-based non-swipe, telemarketing, flea-market, garage and tag sale. Many users of this kit have successfully obtained their own merchant account for their business. $100.00. 200 pgs., 8½ × 11 in.

K-25   ***HARD MONEY COMMERCIAL REAL ESTATE LOANS KIT*** has a 4-hour+ video showing exactly how to get these loans. A fully illustrated manual gives you the forms you need, along with the steps to fill them out so you have a better chance of getting the loan you need. Loans range from $300,000 to $20 million+; close in 1–3 weeks; nationwide lending; minimal documentation needed; short-form appraisals accepted; flexible loan structures. You can use this kit to get loans for yourself, or for others, and earn a nice commission on the transaction. $150. Video and 90-page manual.

K-26   ***EXECUTIVE REPRESENTATIVE SALES PLAN KIT*** allows you to sell all IWS products—newsletters, kits, and books by any normal means (mail order, direct mail, telemarketing, Internet, e-mail, or face-to-face)— and earn a commission starting at 40% of the list price ($40 on a $100 list price) and rising to 50% for life after $2,000 in total list-price sales. You do *not* have to carry any inventory, do *not* have to make any shipments, do *not* have to send a bill to your customers. You are supplied camera-ready ads, along with sample classified ads, plus pre-written promotion materials, and an agreement covering your independent contractor status with IWS. A 5-year subscription to the IWS newsletter is given to you when you become an Executive Rep. $120.00.

K-27   ***AUTO AND TRUCK LEASING KIT*** shows you how to work directly with leasing companies to earn a commission on lease customers you bring to them. This big kit gives you a Startup Manual showing you how to work with potential lease customers and the companies who finance auto and truck leases. It gives you typical lease application forms, ads you can run to find potential customers, plus much more. So if you're interested in working—part-time—as a lease referral commission agent, this kit can help you get started. $100. 150 pgs., 8½ × 11 in.

Besides his longer books, such as the one you are now holding, Ty Hicks has written a number of books he calls *Slims*—that is, thin books slim enough to fit into a person's back pocket or purse. Each of these *Slims* is 5 × 8 inches in trim size. The titles alone are listed below because they—in general—describe the content of each *Slim*.

S-1   ***Build Your Wealth with a Powerful Real Estate Tool—Foreclosures,*** 74 pgs., $12.50.

S-2   ***How to Buy Up to Two Properties a Month with No Down Payment,*** 82 pgs., $12.50.

S-3   ***Real Estate Can Make You Rich—in Good Times and Bad Times,*** 68 pgs., $12.50.

S-4   ***How to Earn a Fast-Fortune Guaranteed Income in a Little-Known Dollar-Rich Business,*** 64 pgs., $12.50.

S-5   ***100 Ways to Make One Million Dollars Quickly in Real Estate Starting with No Cash,*** 78 pgs., $12.50.

S-6   *Secrets of Building Great Riches Fast in a One-Person Business That Is Hassle-Free,* 64 pgs., $12.50.

S-7   *Successful Creative Money Borrowing Techniques for Business,* 96 pgs., $12.50.

S-8   *Big and Easy Moneymaking Ideas for Finders, Beginning Wealth Builders, and Licensing Agents,* 72 pgs., $12.50.

S-9   *Mail Order/Direct Mail Fast Wealth Success Secrets, Including Building Riches in Import/ Export,* 60 pgs., $12.50.

S-10   *Make a Bundle in Real Estate Using Borrowed Money Techniques,* 70 pgs., $12.50.

S-11   *Tips for Using OPM and Mortgaging Out to Make Real Estate Millions,* 74 pgs., $12.50.

S-12   *Sure Steps for Raising Money for Real Estate Wealth Accumulation,* 66 pgs., $12.50.

S-13   *How to Build Great Real Estate Riches Quickly Using Creative Financing,* 82 pgs., $12.50.

When ordered in quantities of 4, 8, or 13, the cost of each of the above *Slims* is $10. Thus, 4 *Slims* = $40; 8 *Slims* = $80; 13 *Slims* = $130. For other quantities, the price is $12.50 each, which includes postage and handling. Order by using book numbers (for example—S-1, S-2) instead of titles. To receive a copy of the IWS 48-page catalog, send $5.00 to IWS, Inc., P.O. Box 186, Merrick, NY 11566-0186.

Tyler Hicks Order Form

For questions on the contents of Tyler Hicks products or international orders, please call IWS, Inc. at (516) 766-5850 or (800) 323-0548.

PLEASE SEND ALL ORDERS TO:
IWS, Inc.
24 Canterbury Road
Rockville Centre, NY 11570-1310

Accept phone, fax or mail orders.
To order by phone, please call 516-766-5850
Mon.–Sat. 8am–10pm EST.
Website: www.iwsmoney.com
Fax, 24 hr/day, 7 days/week to: 516-766-5919

Books

❏ IWS-1	Business Capital Sources	15.00	_____
❏ IWS-2	Small Business Investment	15.00	_____
❏ IWS-3	World-wide Riches Vol. 1	25.00	_____
❏ IWS-4	World-wide Riches Vol. 2	25.00	_____
❏ IWS-5	How to Prepare Export-Import	25.00	_____
❏ IWS-6	Real Estate Riches Supplement	15.00	_____
❏ IWS-7	Radical New Road	15.00	_____
❏ IWS-8	60-Day Fully Financed	29.50	_____
❏ IWS-9	Credits and Collection	29.50	_____
❏ IWS-10	Mideast Banks	15.00	_____
❏ IWS-11	Export Mail-Order	17.50	_____
❏ IWS-12	Product Export Riches	21.50	_____
❏ IWS-13	Dir. of High-Discount	17.50	_____
❏ IWS-14	How to Finance Real Estate	18.50	_____
❏ IWS-15	Dir. of Freight Forwarders	17.50	_____
❏ IWS-16	Can You Afford Not to Be...?	15.00	_____
❏ IWS-17	How to Find Hidden Wealth	17.50	_____
❏ IWS-18	How to Create Real Estate Fortune	17.50	_____
❏ IWS-19	Real-Estate Second Mortgages	17.50	_____
❏ IWS-20	Guide to Business and Real Estate	25.00	_____
❏ IWS-21	Dir. of 2,500 Active Real Estate Lenders	25.00	_____
❏ IWS-22	Ideas for Finding Capital	24.50	_____
❏ IWS-23	How to Become Wealthy Pub.	17.50	_____
❏ IWS-24	National Dir. Manufacturers' Reps.	28.80	_____
❏ IWS-25	Business Plan Kit	29.50	_____
❏ IWS-26	Money Raiser's Dir. of Bank Credit Card Prog.	19.95	_____
❏ IWS-27	Global Cosigners and Money Finders Assoc.	50.00	_____
❏ IWS-28	Wall Street Syndicators	15.00	_____
❏ IWS-29	Comprehensive Loan Sources for Businesses and Real Estate Loans	25.00	_____
❏ IWS-30	Diversified Loan Sources for Business and Real Estate Loans	25.00	_____
IWS-31	Credit Power Reports		
❏	Report No. 1	19.95	_____
❏	Report No. 2	19.95	_____
❏	Report No. 3	19.95	_____
❏	Report No. 4	19.95	_____
❏	Report No. 5	19.95	_____
❏ IWS-32	Good Monthly Income	15.00	_____
❏ IWS-33	How to Buy a Business with No Money Down	19.50	_____
❏ IWS-34	How to Make a Fortune As a Licensing Agent	15.00	_____
❏ IWS-35	How to Run a Profitable Child Care Referral Service	22.95	_____
❏ IWS-36	Successful Financing Techniques for Business and Real Estate	24.95	_____
❏ IWS-37	How to Be a Second Mortgage Loan Broker	25.00	_____
❏ IWS-38	How to Start and Finance a Business that Works for You	24.75	_____
❏ IWS-39	You Can Get Money!	59.50	_____
❏ IWS-40	Options Report	20.00	_____

Slims

❏ S-1	Build Your Wealth with a Powerful Real Estate Tool Foreclosure
❏ S-2	How to Buy Up to Two Properties a Month with No Down Payment
❏ S-3	Real Estate Can Make You Rich–In Good Times & Bad Times
❏ S-4	How to Earn a Fast-Fortune Guaranteed Income . . .
❏ S-5	100 Ways to Make One Million Dollars Quickly in Real Estate . . .
❏ S-6	Secrets of Building Great Riches Fast in a One-Person Business . . .
❏ S-7	Successful Creative Money Borrowing Techniques for Business
❏ S-8	Big and Easy Moneymaking Ideas for Finders, Beginning Wealth Builders . . .
❏ S-9	Mail Order/Direct Mail Fast Wealth Success Secrets . . .

❑ S-10	Make a Bundle in Real Estate Using Borrowed Money Techniques		
❑ S-11	Tips for Using OPM and Mortgaging Out to Make Real Estate Millions		
❑ S-12	Sure Steps for Raising Money for Real Estate Wealth Accumulation		
❑ S-13	How to Build Great Real Estate Riches Quickly Using Creative Financing		

Individual Slims 12.50 _____   8 Slims   80.00 _____

4 Slims   40.00 _____   13 Slims 130.00 _____

Newsletters

❑ IWSN-1	International Wealth Success	24.00	_____
❑ IWSN-2	Money Watch Bulletin	95.00	_____

Kits

❑ K-1	Financial Broker	99.50	_____
❑ K-2	Starting Millionaire	99.50	_____
❑ K-3	Franchise Riches	99.50	_____
❑ K-4	Mail Order Riches	99.50	_____
❑ K-5	Zero Cash Success	99.50	_____
❑ K-6	Real Estate Riches	99.50	_____
❑ K-7	Business Borrowers	99.50	_____
❑ K-8	Raising Money from Grants	99.50	_____
❑ K-9	Fast Financing of Real Estate	99.50	_____
❑ K-10	Loans by Phone Kit	100.00	_____
❑ K-11	Loans by Mail Kit	100.00	_____
❑ K-12	Real-Estate Loan Getters Service Kit	100.00	_____
❑ K-13	Cash Credit Riches System Kit	100.00	_____
❑ K-14	Professional Practice Builders Kit	100.00	_____
❑ K-15	Venture Capital Millions Kit	100.00	_____
❑ K-16	Guaranteed Loan Money	100.00	_____
❑ K-17	Import/Export Riches Kit	99.50	_____
❑ K-18	Phone-in/Mail-in Grants Kit	100.00	_____
❑ K-19	Mega Money Methods	100.00	_____
❑ K-20	Foreclosures and Other Distressed Property Sales	51.95	_____
❑ K-21	Small Business Loan Program	100.00	_____
❑ K-22	Phone-in Mini-Lease Program	100.00	_____
❑ K-23	Fortune Builders Program Kit	300.00	_____
❑ K-24	Merchant Account Kit	100.00	_____
❑ K-25	Hard Money Commercial Real Estate Kit	150.00	_____
❑ K-26	Executive Representative Sales Plan Kit	120.00	_____
❑ K-27	Auto & Truck Leasing Kit	100.00	_____

SHIPPING:

Regular Mail (Please allow 2-3 weeks for delivery):
    $3 first book / $1 each additional book   _____
    $1 each slim / $5 for 5-13 slims   _____
    $6 first kit / $4 each additional kit   _____

Priority Mail (Please allow 1-2 weeks for delivery):
    $5 first book / $2 each additional book   _____
    $11 first kit / $6 each additional kit   _____

Intl AirMail (Please allow 1-2 weeks for delivery):
    $7.00 per book   _____
    $22.00 per kit   _____
    $24.00 per year for newsletter   _____

Intl Surface Mail (Please allow 4-7 weeks for delivery):
    $ 5.00 per book   _____
    $18.00 per kit   _____

Total Books, Slims & Kits **(ORDERS OVER $300–REFER TO MR. HICKS DIRECTLY)**   _____

Total Shipping   _____

                                  TOTAL $ _____

Name _____

Address _____

Phone _____

❑ Check   ❑ Money order   ❑ Mastercard   ❑ Visa   ❑ American Express

MC / VISA / AMEX _____ Exp. date _____ Auth # _____

Signature _____ Date _____ Order taken by _____

INDEX

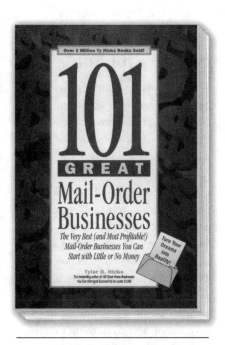

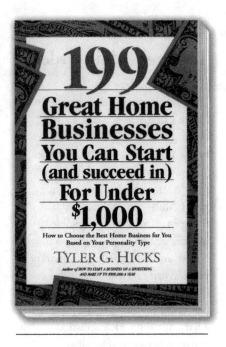